PRAISE FOR GONE

"Marvelously written, exceptionally researched, *Gone Viking III* is a fun ride through Europe and Scandinavia filled with humour and adventure."

—Allan Hudson, *South Branch Scribbler*

"Once again, in his uniquely entertaining way, Bill Arnott enriches our understanding of our world, its places, and its people."

—Timothy Niedermann, *The Ottawa Review of Books*

"*Gone Viking III* is a modern-day saga, a spirited quest with poetic intelligence and a wicked sense of humor. Highly recommended."

—Tor Torkildson, author of *Cloud Wanderer*

PRAISE FOR BILL ARNOTT'S OTHER BOOKS

"Perfect books for the armchair explorer. A true delight from a talented travel writer."

—John MacFarlane, author of *Around the World in a Dugout Canoe*

"Definitely the best reads of the year."

—*CP Review Magazine*

"You won't want to travel with anyone else."

—*The Ekphrastic Review*

"Beautiful imagery. A pleasure to read."

—*The Ottawa Review of Books*

"Arnott weaves an eloquent and delightful tapestry of sights, sounds and scents, creating a sense of timelessness."

—Cheryl Alexander, award-winning author of *Takaya: Lone Wolf*

"Arnott is an erudite and charming guide."

—Canadian Authors Association

"A series of delightful feasts."

—*The British Columbia (Ormsby) Review*

"A colorful travelogue."

—*Perceptive Travel* magazine

GONE VIKING III

GONE VIKING III

THE HOLY GRAIL

BILL ARNOTT

RMB

For information on purchasing bulk quantities of this book, or to obtain media excerpts or invite the author to speak at an event, please visit rmbooks.com and select the "Contact" tab.

RMB | Rocky Mountain Books Ltd.
rmbooks.com
@rmbooks
facebook.com/rmbooks

Cataloguing data available from Library and Archives Canada
ISBN 9781771606462 (softcover)
ISBN 9781771606479 (electronic)

Printed and bound in Canada

We would like to also take this opportunity to acknowledge the traditional territories upon which we live and work. In Calgary, Alberta, we acknowledge the Niitsítapi (Blackfoot) and the people of the Treaty 7 region in Southern Alberta, which includes the Siksika, the Piikuni, the Kainai, the Tsuut'ina, and the Stoney Nakoda First Nations, including Chiniki, Bearpaw, and Wesley First Nations. The City of Calgary is also home to Métis Nation of Alberta, Region III. In Victoria, British Columbia, we acknowledge the traditional territories of the Lkwungen (Esquimalt and Songhees), Malahat, Pacheedaht, Scia'new, T'Sou-ke, and W̱SÁNEĆ (Pauquachin, Tsartlip, Tsawout, Tseycum) peoples.

We acknowledge the financial support of the Government of Canada through the Canada Book Fund and the Canada Council for the Arts, and of the province of British Columbia through the British Columbia Arts Council and the Book Publishing Tax Credit.

For the love of the quest,
and all that you love on the journey.

CONTENTS

"The search for the cup is the search for the divine in all of us, but if you want *facts* and they have none to give you, at my age I'm prepared to take a few things on faith,"

—Dr. Marcus Brody, *Indiana Jones and the Last Crusade*

PROLOGUE

I'm standing at the edge of the earth. Land's End. Behind me, to the right, a series of rough, scalloped sea cliffs, bays in granite and swaths of amber-hued sand. Receding to the left, outcroppings of wave-bashed basalt. Ahead, a meniscus of blue pulls sky into whitecaps, the slightest hint of a distant archipelago, or mirage. I've trekked a hundred miles of coastline, lilting west, to here. And a grin I'm only now aware of clings stubbornly to my face, a prideful smile of accomplishment. Breaking surf and a call of gulls add a maritime score, the juxtaposed essence of isolation, and connection.

I'm viking again. A sense of liberation. Freeing. If these travel exploits are new to you, I've gone viking, voyaging, for a number of years in the wake of history's greatest explorers: uncovering secrets and hidden treasure, meeting remarkable people and making new friends, hoping to gain insight into the meaning of it all. For this iteration I'll travel once more through time, past and present, in my latest and perhaps greatest saga, pursuing the Holy Grail.

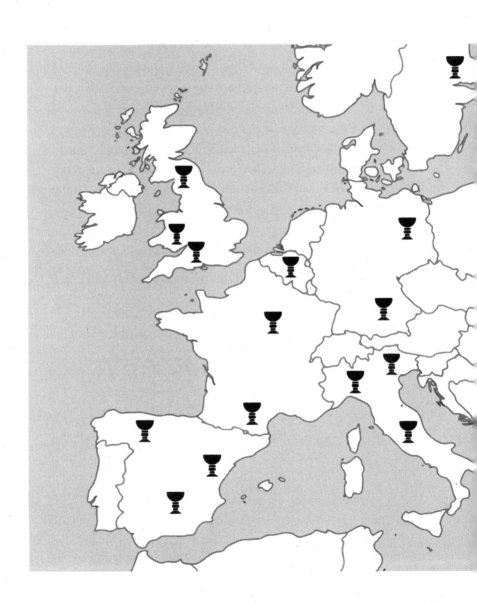

GONE VIKING III:
TRACKING THE GRAIL

INTRODUCTION

The Holy Grail. Monty Python aside, the word, for most, invokes marvel and wonder. Matters of religion, quests and immortality. Kingdoms, knights and chivalry. Akin to Viking Sagas, exploring the unknown, to sail and trek distant lands through swirls of sea and mountain mist. A search, in its way, for the very essence of life.

Legend has it the historically elusive Jomsvikings – faithful to the old gods, battle-hardened mercenaries following strict codes of honour – were forerunners of medieval knights like those of King Arthur's Round Table. These mysterious Norse warrior-pilgrims appear throughout history, from Scandinavia to the Baltic and across Europe, recorded in Germany, Denmark and Iceland. It may be their reputed devotion to a cause that makes them intriguing. Admirable. Christian-influenced versions of these knights also emerge across medieval Europe: German tales of Parzival, Percival in France, and English stories of Galahad, survivors refusing to abandon long and isolating crusades.

Meanwhile, I find myself clicking and flipping through maps, envisioning new travel plans. Fresh excursions. No doubt a seed was sown on previous *Gone Viking* travels as I stood on a windblown cliff in southwestern England, Wales to the north, at the birthplace of Arthur, a rugged expanse of coast, moor and history. But tired, for the moment, of planning the next Grand Tour, I've decided to escape into the embrace of old movies.

Netflix determined I was due to rewatch the *Indiana Jones* films (the good ones, that is). And who am I to argue with their sophisticated algorithms? So I've settled in with salty snacks to relive Spielberg's cinematography, Williams's score and Harrison Ford's adventurous archaeology prof for a bit of fabricated action and entertainment. And before long I'm there, alongside Indy (as I like to call him, as he and I have been friends for 40 years), helping him on his odyssey. A quest, it turns out, he's undertaken with his dad (Sean Connery), to search for the Holy Grail.

Imagine a well-weathered map, last century, filling our field of vision, the white-noise roar of airplane props and a thick red line advancing, making its way along our route as we venture out, embracing the unknown, vagaries of the road our travel companion, the world's mysteries our destination. Unless, of course, we locate the most elusive mystery of all. The Holy Grail.

"I can get it!" Indy calls from my screen. "I can almost reach it, Dad!" What must be the grail beckons, just beyond his outstretched fingers, the earth rending beneath his feet.

"Indiana," his father says in a calm, and calming tone. "Indiana. Let it go."

Only, I can't. Or rather, don't want to. Unlike Indy, my level-headed dad isn't here to talk me down (with a gruff Bond-ish brogue), or to talk sense into me. So I'm left to my own devices, for the time being at least. And as you may know, when left on my own for a period of time, I tend to wander off. Which is what I'm doing now. Setting out on a proper adventure, one I'm certain will be a good story. Like our previous viking undertakings, a true story, with a great many side trips, recollections and mental meanderings. A bit of fantasy, some speculation and, yes, occasional gaps, which I liken to stylized finish on roughly mortared walls. Attractive and somehow conclusive in its incompleteness. In the overall foundation there's a timelessness that makes the whole, I believe, structurally sound. And, in its way, rather beautiful.

PART I:
VIKING CAMELOT

1
BRITAIN

It's a blustery Thursday (Thor's Day), and I've returned to the steep grassy track that leads from a gravel car park to a series of hilltops and cliffs with a broad ocean view, the Bristol Channel spilling into Celtic Sea. A mild gale is swirling cumulous, offering peekaboos of blue, the occasional sundog winking through stratospheric ice. I cinch my hat to the wind, and march into the Dark Ages. According to English Heritage, history and legend are inseparable here at Tintagel, and as I scan the landscape, taking in sea air and ghosts on the breeze, I understand.

Let's go back a millennium-and-a-half or so. The Romans have gone, leaving Britannia once more to the locals and a dwindling handful of Druids. A whiff of Christianity is blowing in across the sea, bobbing this way in leather curraghs, preached with Irish accents by snake-scaring saints. Of course, no one here at the time, or anywhere for that matter, considers the Age to be Dark. That label will come later, penned by monks propagating a neatly scribed blend of truth and nonsense. But for these centuries, the fifth to the seventh, this was a place of remoteness. Again, as always. Mainland that feels like an island.

Rich in resources, this has been a destination for as long as people have been travelling, crafting things and enjoying food. Every seafaring Mediterranean nation came here, quarrying stone, mining copper and tin, and fishing for pilchards, crustaceans and bivalves. With competition for scarce goods and trade, dispute invariably follows. We see this everywhere natural resources are in demand, an eventual creation of haves and have-nots. Inequitable distribution of power. And, most often, rule based solely on might. Which is when heroes and legends are born. Like that of King Arthur. The notion of someone of the people rising up to lead the populace to a better place, a place of peace and abundance. A place like Camelot.

From Land's End, the edge of the earth where our journey began, I'm making my way through the county of Cornwall, now travelling west to east, following coastline, train lines and undulating country roads bordered in hedgerows and ancient dry-stone walls. The land here's been cultivated and farmed for 5,000 years. Produce and grains are diverse and abundant, the dairy exceptional. Cows and sheep seem happy. And why wouldn't they be? Each field seems to roll toward water, offering pristine views in seaside greens and aquamarine. With Penzance and St Ives behind me, I've veered from the coast, the road following higher ground, bisecting this peninsula that makes up the southwest corner of England. Water surrounds the terrain on three sides, its perimeter the Penwith Heritage Coast. Geographer Nick Crane refers to these blank canvas shores when he states, rather emphatically, "For me, Cornwall *is* the explorer's coast." If we keep travelling east into Devon, its border the River Tamar, you can see, geographically and intuitively, why this rugged finger of mainland is considered an island.

I pass through Camborne, Pool and Redruth, the former hub of mining now economically struggling, a triad of towns in need of resuscitation, sardonically referred to as CPR. Northwest is Newquay, a surfers' destination with waves for novices and seasoned wave riders alike, the beaches offering a blend of left- and right-hand breakers. I skirt the Camel estuary, bypassing Padstow, the town famous for seafood.

Tintagel sits on the north coast, our destination for now. Along with Land's End, this remote English stronghold serves as a starting point in our journey. Beneath the current ruins of a medieval Norman castle lies the foundation of an Iron Age fortress, believed to have been the home of King Arthur. If we turn left, we face the coast. Inland, Camelford is directly ahead, reputedly the location of Arthur's last battle, in 537 at a site called Slaughterbridge, where he was mortally wounded by traitorous Mordred. To our right is the vast expanse of Bodmin Moor. In the midst of the moor stands Arthur's stone and a Neolithic circle known as King Arthur's Hall, one of numerous hedges, cists, cairns and hut circles in the area.

A lake called Dozmary Pool meanders through the moor like a murky inkblot. This is where the Lady of the Lake passed Excalibur to Arthur, granting him the right to rule, according to Thomas Malory in *Le Morte d'Arthur*. Following the final battle, on his deathbed, Arthur gives Excalibur to Bedivere, telling him to return the sword to the Lake, or more specifically to the Lady. It may be of interest to note Bedivere had only one hand, the other having been lost in a battle somewhere in Wales. ("What's the sound of one hand clapping?" Zen Buddhists propose. I suggest introducing this guy to someone else with a single hand and seat them next to each other for the encore.) Abiding by Arthur's dying wish, Bedivere returns here, to the lake in the moor, and hurls Excalibur into the water, where it's caught (rather adeptly) by the Lady of the Lake, her silver-clad arm pulling the sword back into the depths forever.

Some versions of the tale have Bedivere disobeying Arthur, unwilling to give up the sword, its beauty too much to part with. Maybe Bedivere figured he'd have a go at being king, what with the sword already in his possession, like popping a crown on your head and letting people assume you're in charge.

Other versions claim the Lady of the Lake was the ruler of Avalon, that mystical isle that's cropped up so often in our viking exploits. Many believe it lay (lies?) just beyond Land's End, and sank into history, perhaps being the city of Atlantis. There's even some science to back up the theory. Currently, the Isles of Scilly sit about 30 miles beyond Land's End across a stretch of Celtic Sea, more or less in the North Atlantic. But not that long ago (geologically speaking) these islands were part of the mainland. At the end of the last Ice Age, an oceanic one-two punch occurred as ocean levels rose at the same time this extension of mainland dropped. The ice cap had been pushing down on the land to the north, forcing the southwest of Cornwall upward, leaving this part of the globe relatively free of ice. Once the ice retreated, the islands were formed. Not simply from increased water, but the combination of water rising and part of the land descending.

So how does Avalon, or Atlantis for that matter, factor into this? Well, a sunken city's been located here – a good-sized town by all accounts, with multiple places of worship. We also know that as the Isles of Scilly were being formed (and reformed) they were populous in the Bronze Age and likely well before that. Inhabitants were boatbuilders, fishers and voyagers, advanced in science and engineering, and constructed complex burial barrows and cairns. From a British perspective it was as far west as one could go toward setting sun, a final resting place for the honoured and revered, that horizon point of no return, as dreamily evocative as Avalon.

Having walked from the car, I'm now scanning this mystical landscape – Arthur's castle at my feet, his last battle site behind me, and beyond that the lake where the Lady from Avalon dubbed him king. Facing the sea, I'm forced to squint into violent gusts and realize I'm gritting my teeth in the teeth of the wind. And I imagine the ghoulish gales that must've kept company with every tower guard through lone watches in the haunted dark of northerly winters.

The castle I'm now looking at is closer in our timeline to the Norseman Rollo's kin by way of William the Conqueror. But beneath these partial walls of rock rest the energy and spirit of Arthur. I step between flagstones and gaze through what were once windows. Rough brick-like sandstone chunks comprise each frame. In the openings are sea views, the water today in sun-streaked shades of peridot and teal. I pass through a doorway – a thick, crumbling slab of wall with an arched throughway. By creeping to the edge of an outcrop, I can peek down a cliff to the shore, a small, jagged inlet known as Merlin's Cave. Later, I'd find myself watching a BBC show with a presenter I don't care for, standing right here with this view. His weather was foul and he looked miserable, which pleased me. But the production values were good and, despite myself, I learned things of interest, aiding us in our quest.

Merlin, as you're likely aware, was an enchanter. A wizard. By all accounts, he resembled Ian McKellen in every Peter Jackson iteration of the Tolkien books. Merlin's backstory is noteworthy. His mom, perhaps unsurprisingly, was a woman. But apparently his dad was an incubus, and Merlin inherited paternal traits of shapeshifting and prophecy, which, although I hate labelling, makes him a cambion. Merlin appears through most versions of Arthur's tale, at times as advisor, prophet and friend. In some he introduces Arthur to the Lady of the Lake, facilitating the gifting of Excalibur. "But wait!" you may be saying. "Didn't Arthur pull Excalibur from a stone?" Indeed he did, in many versions of the story. And in most of those versions, Merlin arranges that as well, guiding young Arthur to the rock-buried sword. In my favourite movie of the tale, both iterations are tidily brought together as Arthur finds the sword in the stone but returns it to the Lady of the Lake as he's dying. Or rather, gets one of his knights to do it.

Other versions state that Excalibur was the sword from the Lady of the Lake, while the one from the stone was in fact another blade, called Caliburn. In our ambiguous blend of history and legend, the sword story is an ancient one, weapons of power being only wieldable by courageous leaders who were pure of heart. The Greeks have their own versions with different swords. Some believe Julius Caesar had one, while Attila was also reputed to carry a sword of power, bequeathed by Roman gods.

At a roundabout in Keflavik, Iceland, a massive stone sword sits thrust in a rise in the roadway with a view to the sea at Reykjanesbær, near a place called Giantess Cave. And at Hafrsfjord, Norway, three towering swords have been partially buried together in grass-covered rock by the water. The legend's pure Viking, recounted in *Heimskringla*, *The Saga of Harald Fairhair*. The year was 872, and three Norwegian tribes were at war. As in so many blood feuds, romantic interests played a part. Very Shakespearean. Helen-of-Troy-ish too, for that matter. But in this Norse history, following a long and nasty battle at Hafrsfjord, peace ensued, along with some predominantly happy marriages. The modern-day swords in the stone represent the coming together of disparate factions and the peaceful unification of Norway into one nation, perhaps a version of "burying the hatchet."

And what would any great legend be without two or three star-crossed lovers? Back to our Arthurian tales, here on the headland at Tintagel. Merlin himself was besotted with his apprentice, Morgan le Fay, Arthur's half-sister. Some versions have Merlin and Morgan as lovers, while others indicate the affair was unconsummated. Then apparently another apprentice won Merlin's heart, a fairy named Viviane. It's somewhat unclear, but Merlin's downfall ensues, the result of his Iggy Pop–ish lust for life (and female protégés), and he's given a choice of prison or grave. He opts for prison, which, it turns out, is a crystal-encrusted cave. The cave at the base of the cliff I'm now peering over.

In the long-standing Viking-esque tradition of plucking Celts to marry and settle elsewhere, from French poems we learn of Tristan, the knight tasked with going to Ireland to retrieve Isolde and bring her here to marry his uncle Marke, who was king at the time. But Tristan and Isolde fall for each other in the process, a range of betrayals ensue and no one, it seems, lives happily ever after. The story was written in the 13th century, but Wagner made it famous with his operatic version in the 1850s, a cutting-edge composition incorporating what's referred to as orchestral colour and tonal ambiguity. Sentiments that perfectly capture this wind-whipped coast and sprawling moorland.

But it simply wouldn't be a proper Arthurian story without Guinevere and Lancelot. Guinevere, as you know, married Arthur, and was queen of where I'm standing now, Wagner's time-spanning score setting a gut-wrenching tone. Guinevere makes her first literary appearance in Welsh records but is best known from Geoffrey of Monmouth's 12th-century *Historia Regum Britanniae*, a British history book written in the same manner as most Viking Sagas, a delicious blend of history, myth and speculation.

Like nearly everyone, Guinevere, it seems, had a predominantly good heart, combined with a well-intentioned nobility. Geoffrey of Monmouth's telling of the tale has Mordred the traitor trying to seduce her. But romantic French versions of the story bring Guinevere together with Lancelot, Arthur's chief knight and friend. This plot twist is further expanded in Malory's *Le Morte d'Arthur*, and the complicated love triangle of Arthur, Guinevere and Lancelot has become the most familiar version, retold countless times in literature, film and, I suppose, werewolf and vampire books.

Lancelot, by all accounts, was a great swordsman (not a euphemism), warrior and jouster. French legends have him as the orphaned son of a king from a lost kingdom, and being raised, interestingly enough, by the Lady of the Lake. Lancelot was renowned as a hero, victor of battles and tournaments, and became one of the greatest knights of Arthur's Round Table. Their common objective, to create a utopian court at Camelot. Leaving us to wonder whether this high crest of rock and scrub grass just might have been the location of Camelot, and what precisely that is. A dream? Aspiration? The medieval version of Kennedy's vision, blending propaganda with troop rallying?

Left with more questions than answers, I skirt a few stones and climb over others to approach yet another land's end, bracing myself against the relentless push and pull of clifftop wind. There's a statue of Arthur, his back to the sea, facing the lake and the moor. It's more of a stylized outline, solid yet wispy, *plein-air* design, landscape literally pervading the king. You can't look at Arthur without seeing the surrounding land and sea. There's an unending swirl of salinated mist, ribbons of fret resembling lance-mounted flags, twisting in northwesterlies. And with this view, this perspective, I believe I can almost see Camelot.

Our spinning orb, slows, for an instant, momentary
as a slender slice of gneiss emerges, on an island
with a lake, and from the lake, a lady lifts

her slender rock-like arm and thrusts a sword
into a country's heart – the rock, the lake, the island
now a kingdom, waiting, waiting to be claimed

Across the sea toward the east
where sickle moon and six point stars
light nighttime sky
and burka-shrouded, fortress-armoured damsels
keep their tumbled lengths of jet hair under wraps
rebuking breaches, laddered walls and sieges

Somewhere in between the two, a supper quietly ensues
a dozen friends, a server and an enemy unknown, as yet,
break bread, and share a laugh, a smile, their subtle consternation
prescient, awaiting destiny, as though they know
this meal is their last, the final one, together
from the centre of the table one man reaches for the wine
tops everybody's cup and then his own
he gives a warm and sad and longing look into his lover's eyes
before he raises burnished challis, toasts his friends, his enemy
and savours one last drink from this. The Holy Grail.

Let's talk a bit about the grail itself. As with so many facets of our saga's history, there are plenty of variations to the tale. Most commonly the grail's identified as the cup, goblet or chalice that Jesus drank from at the Last Supper. No doubt you're familiar with the meal from Leonardo's painting, or Dan Brown's book. And Jesus you likely know from the Andrew Lloyd Webber musical, although he refers to it as a rock opera. Webber, that is. The grail is also considered by many to have been used by Joseph of Arimathea to collect Jesus's blood at the crucifixion, the significance symbolized in Christian worship by way of the Eucharist or Communion. Just to clarify, this isn't the Joseph we see in nativity scenes next to a lamb and the magi, spouse to the Virgin Mary. This is a different one, whom we'll get to know better quite soon.

Some depict the grail as bejewelled precious metal, the kind of thing you'd expect a Viking jarl to hoist from a treasure chest, no doubt a pleasant alternative to drinking from a sideways horn. However, many scholars surmise that at a humble gathering of fishermen and carpenters it's improbable any of the dinnerware would be so extravagant, and the grail is likely a modest drinking vessel, simple in design and composition. Historically, the term grail's been used to describe a range of items, including a plate, dish or platter – in other words, anything used for serving a meal, food or beverage.

In Leonardo's painting, perhaps our most familiar depiction of that gathering, there's no indication of anything resembling a cup or goblet, nor even a jug of wine as far as I can see. There's food on plates, one of which could be our grail, and platters indicating family style dining, but nothing specific to drink from. There are some misshapen dinner rolls around the perimeter, as though holding the tablecloth in place. The grub looks nice, the quantities modest. The room's well appointed, hung with tapestries beneath an attractive panelled ceiling. Perhaps the stemware, a goblet included, had already been cleared from the table, or had yet to be served. Outside, through windows at the back of the room, the day looks pleasant, Israeli or Palestinian hills in arid earthen tones under a cloudless sky. Apparently Leonardo used Milanese subjects as models and inspiration, and I admit the hills behind the diners do strike me as more Italianate than those found around the West Bank.

It's been a few years since I saw the painting up close, albeit through scaffolding, a team of restorers at work with egg-wash and minuscule brushes. So I'm using a web-based image to refresh my memory, enlarging it in a manner I couldn't possibly do in front of the actual one.

And who is this Joseph of Arimathea? He's not in attendance at the supper table. It's believed Joseph was a pious, well-to-do councillor and businessman who took responsibility for burying Jesus after his crucifixion, getting permission from Pilate to remove the corpse from the cross. Joseph is also thought to be Jesus's uncle. According to the *Gospel of Matthew*, Joseph took Jesus's body to a cave, possibly a burial chamber Joseph had already prearranged.

In addition to stories of Merlin, 12th-century French poet Robert de Boron also wrote about Joseph (*Joseph d'Arimathie*), stating that Joseph receives the grail from an apparition of his crucified nephew. So perhaps Joseph didn't have the grail to begin with. However, he has it at this point in the saga, which is where our Arthurian legend, known as the Arthurian cycle, connects directly to the grail. According to de Boron, reiterated through other scribes' sequels, Joseph transports the grail to the UK, quite possibly to Glastonbury. Fellow followers are said to have taken it there, supposedly a party of 12, possibly with Joseph amongst them. Regardless, we now have the grail, in theory, placed firmly in Arthur's homeland, a short distance from Cornwall, in the county of Somerset. And in an intriguing bit of Welsh folklore, Arthur is said to have been buried in a cave nearby, waiting for the right moment to arise when the world needs him most. Sound familiar?

The Welsh-based legends claim Guinevere was laid to rest here as well, and that Arthur was a giant. Archaeological work in the area has unearthed a particularly large human femur, carbon-dated right around our timeline. The leg bone came from someone just over six feet tall, which could be considered a giant, comparatively, in those days. Sadly, there's no usable DNA to pursue the search. But what of the rest of the remains? It's been said because of their proximity to Glastonbury Abbey the bodies were moved for safekeeping when Henry VIII decided that monasteries had to go. The story further claims Arthur and Guinevere were being transported to an undisclosed location in the New World. Vinland, perhaps? But the ship was caught in a storm mid-journey and sank, the remains now allegedly submerged somewhere in the Atlantic.

The significance of Glastonbury warrants further scrutiny. The locale's been a spiritual nucleus since the Stone Age. Megalithic, to be precise. It's the location of the UK's first Christian church. Tintagel and King Arthur's Hall are behind us. Here in Somerset, bearing northeast, we've come to a fork in the road, the A39 veering north while the A361 continues due east. A mile or so ahead is Glastonbury Tor, a conical hill sitting just outside the city centre. This steep pap of land has *also* been called the Isle of Avalon. Yes, the place ruled by the Lady of the Lake, perhaps where her adopted son Lancelot ran and played, no doubt swinging a stick like a sword. So maybe Avalon wasn't off the coast after all. Or perhaps this *was* the coast, in a previous era. One look at the Tor and it's easy to envision it surrounded by water, a solitary peak, the look of a broad grassy lighthouse towering over the town.

But we have other, potentially more promising paths to pursue on our quest, so let's revisit our timeline. Well into our Arthurian saga, Camelot is in disrepair. Merlin's stuck in his crystal prison, the susurration of ocean a woeful water torture. Arthur is heartbroken, seemingly betrayed by Guinevere and Lancelot, two people he loves. Camelot's languishing, the kingdom uncertain. Things look bleak. If this were a movie it seems our protagonists need one final score, an all-or-nothing job to set everything right. What they need, they now realize, is the grail.

And with that, the search for the Holy Grail became the primary objective for Arthur and his knights. Legend claimed the grail was in a mysterious castle, somewhere in wasteland, kept by an incapacitated monarch known as the Fisher King, last in a bloodline responsible for guarding the relic. The Fisher King's recovery was tied to the Round Table Knights retrieving the grail, a circuitous connection that indicates finding the grail would result in the self-actualized enlightenment associated with completing any great quest. Some believed attaining that goal would result in immortality. And perhaps by way of a legacy, it would, depending on how you view the notion of afterlife.

As the Arthurian team sought the grail, each knight soon found himself (all knights at the time in this part of the world were men) on a remote and isolating trek, each path fraught with pitfalls and personal demons. Most failed in the most miserable ways imaginable. But three of the knights – Bors, Percival and Galahad – persevered, deemed to be purest of heart. While Sir Galahad, it's said, was the only one to truly succeed.

So at last we have the grail, we believe, brought from the eastern edge of the Mediterranean toward setting sun, in the direction of Camelot. Joseph of Arimathea's tucked it away for safekeeping somewhere in Somerset, near the landlocked Isle of Avalon, the Lady of the Lake no doubt keeping a watchful eye, a waterlogged blade by her side.

And it *is* safe, in theory, undisturbed for the better part of half a millennium. But back to our timeline. You'll recall, early in our saga, the Romans retreating from Britannia (and most other places) as their empire crumbled. But like burning wood collapsing to ash, fire takes a long time to extinguish. Smouldering charcoal can linger, seemingly dormant, until the right puff of wind reignites it. Which is what occurs across Europe a few centuries later, as legions appear to trade short swords and phalanxes for cassocks and rosaries. The Latin Church by way of a Holy Roman Empire has burst into smoky flame, sending coughing old gods into hiding to bide their time. Meanwhile, from the seventh century on, Islam is growing in groundswells and, geographically speaking, squeezing Christianity from the Arabian Peninsula in the east to the Iberian in the west, the look of a Vise-Grip determinedly closing onto the continent. And in the same way resource demands lead to national expansion, so too does soul-saving conveniently lend itself to the justification of political aspirations.

Here our story jogs ever so slightly, the shimmy of a boxcar catching new rails at a junction. We've got that out-of-work actor who served wine and no doubt cleared the grail from the table at the Last

Supper, the chalice then carted by Joseph of Arimathea across the Channel to England where the Fisher King minded it for a stretch, until Galahad, having attained some version of satori, finally got hold of it. Now, in an Arthurian-esque manner of rejuvenating Camelot, the Knights Templar, iconic Christian Crusaders, have taken over as protectors of the grail.

It's the 11th century. Knights in the area look much like they did in Arthur's time, only now a red cross adorns their mail, and they fight, most often, for crown *and* religion. Warfare is changing. The Golden Age of Vikings is waning, but facets of Scandinavian culture are entrenched across Europe, one of the most significant being newly integrated language (one-third of English has its roots in Old Norse) in addition to increased community density and a delineation of European countries. In my research with a UK-based Norse archaeologist, I was told quite simply, "Europe looks the way it does because of the Vikings. We wouldn't have the countries we do today – France, Germany and Russia – were it not for the Vikings." Redrawing borders following world wars was, after all, merely tweaking things and, in a way, dividing the spoils.

The changing landscape also drove a shift in warfare. Tribe-like skirmishes and raids were becoming a thing of the past. Populous cities begat castles, and castle defences resulted in prolonged assaults, siege weapons such as catapults and trebuchets, and improved technology in crossbows, longbows and long-distance archers. With Knights Templar protecting the grail, and the burgeoning growth of Islam, faith-based fighting continued. The grail, meanwhile, housed somewhere by Templars, was still considered the most precious relic, representing a renewal of some version of Camelot, a panacea for the western world's woes.

This is where our primary characters meld with a tidy overlap of timeline and story, the grail passing tangentially through Arthur's court as the Templars, it's believed, are responsible for its safekeeping. Now Jomsvikings appear again, or still, as Templars reportedly shuttle the grail eastward, their objective to store it away for good. The legend claims that "under cover of darkness, the Templars sunk the grail, in a wooden box, in the lake near Świątki." This is in Pomerania, Poland, as is the alleged Jomsviking stronghold by the present-day town of Wolin. Building on the legend, a stone's been erected a short distance from sand beaches bordered in low hills, ideal for landing longships. The stone, engraved in a neat hybrid of Danish and Polish runes, commemorates the death of King Harald Bluetooth (Harald Gormsson) at this spot, in the Jomsviking home of Jomsborg, This is on the banks of the Dziwna, a channel of the Oder River that joins with the Baltic Sea, typical of Viking longphort terrain we see on rivers across Europe.

Harald ruled Denmark late in the tenth century, his bloodline part of the Knýtlinga Dynasty. King Gorm was his dad. His son was Sven Forkbeard, also a king, and his grandson was King Canute the Great, ruler of Denmark, England, Norway and a bit of Sweden, the whole known as the North Sea Empire. Harald converted Denmark to Christianity, a political move as much as anything, to ensure peace with the surrounding area and conserve resources (land, food, money and lives). Much of Norway was already on board with the new religion, Iceland would officially convert in a few years, and Sweden dabbled in the new faith but clung to the old gods for another two centuries.

Harald may be best known for the Jelling Stones, two massive carved runestones in Jelling, Denmark. The older stone was erected by Harald's dad, the newer, larger one by Harald. Many feel these stones represent the birth of the nation. As with most leaders, Harald's reign had its highs and lows. A runestone in Sønder Vissing, in eastern Jutland, refers to him as "Harald the Good," while Norse Sagas (written in Iceland) paint him with a less admirable brush. In a quote I quite like we gain insight in fairly plain language. The *Knýtlinga Saga* speaks of Harald's grandson Canute, in relation to the family: "Very wise he was, not any more than King Sven, whom he in all was like, or as before Harald and Gorm, who neither were particularly wise." Once you get past the Yoda-speak, you have the impression the kids got progressively smarter. Something we *know* to be true, as each and every one of us has been smarter than our parents, particularly when we're teenagers.

But to offer up a point-counterpoint regarding Harald, I give you this quote from the Saxon leader Widukind, who said of Harald, "He was eager to listen, dilatory to speak." So perhaps more of a thinker than one to act rashly. Bringing to mind the adage of two ears and one mouth; to listen twice as much as we speak. Mind you, as far as I can tell, Widukind died a couple of centuries before Harald was born, making his character reference somewhat questionable.

More reliable sources, however, appear in *The Saga of Olaf Tryggvason* (Olaf Crowbone), the tenth-century Norwegian king we spent time following in previous *Gone Viking* adventures. According to the Saga, composed by Icelandic authors in the 12th century (Oddr Snorrason, Gunnlaugr Leifsson and Snorri Sturluson), Harald spent his early years with half-brother Knud raiding and settling parts of Northumberland, taking the Viking baton from Ragnar Lothbrok's offspring. He then returned to Denmark, and following his father Gorm's death, Harald assumed the throne in 958, ruling Denmark for nearly 30 years.

Beyond his homeland, however, Harald's rule was tenuous. Late in the tenth century, Olaf Tryggvason took over the Norwegian throne while Harald was losing ground to Germanic Angles in the south, specifically the system of fortification known as the Danevirke, or Danework, around 974. Through all of this Harald was forced to submit to Swedish prince Styrbjörn the Strong, passing over a couple of fleets as well as family hostages in the process. But it was the loss of the Danework ramparts that significantly eroded Harald's territory, enabling Germans to settle back into the Schleswig-Holstein region abutting Scandinavia, a geo-cultural border similar to what we see today.

So how does "Harald the Good" factor into our grail quest? I glossed over this regarding the royal succession, but Harald's son Sven didn't so much assume the throne as in fact wrest it from his old man's grasp.

An insurgence occurred and Harald was mortally injured fighting off his son's rebellion. This occurred in either 985 or 986, depending on who you ask. But what's most relevant to our tale is that according to medieval German chronicler Adam of Bremen, King Harald died of his wounds in Jomsborg. That's right, home to the Jomsvikings, and what we suspect to be the most recent resting place of the grail.

Some believe Harald's body was laid to rest in his homeland, in Roskilde Cathedral, a short stroll from what's now a Viking ship museum on a fjord that feeds into the Kattegat Sea. However, we have evidence indicating otherwise, gleaned from a combination of old records and the work of Swedish archaeologist Sven Rosborn.

In 1841 a group of kids were playing in the Polish village of Wiejkowo, in what's now part of Wolin, site of Jomsborg, when the oldest of the gang, 12-year-old Heinrich Boldt, stumbled onto a crypt entrance at the ruins of a local church which was then a construction site. As kids will do, they kicked around a bit, then got bored and took off. But upon further examination, the crypt revealed a buried Viking hoard, which remarkably was left undisturbed, pretty much, for the next hundred years. Until 1945, when Polish soldier Michal Sielski and his brother Stefan also happened upon the crypt and chose to haul out the treasure. The booty included small discs, with the look and feel of crudely made buttons, which is what they were mistaken for, and got stored away amongst heirloom bric-a-brac and old sewing supplies. Some time later, Michal's 11-year-old great-granddaughter selected a particularly shiny one to take to show-and-tell. Her history teacher suspected she was onto something and notified the media. This was in 2014. The shiny button, it turns out, is what's now known as the Curmsun Disc, and is in fact a stamped gold coin. What's written on the coin may be our missing link, proving King Harald Bluetooth was interred here at Jomsviking headquarters, reported home of the grail.

The coin is stamped on both sides. The tail side (reverse) has a cross with four dots, common on tenth-century coins. The head side (obverse), however, has six tidy lines of block letters that read, "+*ARALD*

/ *CVRMSVN*+ / *REX AD TAN* / *ER*+*SCON*+*J* / *VMN*+*CIV* / *ALDIN*+,"
which is a transliteration of spoken Old Norse into written Medieval
Latin. It means "Harald Gormson, King of Danes, Scania, Jomsborg,
bishopric Aldinburg." In other words, this is Bluetooth's property, he
being King of South Sweden, Jomsborg, and the town of Oldenburg,
that bit of Holstein Germany reliant on the Danework, and this coin
belongs to him. It's one of the last examples of a coin inscribed with
translated Old Norse. The exclusively spoken language, captured in
infrequent runes, was already on its way out. But this particular piece,
along with the rest of the hoard, is the kind of thing one buries with
royalty, ready to be spent with mead-fuelled abandon at the gaming
tables of Valhalla. (Just because he converted the country to the new
religion doesn't mean he no longer believed in the ancient gods. As
Icelanders often say, "Why disbelieve anything? It could all be true.")

But back to our Templars hiding the grail "in the lake near Świątki."
A short distance away from Harald's Jomsborg marker stone, Świątki's
lake has vanished over the past millennium, the village now surrounded
by marshy ground where the lake once was. So, is the grail still buried in the area's swampland, or submerged in what's become a cluster
of outlying ponds? Impossible to say. But now we know, almost certainly, this was Jomsviking terrain, the Scandinavian voyagers traversing the planet as proto-crusading pagan knights, in a time-bending
way Arthurian in their grail quest. The enticing overlap in both time
and place leads us to believe that, at some point, these uniquely chivalrous, cosmopolitan Vikings *were* possessors of the grail.

Before we get ahead of ourselves, we need to pop back to Arthur's
homeland and introduce a couple of (somewhat) new characters, both
pivotal players in our saga. Let's start with Saint Michael, someone I
quite like, as he stars in each of the three pre-eminent faiths in this
part of the world: Islam, Judaism and Christianity.

Saint Michael was an angel – a kickass one – a white-winged warrior wielding a blade much like Excalibur (or Caliburn). High rank made him an archangel. And he apparently gave Satan's red-jerseyed team a proper thumping when their forces clashed at a series of violent donnybrooks in heaven. He's been credited with defeating an array of Satanic iterations, from archangel Samael to monster serpents and dragons. Michael's also seen as a healer, responsible for forces of nature and defender of good from evil. And it's that notion of overcoming evil, light vanquishing dark, that's so often represented as dragon slaying.

Saint Michael is often affiliated with Saint George, particularly in British military history. The esteemed Order of Saint Michael and Saint George is a prime example, an award based on the chivalry and honour associated with Arthurian knights. So let's meet George, patron saint of England, his background intriguingly rich with seeming contradiction.

George was born in the third century, at the height of the power of Rome. His mom was a Palestinian Christian with Greek heritage, his dad Turkish-Greek, also Christian, who fought in the Roman army, their heredity intricately interwoven through geography and religion. George followed in his dad's footsteps, joining the Roman army (like they had a choice) but rose in rank to serve in the elite Praetorian Guard, personal bodyguards to the Roman Emperor. George, however, refused to renounce Christianity, one of the requirements of service, and was put to death. For this, in part, he became a military saint and symbol of chivalry, still prevalent to this day. And somewhere in his short life history, like Michael, George too was credited with slaying the pesky dragon, an embodiment of evil. This particular accomplishment, however, didn't surface on George's resume until the 11th century.

The power of Saint George grew in England, particularly in the military. It became a battle cry: "For God, England and Saint George!" Shakespeare even coined a spin on it in *Henry V*, in which the king, in typical modesty, rallies his troops with, "For God, Harry, England and

Saint George!" In other words, "For *me*...oh yes, and god and country and the rest of you lot!"

The film *Excalibur* includes a scene that adds a relatable human element to the ritual. Arthur is a young squire at the time. They're preparing for a tournament and poor Arthur's misplaced his knight's sword. In a panic he searches the camp, desperate to find a blade for his master, when he stumbles upon the sword in the stone, which he pulls from the rock, but gets caught in the act.

"Put that back!" someone scolds. "You can't do that!"

So Arthur puts Excalibur back in the stone. But by now the hub-bub's attracted a crowd, and a few knights push in, each trying to tug the sword from the stone, which of course they're unable to do.

"You can't possibly be king!" someone says to Arthur. "You're not even knighted!"

And with that Arthur slides the sword rather effortlessly once more from the stone to collective gasps, and gives it to Uryens, the nearest knight, who, I might add, was being a jerk to Arthur.

"You're right," Arthur says to no one in particular. "I'm not yet a knight. Here, Uryens. Make me a knight." (A knight can knight an-other knight. Now, say that three times fast.)

Merlin pushes in. "What's this?!" he demands, remarkably sur-prised given the fact that he's a prophet.

Arthur kneels and passes Excalibur to Uryens, who now has the sword, raised, at Arthur's neck. For a tremulous moment Uryens hesi-tates, leaving us fearful as to what might happen next, but then Uryens touches the blade to Arthur's shoulders – once, twice, three times – and declares, "In the name of God, Saint Michael and Saint George, I give you the right to bear arms and the power to mete justice."

To which Arthur replies, "That duty I will solemnly obey, as knight and king." (Huzzah!)

So we have Michael and George in our story, dragon slayers guiding soldiers and knights in their quest for the grail, and perhaps a renewed iteration of Camelot. Now let's get back on the trail. In a tangential trek from Arthur's home, I'm following the dragon slayers, a meandering path bearing east (for now), following diverse topography bridging borders and faiths that'll take us from the land of Round Table Knights to the Crusades' last bastion of Islam.

On a previous visit to this remote stretch of Britain I ventured out on a miserable March night to climb a rise in the headland fronting a cemetery and sea, to Barnoon Workshop, a compact building in white and blue mimicking waves and capping the hill like a crown. (Since then, the workshop has relocated to the Quay.) It's a haunt I love – place and people – a respite for music, visual art and shared creativity. The Tate St Ives sits just down the slope, its turret-like walls a welcoming bastion of modern art. On another occasion I drank local bitter with new friends as we rang in midsummer, the pagan ritual acknowledging summer solstice. That night the final sun of spring set in bands of violet, purple and peach, easing into eerie calm sea. The night in March, however, there'd been no sign of sun in what seemed like forever. And I chose instead to veer from the roadway. I was on foot, a travel guitar slung over a shoulder, a packet of chocolate biscuits in hand, my offering to the gods, or in this case my artist friend and rock-and-roll guru Pete Giles, a.k.a. Bobby Wotnot. Scrambling down worn concrete in the dark, I crossed a wide crescent of soft, deep beach, each step the prolonged and grasping feel of quicksand. The froth of breakers gave a dim whitish glow, as though the softest night light of moonbeams were my guide. The tumble of waves, too, served as aural signposts, with a rattle and clack of sea stones thrown on the shore of Porthmeor Beach. What I experienced I call a "Gobletful of Porthmeor Rock and Roll." It's in the poetry collection *Forever Cast in Endless Time*, and goes like this:

Walking sandy shoreline joining pincer-points of land
a rocky crab-claw grasping at Atlantic
limpets, whelks, and cuttlefish-bone litter wave-tamped shore
with discs of slate like Lilliputian blackboards

sun set some time ago, I shuffle through the black
angled slope of beach my guide and line of breaking waves
something different in their sound, this evening somehow new
a noise like throwing countless dice at walls in shadowed lanes

each rising surge of water tumbling on the shore
tonight, is spinning fist-sized rocks like Stone Age chorus lines
rows of Neolithic dancers kicking with the tide
their score the roar of wind and wave, their band the sea and shore

these walking rocks, this rolling stroll, the sound surrounds me all
    around
somewhere a Bronze Age man my age smiles at the symmetry
more land was near when he was here, sea lower, far away
what we'd call Lyonesse, in time, where Guinevere was lost

to Lancelot, besot with Gwen, beseeched his men, for freedom ran
across the sand, from Camelot, beyond the End of Land
where Percival, and every knight, were able now to rest
each wayward haggard wanderer laid down in western barrows

with a dusty chalice boxed and stored in someone's attic
finally at peace, like you, like me, and all we see
or long to be, on nights like this, at one
ensconced, in endless darkened sea

A new day, the cusp of a balmy season, and I'm meeting my friend Clem
who lives nearby. He said he wants to show me around Penwith, and
although I've hiked the perimeter, endless points of interest still lie inland. Having a local guide whose company I enjoy seems an ideal way
to spend a sunny afternoon. We're strapped into his vintage car and he's
keeping me entertained and informed as we bomb along country roads

with views of moorland and sea. We have a few hours to enjoy before we're due to see a show at the Minack Theatre, where a band of mutual friends will perform Celtic folk rock on the clifftop seaside stage.

We start in Zennor, a place you may recall from a previous *Gone Viking* excursion, in which I hiked the coast path to the medieval pub and met a colossal strand of snot followed a short while later by the man from whence it emanated. This time around, Clem and I are exploring St Senara's Church. What we're looking at (and walking around) is a squat, stone building with a Norman look, built in the 12th century. But the church that was here before this was completed at the time of King Arthur, in the sixth century. A circular cemetery surrounds the chapel, used for burials since the Bronze Age, and I wonder how many knights are down there, lying beneath our feet.

The church is open and we poke around inside. There are a couple of other sightseers speaking in hushed tones and someone doing their best to pray in the cramped space. Along one compact wall is a 600-year-old pew, its bench-end intricately carved with a likeness of the Zennor mermaid. It's now known as the Mermaid Chair. The story of the mermaid's a good one, reminiscent of transitional pagan-Christian art, blending ancient lore with the new faith.

The legend claims the mermaid (although no one knew that's what she was at the time) attended church here, not frequently, but regularly, and would sing with the choir. Her voice was angelic and she never seemed to age, not unlike Stevie Nicks. Then a local lad named Mathey (Matthew) joined the choir, with a voice, apparently, as lovely as that of the mermaid. One day after service they were seen holding hands, strolling toward the sea, and were never seen again. Until one Sunday, a few years later, when a ship cast anchor in the bay. The sailors aboard said a mermaid surfaced, called to them, and explained their anchor was blocking the door to her home, keeping her from her children. The sailors obliged by weighing anchor and moving on to new moorage, but not before one of the ship's crew recognized her as the ageless singer from Zennor church, the one last seen hand-in-hand with Mathey.

The Mermaid Chair is where she sat when she came to pray and to sing. (The carved bench-end was added later.) But I can't bring myself to sit in it. Somehow it doesn't seem right. So instead I admire the workmanship. The wood's carved with fish, and the mermaid's holding a comb and hand-held mirror, admiring her reflection. Her hair, by the way, is fabulous.

Clem and I move on to a simple café next door for a cup of tea. Songbirds flit by and a couple of hikers cross the road to the moor and a hilltop Stone Age quoit. Clem and I share photos on our phones and swap stories. He's been a bit disappointed lately, he explains, as he's not quite as physically capable as he once was. Clem's 85. And explains he can no longer do a free handstand but has to rest his head on the ground while he does it, creating a tripod with his palms. I smile as he tells me. I'm quite sure I could *never* do that, with or without my head on the ground.

As we look through more photos, he shows me a few from a party he recently attended – a birthday celebration for a pal of his. In the pictures, helium balloons decorate a table, with three numeral ones in mylar tied next to a cake.

"These are great," I say. "But I don't understand the one-one-one."

"Oh, right," Clem says. "My friend was celebrating his hundred-and-eleventh birthday."

Naturally I think of Bilbo Baggins's eleventy-first celebration, but what comes from my mouth is, "Wait, what? A hundred-and-eleven?!"

"Yes," Clem chuckles. "He's the second oldest person in Britain right now. But between you and me, the older chap's not looking too well. My friend's got his fingers crossed!"

"Huh," I manage to say, wondering what *does* one do with a dozen birthday cards from the reigning monarch?

We tour around some more, get lost at a couple of roundabouts, reorient ourselves and make our way to the show, where we grab goat curries from the concession and settle in on carved stone seats with rented cushions. There's a good crowd, maybe 300. It's a clear evening and sun's setting just past Land's End. The temperature drops alarmingly and breeze off the water has us shivering despite multiple layers of clothes.

When the band comes on, the singer makes a grand entrance, descending curved stone steps that seem to hover above the ocean. She's wearing an elegant gown with a slit high up the thigh. They finish the opening number and she bolts from the stage, returning moments later in jeans and a parka. The crowd laughs and gives her a standing ovation.

The first time I hiked this stretch of sand and rock coast a short distance from the Minack, I gradually became hypothermic, my deadening digits resembling sausages straight from the freezer. We got up early, Deb and I, having slept fitfully in a smoke-saturated room with an open patio door that let in gusty squalls and, as we gagged down stale biscuits and coffee, relentless hail.

We had technical gear, covered packs, rain pants and jackets, all of which were soaked through in minutes. Our packs were too big, turning us in blustery wind like sails, and we staggered along the shore, following a three-mile curve of coast. Away to our left, a wall of frigid mist hung directly offshore like a surgery curtain. We did our best to make light of the situation, forced humour as stale as our breakfast, neither of which offered much sustenance. Doubled over, we zigzagged west from Marazion toward Penzance, our plan being to round the headland and make our way to Lamorna through Mousehole (pronounced "*Mow*zle," with Mow like the first syllable of Maui).

Had the weather been clear (and above freezing) it might've been a lovely view of the flagstone crossing to St Michael's Mount, a tidal footpath that submerges the walkway isthmus twice daily, turning the castle and surrounding gardens into an island, like Normandy's Mont-Saint-Michel. Both places were given to the Benedictines, this one believed to have been the site of a monastery since the eighth century. In an interesting twist, this locale is often confused with "St Michael's on the Mount," the church at Glastonbury Tor, our Lady of the Lake's Avalon home, where Lancelot might've been raised.

In spite of Henry VIII's dissolution of monasteries, St Michael's Mount remained a pilgrimage site, having been granted an indulgence by Pope Gregory in the 11th century. An indulgence, by the way, is a remission of punishment in the Catholic faith. Not so much a get-out-of-jail-free card as a get-out-of-jail-sooner card, on a reduced sentence plea. Historically, pilgrimage and hefty donations were the surest ways to be looked upon favourably from on high. But for those not financially flush, pilgrimage became the most viable option for reserved seating at the good table in the afterlife.

Now, where were we? Ah, yes, our sub-zero trek from St Michael's Mount, a hellish start to our journey of indulgence. As my teeth chattered uncontrollably and I lost feeling in extremities, I thought of those nasty Everest photos of climbers losing toes and noses. Sure, I could set myself up for that timeless gag: No nose?! How do you smell?! *Well, it depends on what I've eaten, and if it's bath day.* But that struck me as a hell of a price to pay for a mediocre joke I could probably share regardless. So we stumbled into Penzance and caught a taxi to haul us and our outsized packs to the smugglers' haven of Lamorna Cove.

Before we leave this memory-lane side trip, let me share a couple of fun historical tidbits. Some time after the Middle Ages, this part of the world became a hub for smuggling. There are a few reasons for this: increased taxation, this area being politically and geographically isolated, and the fact that the local economy and culture felt (feel?) more closely connected with elsewhere, not unlike long-standing Scottish–French relations bypassing London. But as war between England and France resumed, or continued, anyone in Britain who bought stuff from the French (thereby supporting France financially) was considered a traitor to the British Crown. However, when your gin and brandy suddenly triple in price, it's a heck of a motivator to buy direct. Combine this with the fact that the area's made up of jagged coastline providing countless bays and concealed moorage, along with a populace experienced in navigating the waters, and you've got yourself the makings of a flourishing smuggling industry.

With England's resources going toward financing the war and its navy, there wasn't much in the way of policing of this sort of behaviour, yet. But the very nature of smuggling, along with the potential penalties if caught, still made a clandestine approach essential. Business was conducted, most often, under cover of night, with ship-to-shore exchanges happening in inlets and small bays using rowing gigs, dories and hooded lanterns. Shippers got increasingly creative in concealment and ship design, building false bottoms and hidden storage holds. And it's from here we get the expressions "all above board," meaning not concealed below decks, and "the coast is clear," which is fairly self-explanatory.

In Lamorna I undertook a mini-pilgrimage by trekking to the Smuggler's Cove Pub, figuring I'd need to give a wink or secret handshake to get a swig of untaxed gin. But the place made our smoke-infused room in Marazion seem evergreen fresh by comparison. So instead I traipsed away from the water for a fully taxed drink at a place that didn't smell like three centuries of unfiltered Player's Navy Cuts.

The next time we trekked around St Michael's Mount it was a gorgeous day: hot sun, cerulean sky and languid, cotton ball clouds. We behaved like proper pilgrims, shoelessly sloshing our way through shallow sea to the castle perched on a dais-like plinth of offshore rock. It was the start of summer, and gardens surrounding the castle were layered in lush greens and impressionist shades of blossoms. Succulents clung to steep banks while planted flowers craned through greenery and creeping vines. Songbirds vied with gulls for lead vocals, an Eden-like hum of fauna swirling above flora.

Following a modest climb and circumambulation of the island, we settled in for tea and scones, ensuring we put jam on first, then cream, as they do here in Cornwall, not like those madcap Devonians who insist on putting jam atop cream. We meandered around the castle parapets, savouring views of blue and a seemingly distant shoreline. I kept an eye on the time, wanting to walk back to the mainland ahead of the tide and not rely on the small passenger ferry. From the Marazion shore, I could make out the pilgrims' path of St Michael's Way veering inland, over the fat of the peninsula, in the direction of Knill's Monument.

John Knill was an 18th-century Cornish mayor who erected a 50-foot granite obelisk to commemorate, well, himself. In most records he's described as being eccentric, which as we know is a polite way of saying crazy but rich. In spite of his final wishes, or perhaps because of them, the locals buried him elsewhere. His towering monument, however, still tops the high point of Worvas Hill overlooking St Ives and serves as a landmark (in clear weather) for a broad sweep of the surrounding area. I've trudged through snow at the site, a rarity in this part of the world. It was another moment in which I felt my pilgrim-like pursuits were putting me to the test.

The British Pilgrimage Trust calls this stretch a micro-pilgrimage, delineating the trek as a 12- or 13-mile tramp from St Michael's Mount to the village of Lelant. Lelant is on the Hayle Estuary, which feeds into St Ives Bay. As well as being an ancient site for salt harvesting, Lelant is significant to our saga in a number of ways. There's evidence indicating it was a Roman fort as well as the burial place of Saint Euny, the monk some credit with bringing Christianity to Cornwall from Ireland. But older legends claim a local Celtic woman named Anta was the first to teach Christianity here, an early version of the new faith, a nudging shift from druidic ways, circumventing the gods Rome left behind. The transition is still evident in ornate, curved Celtic crosses that share prominence alongside the simple right angles of the Church of England.

Lelant is also key in that it served as a port for pilgrims making their way south to Spain's Cathedral of Santiago de Compostela, known as the Way of Saint James or Camino Way, and St Michael's Way is part of that Camino de Santiago. By landing at Lelant and trekking overland to St Michael's Mount, pilgrims were able to bypass rugged coastal track that undulates around Penwith, not to mention avoiding tumultuous water at Land's End. Yes, that choppy stretch of Celtic Sea that surrounds the Isles of Scilly, our Ice Age islands that neighbour one version of Avalon. It remains one of those water crossings where passengers fight more for sickness bags than life preservers.

Now Lelant is a small, pleasant village with good pubs, coastal walks and golf. Traipsing here on a few occasions, I've slogged through soft sand on the beach, dodged rising tide and explored bits of shipwreck. Other times I've marched along pathway carving through yellow bloomed gorse that exudes an exotic, tropical aroma of coconut and mango. The sandy dirt path's often littered in snails, their shells a swirl of amber and black, descendants of those the Romans introduced as simple, sustainable protein. The wide finger of land between footpath and sea is a series of towering dunes, marram grass holding embankments in place. And it's these walls of shifting sand that are said to have buried the transitional church of Saint Anta.

Along the way are signposts with gold-painted acorns marking the coastal path, until you encounter the next set of markers, engraved with a stylized scallop shell, the look of a lighthouse subduing the dark, in a way dragon slaying. This is the symbol of the Camino Way. Which officially puts us on the pilgrims' path, our destination Spain, resting place of Saint James. And, I now realize, a possible home to the grail. Which we'll examine soon enough. But first, we need to traverse a good chunk of Europe to get there.

2

BELGIUM AND FRANCE

Flying away from England, we've made a swooping turn south. Below, the West Country stretches to Land's End, sparkling in afternoon light that glints off the sea. Across the Bristol Channel I see rugged Welsh coast, reaching toward Ireland. And I'm awash in a bliss I don't fully understand, perhaps the result of being airborne in sun. Or saying yes to a refill of wine.

I plot the north coast of Cornwall with the width of my index finger and believe I can spot the jagged bit of land where Arthur's castle once sat, staring wistfully over the water. The south portion of Wales, which we're now directly above, up from Cardiff and Newport, is the site of Caerleon, what's known as King Arthur's Table. Geoffrey of Monmouth pegged it as such, the place the knights met to organize quests. But the circle of stone walls and grass has been identified as the Roman amphitheatre of the fortress of Isca. In further Welsh writings the site was called Arthur's Court, and despite archaeological evidence proving otherwise, it's still considered by many to be as authentically Arthurian as the Cornish castle we just came from.

The Welsh flag does nothing to disprove the Arthurian cycle, a red dragon on a green and white background, the dragon a symbol of Wales for a thousand years. Green and white are the colours of Tudor, the flag carried by Henry VII to St Paul's Cathedral in the 15th century, acknowledging Tudor Welsh heritage. But a part of me sees something more, beyond the pride and the dragon, almost taunting Saint George, perhaps glorifying the one that got away.

While gazing dreamily down on Welsh Marches, the borderlands, I'd be remiss not to mention King Offa. Offa ruled Mercia, a vast English chunk next to Wales, for 40 years, from 757 to July of 796. (Sadly, no song was written about the summer of '96. The eighth-century rhyming scheme doesn't work nearly as well as the 20th-century summer Bryan Adams sang about).

King Offa of Mercia fits neatly into our mosaic for a number of reasons. Firstly, despite being a frequently overlooked monarch, he was probably the most influential Anglo-Saxon king before Alfred the Great arrived a hundred years later. Offa made no bones about delineating church and state, to a degree. Following a prolonged squabble with the Archbishop of Canterbury, Offa had the Pope divide the archdiocese of Canterbury in two, effectively reducing church power while ensuring he had an ally in at least one diocese.

Secondly, following decades of conflict with the Welsh, Offa had a barricade constructed, separating his kingdom from Wales. Known as Offa's Dyke, it's a massive ditch with a raised earthen wall running the length of the English–Welsh border. From an engineering perspective, it's nearly as impressive as the Pyramids or Hadrian's Wall.

Lastly, in the same manner as King Harald and others stamped coins, King Offa too was a great printer of money, coins being not only a means to standardize currency for economic efficiency and ease of trade, but each shiny disc being its own little piece of political propaganda. And here's what sets Offa apart. Most coins, like the one from Harald's Jomsborg hoard, were struck based on Roman models, naming the monarch du jour on the obverse, occasionally with additional info, the way American money declares "In God We Trust." But as well as making new penny coins consistent with common currency in circulation across Europe, Offa also printed dinars – Arabic–English coins – or at least one that we know of. Offa's lone gold dinar, housed in the British Museum, is stamped with OFFA REX (King Offa), which is encircled in Arabic that roughly translates to "There is no deity but Allah, and Muhammad is the apostle of Allah." Like pennies at that time, dinars were the most common (and therefore important) coinage in use around the Mediterranean. So here we have forward-looking, politically and ecclesiastically motivated Offa letting it be known that not only is he king of where he is, but he's also a (self-proclaimed) player in global finance and trade. In other words, money talks, no matter where you come from or who you pray to.

An interesting side-note in the study of ancient coins is that far more die-casts and stamps exist to make forgeries, while few legitimate minting tools have ever been found. Based on its design, we can be fairly certain Offa's dinar, although legal tender, was copied from an original, as the Arabic script is backwards.

Meanwhile, far below, Wales has grown coy under a blanket of cottony cloud, while our plane seems to have finally chosen its flight path. We've left British airspace (I guess), and I can just make out another channel, *the Channel*, widening as we bear north, until I see nothing but water. Making our way toward Brussels, we're heading into the heart of Flanders, the populous north half of Belgium. The link here is that this part of the continent witnessed a tidal wave of emigration to Britain, comparable to the exodus of Viking settlers from Scandinavia. A thousand years ago, the population of Germanic Dutch-speakers in this fertile pocket of western Europe grew faster than the land could accommodate. For this reason, an exodus of Flemish, or Flemings – skilled farmers, merchants and labourers – relocated to the arable lands around Offa's Dyke. And as William the Conqueror increased his grasp, slowly but surely encroaching on Wales, Flemings became a politically shrewd pool of immigrants, not only driving the economy but creating a peaceful buffer between the feisty Welsh and the rest of William's England.

Finally screeching down into Belgium's capital, we begin the tedious wait for our luggage. Not sure why; possibly labour contracts, but Brussels International has, I believe, the world's slowest baggage handlers. After what feels like a week of waiting at arrivals, we gather checked bags and head into the country.

When Julius Caesar added this real estate to Rome, they called it Gallia Belgica. He found it economically lacking but comprised of resolute patriots, locals unwilling to simply let Rome take over. For some inexplicable reason Belgians were uneager to be subjugated, ruled and taxed by foreigners with scrub-brushes topping their helmets. But a few dozen legions marching through town does tend to make a compelling case to just go with it, and start learning Latin.

At our accommodation, I settle in and unpack. Wait, this isn't my bag! No matter. I find something that fits, a flattering dress in autumn tones, and we head out to explore. My hikers look silly with the frock but my calves really pop, so I carry on.

South of us is French-speaking Wallonia, larger geographically with a comparatively small population, still hurting economically, much like when Julius arrived. But we're sticking to the northern part for now, where Dutch-Belgian and English make up most of the conversation. The local flag's not dissimilar to the Welsh one, only here it's a lion rearing on a background of yellow, a beast with a decidedly dragonish appearance, its tongue or possibly flame licking out in a fiery lash.

Following a pleasant drive through broad fields of freshly turned soil, we come to our destination: Roman ruins from the first century, dated at around 50 A D. We park and wander the site, broken flagstones that were likely the entryway or terrace of a villa, assuredly someone of high rank or wealth, tied closely to Rome. Being here is another time warp, the same sensory connection I feel at every ancient site. This one preceded Arthur by a few centuries, the historical remnants here of wealth, privilege and foreign rule quite the opposite of the Arthurian cycle. But Flemings no doubt had their own version of a sword-bearer legend, a hero to fight forces imposed from abroad.

As intriguing as these ancient flagstones are, with more research I learn they're only one of a hundred Roman sites across Flanders. And whether it was that influx of Italian capital or political coordination, a few centuries later Flanders was an economic powerhouse. In the Middle Ages, the canal and river port towns of Bruges and Ghent became some of Europe's richest, most urbanized centres, a crossroads for the Hanseatic League, a commercial confederation of guilds across northern Europe. Weaving wool, making lace and shipping goods drove the economy, which continued into the Industrial Revolution, with

Flanders leading the continent in manufacturing and trade. Even now, Flanders remains one of the wealthiest spots in the world.

To do this place justice we explore one of those centres, the UNESCO World Heritage Site of Bruges, which makes an appearance in the *Anglo-Saxon Chronicle*. With an eye now to tourism, Bruges has maintained (or reclaimed) all its medieval glory. Buildings, it would seem, are exactly as they were half a millennium ago. Stone and brick structures with towering belfries border tidy canals, the whole striking me as a quaint and better-preserved Amsterdam. Along with fancy chocolates, lace-making remains one of the main draws, a delicate process unchanged, more or less, for the past 500 years, still managed and operated predominantly by nuns.

Strolling past windows of chocolate and lace, I make my way to the centre of town, in the midst of a ring road and looping canal. What faces me now is the Basilica of the Holy Blood, a compact church with an entryway that seems arabesque, the look of a two-dimensional onion dome. The building was originally Romanesque in design, transformed over time to Gothic. But when I climb the steps and peer inside, interior décor's decidedly Catholic: rich brocade, vibrant enamel and paint, stained glass and an abundance of gold. Constructed in the 12th century, the church is where Thierry of Alsace, Count of Flanders and decorated Holy Land crusader, returned to house a relic of the blood collected in the grail by Joseph of Arimathea.

The actual relic is a vial containing what's said to be a small piece of cloth Joseph used to blot blood when he removed Jesus from the cross, part of the process of cleansing the body for burial. This is recorded in the *Acts of Pilate*, derived from Hebrew and written by Nicodemus, considered an associate of Jesus. Following the crusade of 1147–1149, Thierry's brother-in-law Baldwin III of Jerusalem presented Thierry with the relic as a reward for his military service, no doubt to the sound of colleagues grumbling about nepotism.

So perhaps the grail wasn't exactly used to catch a flow of blood like fountain soda at 7-Eleven, but instead as a receptacle for this venerated swatch of stained fabric. The whole piece is a work of art, substantial in size, capped by two gold coronet crowns set with gems. The vial's made of rock crystal and suspended in a glass canister, giving us a relatively clear view of the cloth and the blood, which was said, for a time, to liquify at noonish on Fridays. In 1310, Pope Clement V granted indulgences to pilgrims who travelled here to see the relic. And for a moment I wonder if this elaborate piece could itself be the grail, but testing has shown the vial was crafted in the 11th or 12th century as a perfume bottle in Byzantine Constantinople, the great Viking city of Miklagard. Which fits our timeline of Thierry receiving it and bringing it here.

Feeling I've placed another puzzle piece in our jigsaw, I can't help but think that with all these indulgences I'm racking up as a wandering pilgrim, things are looking pretty good for the future. Perhaps the maître d' in the sky might yet wave me up from the back of the queue for that coveted table with a view.

South of where we are is the Duchy of Luxembourg, a relatively tiny place but one with an outsized history. This small parcel of land produced a succession of Holy Roman Emperors, originally known as Emperor of the Romans and later as the German–Roman Emperor. For a few centuries in the Middle Ages the role was held in conjunction with the titles King of Italy and King of Germany. In other words, the person in charge around here.

The area has indications of human habitation dating back 35,000 years, among some of the oldest in Europe. Celts settled the area ahead of the Romans over 2,000 years ago, living on tributaries of the Rhine and Meuse rivers that flow into the North Sea. When Julius arrived, conquering Gaul and part of Germania, he snapped up this prime land as well. Compared to the Roman experience elsewhere, the annexation went smoothly, with Celts living peacefully for four centuries under the Pax Romana. When Rome eventually retreated, Germanic Franks moved in, their language essentially what's spoken here today.

Location (location, location) is what made it important, strategically placed between Germany, France and Belgium, and close to the Netherlands, all major traders with invaluable waterways. These liquid roadways not only connected the region to the rest of the world but enabled Norse, Swedes and Danes to row *this* direction as well, traversing most of the continent.

Serving as another crossroads, Luxembourg is effectively a geopolitical market-cross in northwest Europe, and for this reason a substantial stronghold has been here a very long time. The most impressive fortress was built on a rock outcrop known as the Bock, its ramparts increasing in size and fortification over time. It's been called the Gibraltar of the North, controlled by Habsburgs for centuries. And it's the Habsburgs who play into our saga.

The Habsburg Empire, ultimately known as the Habsburg Dynasty, was closely affiliated with the Holy Roman Empire and ran things across much of Europe through the Middle Ages (and beyond), encompassing Austria, Germany, the Netherlands and Spain. Here the term empire refers to a union or cooperation of crowns, functioning in judicious coexistence with Rome, reminiscent of King Harald's (and others') politically driven adoption of Christianity. True separation of church and state, it would seem, was not yet a priority.

Let's hang a left (on the map) into France for a while, a country as intricately linked to the grail as Arthur and Saint George's England. At this point our grail legend picks up in the 12th century, when French poet Chrétien de Troyes first wrote of Lancelot and Percival. Chrétien's heroic verse and tales of romance had become all the rage amongst noble courtiers at the time. But his most ambitious project, *Perceval, le Conte du Graal* (*Percival, the Story of the Grail*), remained unfinished, leaving us to wonder what else he knew, and what mysteries he intended to unravel. His work is considered the earliest written account of the grail, and he specifically refers to it being a plate or dish, rather than a cup.

Despite his story of the grail being frustratingly truncated, it was picked up and added to with a whopping 54,000 additional lines contributed by others, the whole becoming what's known as the *Four Continuations*. This work was then utilized by German knight, poet and medieval singer-songwriter Wolfram von Eschenbach, who identified the grail as a stone, perhaps fuelling the notion of the sword and the stone. Going forward, we'll find further examples of the grail being referred to as a stone. Whether alluding to a grail stone was literal, encoded or somehow allegorical remains uncertain. But what I like to take from this (and you can too) is that in the event *this* book should end abruptly, fear not. Others are sure to pick up the pieces and turn it into a comprehensive albeit disjointed story.

Meanwhile, at almost the same time, Robert de Boron was writing *Joseph d'Arimathie*, in which we learn of Joseph getting his hands on the grail. But here in France, a Lancelot grail cycle develops into its own storyline, in which Galahad is believed to be Lancelot's son. This is also known as the Vulgate Cycle, wherein Galahad surpasses his dad's knightly accomplishments and eventually becomes the grail bearer. Subsequent authors have Percival linking up with Galahad and other travel companions toward the end of the grail quest, where they witness Galahad's ascension into heaven, directly to the VIP table.

Arthur Hughes, the Pre-Raphaelite artist, captures it, or at least the moments leading up to it, in his 1870 painting *Sir Galahad, the Quest for the Holy Grail*. In the piece, Galahad and his white steed, visibly knackered, stumble their way along a path through brambles and spear-like rocks. They still look marvellous, mind you, Galahad's red cape flowing in the breeze, gold plate mail polished to a sheen, but he leans heavily on his lance. Three angels swoop toward our hero, over trees, under stars, hand-held censers swinging from chains. The look, overall, is one of exhaustion, and imminent conclusion. What I don't see, however, is the certainty of completion. It remains more quest-like than conclusive, as though we've yet to reach the finish line. And what stands out to me more than anything, easily overlooked in the painting's lower right corner, is a frothy splash of water on rock. Is it a burbling brook, or the cusp of sea? And if sea, *which* sea? What Land's End is this, exactly? Which leaves me desperate to pull back, to see a bit more of where this is. It's another puzzle completed but with the edges arriving too soon.

I suppose we'll have to satisfy ourselves with a couple of theoretical sides to our Rubik's cube finished, for now. In the meantime, if you don't mind, I'm going to spend time on my own, exploring Paris. Obligatory croissants, strong coffee and a nagging urge to smoke Gitanes. Not that I smoke, mind you, but I believe I'd be good at it. I know when I was 12 and tried it, I looked incredibly cool. Once the coughing subsided.

Some time later, now reconnected with Deb, we head out from the French capital to visit friends in a leafy green suburb. Their home resembles what I imagine ancient Roman villas were like when first built, their remnants the well-trodden rubble we explored in Flanders. Here the property lots are large, trees well aged in a colourful blend of chlorophyll – purple and green – Japanese elm, maple and oak. To turn this gathering into a party of sorts, our hosts have invited the neighbour to supper. I'm keen to practise my French, the neighbour eager to work on his English. So we compromise and stand in silence, smiling, nodding and methodically working our way through a wheel of brie the size of a tractor tire. The squeal of youngsters running and playing emanates from another yard through a hedge. Sun sets and the next-door noises increase in volume. Despite not knowing the words, there's no mistaking the intonation of pleading children and tired parents.

We sit down outside in the dark to a meal of mostly raw chicken. The lack of light keeps us from noticing, aside from the mouth-feel of poultry sashimi, reminding me of an episode of Anthony Bourdain's travel show where the diners are served uncooked chicken, simply butchered, deboned and served on a platter.

"Aren't you worried?" he asked his dining companion.

"About what?"

"Um, you know. Salmonella?" he said, as tactfully as possible.

"Oh, no. The chicken is very fresh."

"Ah," Tony said, and proceeded to eat and, we're left to assume, not get sick.

Unlike us. Our chicken was not "very fresh." If there's one thing I remember from culinary school, it's to cook the fucking chicken. However. In hindsight I feel we were excellent houseguests, not becoming violently ill until we were elsewhere (and then writing about it). Long story short, when being examined by a doctor when you don't speak each other's language, suffice it to say I'll do quite well if I ever play charades and have to portray the grisly physical effects of acute food poisoning.

I explore (a small bit of) the Louvre, joining the throng to see the *Mona Lisa* and headless *Nike of Samothrace*. Then a stroll down the Champs Élysées to the Arc de Triomphe, with a backtrack to the two spans of Pont Neuf, where I imagine Ragnar Lothbrok rowing his fleet in 845, the sweeping serpentine of the Seine reminiscent of the last few bends in the Thames. While the rest of Paris celebrated Easter, Ragnar and his entourage hauled away a staggering 7,000 pounds of silver and gold in the form of tribute, which is a genteel way of saying extortionate shakedown. In an interesting side-note, stories of Ragnar claim he was a slayer of serpents, perhaps like the dragons our saints battled in Arthurian England.

SWITZERLAND AND GERMANY

So how does Switzerland play into our saga? In a couple of ways, as you'll see. Firstly, this unwaveringly neutral, landlocked country serves as another crossroads for its large, western European neighbours: France, Italy and Germany. Which you can see, and hear, when you travel through this relatively compact area. Each language becomes prevalent as you near respective borders. Travelling around the country I feel as though I'm on a Ouija board, sliding this way and that at the end of uncertain hands, drifting culturally between French, German and Italian, with an occasional pocket of Romansh. English, however, is spoken everywhere. And I like the way the border with France bisects Lac Léman (Lake Geneva), a slender finger of water that doglegs, as though some fair-minded portioner said, "I'll slice, you choose."

The country's famous for watches, chocolate and banking. It's a wealthy nation with a high standard of living, one of the first places to experiment with simply paying people a living salary. Not welfare; not minimum wage. Just the government paying folks so they can enjoy a decent life and not go to work.

Despite its seemingly passive nature as a nation, it's the Swiss Army that's brought me here. Obviously they have those knives that enable you to trim your nails while eating, which although gross is quite convenient. But it's actually the Swiss Guards that represent a link in our tale, the elite little army of Swiss nationals who guard the Pope, something I view as an updated model of the Roman Emperor's Praetorian Guard, where George worked before moving on to sainthood and dragon slaying.

The notion of hiring highly trained mercenaries from abroad to protect the person in charge has a long history, the idea being, in part, to eliminate local prejudice and reduce the likelihood of old grudges. We saw this with the Varangian Guard, Viking warriors hired from Scandinavia to protect the Byzantine Emperor. Alexander the Great had a version as well, with his Macedonian Somatophylakes. And like Alexander's personal bodyguards, Swiss Guards were originally selected from the nobility. Imagine if Wills and Harry carried on their military training, became more like Jason Bourne, then got a well-paid gig elsewhere. And although elements of that continue, Swiss Guards no longer (necessarily) come from noble stock. Current criteria include a formal education, a height requirement and devout Catholicism, a sharp 180 from George's time.

The Swiss Guards (who aren't here, but at the Vatican) may be best known for their Renaissance-era uniforms, one of the oldest unchanged military outfits anywhere, which they don for special ceremonies. Outfitted with blue doublets with ruffs and berets, striped tunics in Medici colours – red, yellow and blue – and extravagant, ostrich-plumed helmets, each soldier's equipped with an axe-topped pike, a long, lethal weapon used (in the day) to bring down cavalry. In a fun nugget of word history, the tuft of feathers in the headdress is called a "panache."

We'll get a chance to see these hired guns (or hiked pikes, I suppose) in action soon enough, when we make our way to Rome. But that's another day. For now, let's explore this peaceful pocket of planet. Flying into Geneva, I enjoy a bird's eye view of the Jet d'Eau, Geneva Water Fountain, a 140-metre-high jet of white water blasting from the southwest corner of Lake Geneva. From up here it looks like one of the white feathers in the deep blue beret of a Swiss Guard. I check into a hotel, have a nap to shake off residual jet lag, and start my day (midday) with the best cup of hot chocolate ever, knowing I'm now ruined for cocoa anywhere else, ever again.

The streets of Geneva are clean and orderly, architecture a blend of medieval and modern. I have a cheese fondue, which feels like the thing to do. And decide I quite like the idea of a big bowl of cheese for supper. If I make this a dietary staple I can't imagine needing to save for retirement. Maybe have another go at Gitanes while I'm at it.

I spend time in Lausanne (highlights: potato rösti and a dusty old record store, where I treat myself to the Police's *Reggatta de Blanc*, because a vinyl LP is such a convenient souvenir to stuff in a backpack). Then I visit the capital (federal city) of Bern, medieval architecture hugging the banks of the Aare River. It feels, I suspect, much as it did when the town came into being in the 12th century, right around the time Robert de Boron and Chrétien de Troyes ignited our Arthurian and Lancelot cycles on the French side of Geneva's feather-fountained lake.

Now I've found what I consider another tidy link, bridging our saga with a bit of modernity. I'm riding a slick commuter train along the lake's north shore, travelling east to Montreux. It's a resort town, nestled in a bay with the Alps looming in the distance. Mary Shelley, her hubby Percy Bysshe, and Lord Byron hung out here in the summer of 1816, when Mary came up with the outline for her novel *Frankenstein*. But beyond the literary connection, I have my own tangential pilgrimage to complete, one every rock-and-roll fan can appreciate.

If you've ever picked up a guitar, the first lick you played, without fail, was the opening three-chord riff of Deep Purple's "Smoke on the Water." The lyrics refer to coming out to Montreux, here, on Lake Geneva's shoreline. It's where the band came to record that classic album. It goes on to explain the true story of a building burning down, forcing the band to move their recording session elsewhere, but giving them the fodder for a career-making tune. Not sure if this particular pilgrimage earns me a papal indulgence, but the *personal* indulgence is worth it. I celebrate with pizza, Kronenbourg and a lake view, where the now famous building once stood.

From Montreux, I follow the shore to the end of the water. To the south, Mont Blanc straddles France and Italy, while a short distance east the Matterhorn stands astride Italy and Switzerland. Iconic landscape. But the reason I'm here is Chillon Castle, the Château de Chillon. Unsurprisingly, this place was established by Romans, as it sits at another key throughway, in this case a channel to France and Germany through Burgundy and Vaud, with the Rhône beelining to Italy.

Chillon itself is a small limestone island, and the ultimate lookout, a panorama of water and mountain. And while it's been a key military locale since the time of the Roman Empire, construction of what I'm looking at now began in the tenth century, when Harald Gormsson was accumulating coins and raising his son Sven, unaware the boy was unwilling to wait for his dad to relinquish the throne. And if we *really* want to date this place, excavation has revealed stuff dating back to the Bronze Age. But the first written records pertaining to the castle are from 1005. Soon afterward, the House of Savoy ran things, keeping order with a fleet of ships on Lake Geneva.

This castle is a touchstone, encapsulating the Jomsviking era, in proximity to Rome, at the start of the Crusades, all of which connect to our grail. Crossroads, therefore, in more ways than one. Now classified as a Swiss Cultural Property of National Significance, the castle's a hub of tourist activity, and has been for a couple of centuries. Poets love it, and I admit it's a romantic setting. Byron made his way here for inspiration. Victor Hugo as well. Even Alexandre Dumas. Which brings to mind a classic radio faux pas we laughed at years ago when a live, on-air announcer, doing her best with unfamiliar names, made a phonetic leap to introduce the work of one "Alexander Dumbass." Now that's all I see (or hear) when we speak of the famous French writer.

I join a clump of tour groups and creep about the castle for a while. Thick stone walls exude a penetrating chill, and ancient aromas seep from the rockwork. A few centuries of armour and weapons are on display, suits of plate mail that appear child-sized, but of course were the size of knights in the day. A wall is hung with maces, swords and morning stars, with a cluster of pikes resembling a terrifying rack of pool cues.

Despite the history on display, everyone, it seems, is here to see the dungeon, what the castle became known for in the 16th century. We descend and the temperature somehow keeps dropping as we duck under lintels and beams. Each stone stair is now round from a thousand years of traipsing feet. In the lowest and deepest part of the dungeon we see centuries-old manacles, rusty and worn, and I'm sure I'm not the only one who feels the icy presence of long-dead inmates.

Perhaps the most famous prisoner here was 16th-century monk François Bonivard, deemed a religious enemy by the dukes of Savoy. Imprisoned in 1530, Bonivard spent six years pacing this tiny enclosure of frigid rock. And I stand silent with a handful of strangers as we stare at the dusty floor, where a groove is still visible, carved from the monk's shackle-chain as he paced, a deep-rutted scar in the stone.

Now, I'm afraid to say, we come to a dark period in our saga. It may surprise you to know that in pursuing the grail our tales of death, prison and torture aren't entirely rosy. I'm back in a plane, temporarily, flying over Germany toward Munich. As comedian Norm Macdonald said in explaining his fear of Germany, "Now, I don't know how many of you are history buffs, but..." And yes, last century, when much of the world took the lead from Saint George (and Michael) to hack away at a new kind of dragon (with a small, bad moustache), the grail again sought the spotlight.

"The quesht for the grail is not archaeology, it's a race againsht evil. Do you undershtand me?!" says Dr. Jones Sr. (Sean Connery) to Indy. Which assumes our grail search has us outwitting Nazis to find it. Not entirely relevant to our saga, but fun to say in the voice.

In that vein, directly below our flight path is the German town of Michelstadt, home to one Otto Rahn. Born in 1904, Rahn excelled at school, went to university to study archaeology, and had his own version of an Indiana Jones-type professor and mentor who inspired him to pursue his passion, that being the study of Percival and the grail.

Which Rahn did, with extensive, controversial research into Catharism and what's known as the massacre of Montségur.

Part of Rahn's studies focused on Lohengrin, Percival's son, who plays a larger role in German Arthurian literature. Lohengrin, also considered a grail knight, may be best known for this unusual mode of transport, a boat pulled by swans. And in this literary blend of the Arthurian and Crusade cycles, Lohengrin's dad, known as Parzival around here, takes over as protector of the grail from the Fisher King, assuming the moniker Grail King. This comes predominantly from a version of the tale penned by Wolfram von Eschenbach (our German poet-musician-knight) and became the Wagnerian opera *Parsifal*, a few years after *Tristan und Isolde* hit the stage.

So let's delve into the meat of Rahn's grail research, specifically Cathars and Montségur. Catharism is Gnostic or dualist in nature, a hybrid faith combining religious scriptures with traditional beliefs, reminiscent of Icelandic Vikings at the turn of the first millennium as Christianity enveloped west Europe. The Icelandic Althing (parliament) decreed the nation would officially be Christian, in keeping with King Harald's prudent policy-making amongst Danes, as it was the most effective way to maintain peace. But it was generally understood anyone could worship whatever gods they chose, as long as they did so privately. A version, I suppose, of don't ask, don't tell. In its way, it was progressive and inclusive. People would be judged on their actions, not some convoluted notion of who or what they prayed to.

The Cathar view of things, however, was essentially black and white, literally, as they felt two gods existed, a good one and a bad one, as though both George *and* the dragon had recurring roles to play in the order of things. Followers of the faith (in theory) lived their lives doing their best to be "perfect," which to Cathars meant something along the lines of attaining knowledge and being adept at their teachings, with an eye toward enlightenment.

Considered more relaxed than the rigidity of Catholicism, the new religion caught on, taking hold across northern Italy and France.

Which, as you can imagine, ruffled feathers (panache) in a big way in the Vatican and Rome. The Cathars likely pushed things a bit as they claimed the New Testament aligned with the good, the Old Testament with the bad. And went so far as to refer to themselves exclusively as Good Christians. So perhaps not *that* relaxed after all.

It was this, in part, that sounded alarm bells at papal head office. It was the 13th century and Pope Innocent III was running things, now more than a little concerned by Catharism's growing popularity, particularly amongst wealthy power brokers in France. So he sent an envoy to talk sense into supporters of the religious upstarts. The envoy, or legate, a fellow named Pierre, travelled to France and with a rather heavy hand excommunicated Raymond VI, who was the Count of Toulouse and Marquis of Provence, the reason cited being excessive leniency toward the Cathars. Tolerance, it seems, would not to be tolerated.

Then, in what can only be considered a retaliatory, "Fuck *me*? Fuck *you*!" response, Pierre the undiplomatic diplomat was killed before he could return to Rome. Upon learning of this, the Pope, done with negotiation, deployed vengeful troops in what was labelled a crusade, the Albigensian Crusade. Its objective? To eliminate Cathars. And with that, we see the shift in crusades within Europe itself toward political-religious warfare. In other words, a holy war. Making this the earliest days of the Inquisition.

Soon afterward, a particularly grisly event occurred in the French town of Béziers. The Pope's new envoy was military commander Arnaud-Amaury, a no-nonsense Cistercian abbot who led this particular campaign. A siege ensued, in which the Catholics of Béziers were told they could leave the walled city and be unharmed. But in a remarkably telling twist, local Catholics declined, opting instead to fight alongside Cathars against the army from Rome.

With some clever maneuvering, papal forces broke the defences and accessed the town. As troops stormed in, Arnaud-Amaury was asked by his fighters, "How do we tell Cathars from Catholics?" To which

he famously replied, "Kill them all. The Lord will recognize his own."
It was a massacre, in every sense of the word.

The Cathar Crusade continued, buoyed by an incentive to French
lords that there were plum pickings to be had amongst the lands of
Cathar sympathizers. What happened next is what most intrigued
grail researcher Otto Rahn, who, as it turns out, had gotten a job as an
officer in the ss. His boss (not that one, the other one) was a known
occultist, keen to see what Rahn's ongoing work might reveal. And
it was at this time, following the massacre at Béziers, where we catch
another fleeting glimpse of the grail.

Technically speaking, the Cathar Crusade ended in 1229 with the
signing of the Treaty of Meaux. But conflict dragged on. One of the last
strongholds of the Cathars was the castle at Montségur, in the Pyrenees,
bordering France and Spain. The fortified Château de Montségur sits
atop a steep limestone rock, seemingly impregnable. For nine months
the Cathars were besieged, now by a new wave of troops made up of
French royal forces fighting not only for the church of Rome but local interests and personal gain.

Montségur became a symbol of resistance, with sympathizers sneak-
ing supplies into the castle through a complex series of hidden tunnels
and passageways. Meanwhile, out on the sheer chunk of limestone,
Basque mercenaries fighting alongside the "crusaders" managed to
bivouac in a slight dip just east of the summit. From here the attack-
ers were able to construct a catapult and bombard the castle.

Finally, in the spring of 1244, Montségur surrendered and 200
Cathar perfecti exited the stronghold, led by a bishop named Bertrand
Marty. They solemnly made their way from the castle to the place where
they were to be burned at the stake. As catapult boulders had smashed
bulwarks for the preceding two weeks, the Cathars had been fasting
and praying. Now they were ready. Walking together to their death
sentence, the Cathars told their executioners no stakes were required.
And in a remarkable show of something bordering on cultish devotion, they climbed onto the pyre and voluntarily died in the flames.

What Rahn (and others) were most interested in with respect to this moment in history is the fact that not *all* the perfecti went to the pyre. Three or four, it's said, snuck out through the same carefully concealed passageways that kept them in food for nine months. And why, exactly, did those Cathars leave? What task could possibly be so important that they'd forgo an assured fast track to their good place? The reason, it's believed, was treasure. A specific, mysterious treasure that needed to be shuttled away, kept from the royals and Rome. Something worth risking *everything* to protect.

In 1933 Rahn published his findings. His book, *Crusade Against the Grail: The Struggle between the Cathars, the Templars, and the Church of Rome*, is still popular today, and considered as much reference material as it is quasi-fiction. Having explored networks of caves beneath the Pyrenees, Rahn pinpoints what he believes to be hidey-holes and places of Cathar refuge. Considering the muddying of political and faith-based waters occurring at the time (you'll recall local Catholics supporting Cathars), Rahn felt certain this was the moment the grail passed into the hands of the (new) crusaders. Not the "Inquisitive" ones from Rome, but the Arthurian-esque ones, those pure-of-heart Templars akin to Jomsvikings. Protectors of the grail.

To support his thesis that Montségur was home to the grail, Rahn cites Eschenbach's *Parzival*. In the same way 20th-century Viking Thor Heyerdahl used Snorri Sturluson's *Ynglinga Saga* to validate his search for Odin and Scandinavian origins, Rahn viewed *Parzival* as historical rather than speculative fiction. Using Eschenbach's text, Rahn refers to the fact that the grail castle in *Parzival* is Monsalvat, meaning "safe mountain," the exact translation of Montségur. And the treasure from there is referred to as the "stone from the stars," again believed to be code for the grail, which we've seen in references to guardianship by the Knights Templar.

Following his research and publication of the book, Rahn was promoted to archaeologist in the SS. And yes, we can be fairly certain Rahn was Spielberg's inspiration for the Nazi archaeologist in the first Indiana Jones movie, the one whose face melts off in a horrific and satisfying manner.

So here we are, in the south of France, the Cote d'Azur just east of us, where Björn Ironside (Ragnar Lothbrok's son) added to his longship fleet and lined already bulging pockets on his Mediterranean viking campaign of 859–861. Up ahead is the Rhône and the city of Arles, where Van Gogh painted sunflowers and a Roman amphitheatre still stands at the river mouth by the sea. Naturally, we have to go to Rome, as all roads lead there, apparently. Not only do I need to explore that hub of successive empires, but Indy went to Italy in *his* grail search we well, which seems as good a set of footsteps to follow as any.

But we're awfully close to Spain at the moment. It actually *feels* Spanish, even on the French side of the Pyrenees – hot and dry, with olive groves. They have bullfights too, in this part of France. Illegal in the rest of the country, here they still hold what're known as the "bloody" ones. Not the Bugs Bunny type where you smack the bull on the nose with a dueller's glove, but the nasty ones that make you cheer for the bulls at Pamplona. I'm also curious about those ingenious Basque mercenaries, responsible for turning the tide at the fight for Montségur, flushing out Cathars, which, we suspect, spooked the grail into hiding elsewhere. Plus, I understand Basque cuisine to be amongst the best anywhere.

Between you and me, I've actually gone home for a spell, done laundry and returned for a literature festival and some multimedia gigs. But we're back where we were, seemingly a moment ago, to pick up where we left off. A pocket of geography that looks as though it could be an overlap of France and Spain, here at the narrow, easterly part of the Iberian Peninsula. But with distinct regions of fiercely proud, ancient cultures of Catalan and Basque, not to mention a predominantly Castilian population, this area is far from congruent.

Ⲩ

SPAIN

It's an unusual reunion as I stroll through arrivals from a domestic European flight to a bus loop where Deb is waiting. She's just crossed the Atlantic to join me in Spain, a lovely albeit tired start to our latest adventure, together, as we board a bus in the rain, this one to haul us an hour east from Bilbao to the coast at San Sebastián.

I hadn't put sufficient effort into familiarizing myself with Basque – words and place names in no way akin to Spanish – and my travel confidence is waning. However. With a few frustrated attempts to decipher a map, darkened streets, a lock box and a few flights of stairs, we manage to gain entry to a small but clean, acutely white rental unit, the feel of a nicely appointed sanitarium cell, with city view. We stumble out in heavy rain for rations, the hour late (on a Sunday) and our option (singular) is a convenience store that's about to close. With heavy sighs (ah, the glamour of travel) we enter the tiny market store, doing our best to contain the drip of umbrellas. What greets us, perhaps unsurprisingly, is a convenience store unlike anything one might find elsewhere. The compact space is stocked with an exceptional array of Iberian ham, tinned sardines and octopus, cheese and morcilla, the Spanish-style blood pudding. With crackers and a bottle of rioja, we piece together a rather gourmet feast. Back in the dry comfort of our new little home, we eat well, and sleep.

In the morning we meet our smiling driver–guide, Irene, a Basque woman with a tousle of hair in russet and blond that matches the landscape. We get comfy in her car and head east, following winding, rugged coastline and crossing the Spanish–French border to the surf mecca of Biarritz. An elegant seaside town on southwest France's Basque coast, Biarritz has been a resort destination since European royalty began visiting in the 19th century. It's a popular surfing site too, with long, sandy beaches and surf schools. On a rocky outcrop, jutting into the Bay of Biscay, is the Rocher de la Vierge, symbol of Biarritz, a spike of headland topped with a statue of the Virgin Mary.

As we arrive, surf curls leisurely from the west over wide, flat beach. Beneath an overcast sky, rollers gleam in silver and gunmetal blue, their pace the pulse of the world. From a clifftop we watch a solitary surfer straddle his board, rising and falling, the endless wait for a better wave. Two swimmers walk to the shoreline, a long trudge across wet sand. It must be 500 metres just to reach the water. I shiver in the chill of the mizzle. We descend into town, take shelter under a patio umbrella and drink strong espresso with a view of a sombre sea.

A short walk, another coffee, and we're back in the vehicle, heading south, into rioja wine country, gaining elevation as we go. The land dries into arid hills, what I associate with Hemingway's stories set here. Intermittent pockets of green dot the landscape, a blend of microclimates and irrigation. We park and enjoy a proper hike on undulating dirt trail that soon leaves the road far behind, climbing to the site of an Iron Age fort. Later, I'd watch a documentary in which the traveller asks the historian, "How do we know it was a fort?" To which she smiles and says, "Oh, we rarely do, but it's far more exciting than calling it a farmhouse, which most of these bumps were." Quite right. Let's stick with fort.

In the distance, farmland's woven with vines and dotted in wildflower splashes: coral-orange and white with vibrant yellow and fuchsia. Another quick drive, another brisk tramp, and we link up once more with the Camino, our pilgrim path that started at St Michael's Mount, that timeless stretch of seaside where I scrunched through sleet, snow and high-UV sun, all within moments. This poem, "Camino, Clams, y de Compostela: St Michael's Mount to St James Grave," which also appears in *Forever Cast in Endless Time*, captures, in part, that ramble from there to here.

I summit in old crust snow, expired, soured, turned
beyond, below, a crescent tinted sand-dune shore
in hues of almond-husk that bend and stretch forever
discarded, to late winter elements, a chill to permeate

eider, wool, and ligaments, beneath old soles
a blend of mud and ice-skimmed loam, the way
of pilgrims, slipping, sinking, blinking, hoodwinked eye
on signposts glancing ever east, and west, like Sauron

as the hobbits near, barefooted ring-worn pilgrims
while a redhead rides a painted clamshell, saintly crossing
west Galicia, home to Guthred for a spell
before more maverick moors moved in

broke oaken booze-soaked casks, these infidels
beneath a thumbnail moon the look of distant beaches
curved in prayer-like mats of downward heathen dogs
behind me, dragon slayer's mount

Celt crosses, circled Druid stones
a slosh of pious feet through low-tide estuary
echo like an invocation, rosary, akin to worry beads
the sound of footsteps, balls on abacus

we multiply, by tens, carry the (chosen) one
go forth and multiply, divided nobody will conquer
holy ways and holy wars and holy shit
these socks are full of holes, from travelling this far

and eating nothing more than holey wafers, half-ass tapas
lembas bread and wine – the copper taste of corpses
and of promises reneged, across an ocean, hemisphere
the clam-like scallop eye it rolls, looks askance, nods from passing
    nuns

a woman in a niqab smiles, I think, a crinkle in the eye
as snow's long gone from Michael's Mount
and Ararat's gone dry as sun-bleached crucifixion bone
but here, in costa verde Spain where language, land and pintxos

rally from behind, defeat the continental church and currency
in penalty kick shootouts, running from the field, the bulls
these blisters buried in my boots now seep rioja red
I cross myself and mutter inshallah

remove my dusty shoes, a money changer's belt, suspenders
toss away a weathered mat and carry on, my goal!
blurred wind, Atlantic mist, the colour, scent
of westward Avalon...

as a bivalve shatters underfoot, a solitary pilgrim treks the other way
circumambulation an imagined destination, zero pearls reside inside
   this home
of hollow brittle walls with bits of mucous-meat that hold it all
   together
reminiscent whiff of history, of saline, sandstone battlements, and
   sea

The Camino insignia appears everywhere here in northern Spain.
Occasionally it's a simple wood carving, at other times attached to
signposts and painted ceramic tiles hung from homes, or inns, and at
crooked forks in the road. It's the familiar sideways scallop shell, resembling beams of light radiating from the left, as though a guiding
lighthouse, or the ever-watchful eye of Tolkien's villain. The Camino
has always been a spider's web of footpaths, roadways and trails that
snake across the terrain like capillaries, linking arteries and veins to and
from some figurative, symbolic heart. Unless, of course, the remains

of Saint James at Santiago de Compostela Cathedral include his *actual* heart. Preserving hearts was, after all, amongst the earliest examples of mummifying select bits of the revered.

Along with walks to Rome and Jerusalem, the Camino remains one of the world's most well-trodden pilgrimage paths, earning a plenary, or absolute, indulgence. Most modern-day trekkers, mind you, are far from devout. British long-distance walker Ian Broderick, a lifelong pilgrim, explains in a BBC interview, "Defining pilgrimage is a complicated thing. It can mean many things. And the modern pilgrim isn't a purely devotional Christian. We walk with more intention of discovery. A lot of people say pilgrimage mimics life: it's difficult, it's tiring, there are events that surprise us, and there are no hiding places on a pilgrimage, if you're honest with yourself."

I have to agree, and consider our trek primarily secular, motivation a range of rationale, from spirituality to the lure of a quest and love of being active outdoors. Regardless, remarkable journeys of, shall we say, ambiguous or varying indulgence, are invariably worth the endeavour. If we were to impersonate Phileas Fogg at this moment and clamber into the basket of a hot-air balloon, lifting and drifting over this hilly terrain, to the east we'd see France, Italy and an alpine slice of Switzerland. South of us is the meat of the Iberian Peninsula, Roman for a spell, then Gothic, Moorish, and now a blend of religion, atheists and agnostics, with two-thirds of the population aligning with Catholicism. West of us is the Atlantic, where Vikings were fleetingly in charge and Saint James (and his heart) are interred. But here throughout Spain, key locales continue to surface. In addition to pilgrim destinations and relics, we find some of the most revealing clues yet in our search for the grail.

A short distance south of where we are, toward the border of Portugal, is the province of León. In the region's centre is its capital city, also called León. And in the centre of *that* sits the Basilica of San Isidoro. Once a Roman temple, then a monastery to John the Baptist, this clunky basilica of sandstone has stood for a millennium. In the

11th century it was dedicated to Saint Isidore, archbishop of Seville, an academic theologian who ran things around here prior to Moors being in charge. The basilica houses a compact museum with a solitary item on display. The item, set on grey marble under glass, is the Chalice of Doña Urraca, believed by many to be the Holy Grail.

The chalice looks like a piece of furniture, heavy striped onyx in crimson, white and jade, wrapped in gold, set with bubble-shaped jewels and gemstones. It was the property, for a while, of Urraca of Zamora, daughter of Ferdinand 1. And like any item alleged to be the grail, the cup's attracted a great deal of attention, speculation and opinion. But it was only purported to be the holy relic in 2014. Prior to that, there's no reference to this being the *actual* grail, although the cup's been here for over a thousand years.

Two local researcher–authors, José Ortega del Rio and Margarita Torres Sevilla, state emphatically in their book *The Kings of the Grail* that this gaudy item's the real deal. Other historians and grail experts, however, were quick to disprove the two writers' claims. Artisanal features alone – goldsmithing and gem inlay techniques – would date fabrication of this piece to the Middle Ages. But despite the controversy, clergy jumped aboard, put the cup on display, and the church has never been busier. Too busy, in fact. Since *The Kings of the Grail* was published in the spring of 2014, crowds have flocked here, forcing the basilica to set up a separate, dedicated museum space where the grail is now, part of an adjacent tower and library.

Del Rio and Torres insist they can trace the cup's origins to an early Christian community in Jerusalem. From there, they explain, Muslim traders travelling by caravan transported the chalice to Cairo, where it was subsequently gifted to a Spanish emir, payment or thanks to the Spaniard for coming to the aid of famine victims in Egypt. After this, the authors say, the cup was regifted to Spanish King Ferdinand as a peace offering or show of tribute. Ferdinand then gave the chalice to his young daughter Urraca, who no doubt just wanted a pony.

The body of the chalice, according to the authors, can be dated to one or two centuries before the time of Jesus, which would indeed put it in the right time frame. The heavy gold and gem work would've been added later, they say, increasing its value for subsequent gift giving, based on intended recipients, as it made its way in the direction of León. "The only chalice that could be considered the chalice of Christ is that which made the journey [from Jerusalem] to Cairo, and that is this chalice." The authors then add, however, there's no way to know for certain if Jesus ever drank from the cup.

Oxford history professor Diarmaid MacCulloch, who specializes in this sort of thing, calls these Spanish theories "idiotic" and lists 200 examples of cups and dishes that "vie for the title." But a few investigative doors are left invitingly ajar, as though everyone involved still *wants* the genuine article to be out there, somewhere. Despite opinion and conflicting research, pilgrims still come to León in droves. The basilica now features a virtual grail experience, where visitors can rent VR (virtual reality) glasses and "handle" a simulated, 3D version of the chalice.

Now, a quick intermission. Think of it as a chance to grab a snack. Which provides an opportunity for me to expand on those compass points and slivers of recollection that radiate from where we are. Last time I was here we veered southeast to spend a few days in Barcelona. Our first order of business? To skip the Dali museum. Reason being, I'd experienced a lifetime's worth of flies stuck to stuff and melting clock visions when I was a drummer in a southern rock band. (Seriously. We were called Three Pairs o' Boots.) Plus, having kept company with Dali's *Christ of Saint John of the Cross* at Glasgow's Kelvingrove in our first *Gone Viking* saga, I couldn't imagine witnessing anything more impressive. Religion aside, it's a spectacular piece. It almost distracted me from the museum's extensive Viking exhibit. Almost.

In Barcelona, we focused instead on the work of Gaudi, strolling from his Sagrada Família to Casa Batlló and the watery ceramics of Parc Güell. At this stage of life few things shock me. But what I saw that day shook me to the core. In the centre of the park – a homage to gardens and architecture, and the symbolic heart of Catalunya – where proud locals have fought 2,500 years for independence, outlasting Phoenician, Roman and Muslim invasions, not to mention communists, fascists, and ironically well-organized anarchists, I watched in horror as a hundred Catalans line danced to Billy Ray Cyrus's "Achy Breaky Heart," warbling from a scratchy PA. It was then I knew the end of civilization was nigh.

Following one of our thrice-daily meals of jamón on crusty baguette, we wandered picturesque Plaça Reial and Las Ramblas, where spray-painted buskers stand motionless, expecting money. I fought the urge to push them over. Perhaps the art form of doing diddly-shit is lost on me. When I did nothing, awaiting pay, at least I wore a suit and sat in an office.

Having survived a much milder round of food poisoning (thus the three squares of jamón baguettes), we boarded a rickety commuter train that rattled us south along the Costa Brava – windswept views of cyan surf and gravel beaches. This nook of the Mediterranean is the Balearic Sea, and the Illes Balears (home to party destination Ibiza) sit a short distance offshore, like stones being skimmed toward Italy and France, jumping toward Sardinia and Corsica.

Our train followed the coast, where Björn Ironside sailed with his brother Hastein on their ninth-century campaign. To the northeast, on the curve of France's south coast, is the mouth of the Rhône, flowing from the Alps through Lake Geneva. The river forms the deltas of Camargue at the city of Arles, where Hastein and Björn wintered their ships. But ahead of us, down this east coast of Spain, lies another fat crumb on our path, leading to what could be the actual grail, in the seaside city of Valencia.

After Madrid and Barcelona, Valencia is Spain's third-largest city. Another distinct pocket of culture and history, and a hub of commerce, this port is the Mediterranean's busiest. Container ships clog the river mouth like a log boom. I can imagine the Lothbrok brothers' fleet of a hundred ships making their way through this water, where the Turia River enters the sea. I learn that the city's classified as gamma level and wonder for a moment if that has to do with superheroes getting bitten by radioactive bugs, but in fact it means this place links regional economies to a vital global network.

Most sources claim Valencia was founded by Romans in the second century BCE, before being ruled by Berber and Arab Moors in the 700s, a century before the Northmen were here. Its key placement on the map has always put the city in play, a token of power, changing hands between rulers, religions and shifting political interests. It was Spain's capital in the 1930s, in the midst of its civil war. Hemingway came through at the time as a newspaper correspondent, although he spent much of his time in Madrid. Despite the violence and turmoil, or perhaps *because* of it, it was one of his favourite places. He called Spain "the last good country left." Whether his love of the place was based on landscape, culture or cheaply priced cognac, we can't be entirely certain. But even in a country of radical diversity, Valencia still stands apart, receiving UNESCO status a few years ago for Intangible Cultural Heritage. World Heritage Sites usually relate to historical or geographical significance (buildings, artifacts, monuments), but here, intangible heritage pertains to tradition, customs, language and folklore.

In the heart of the city, set in a series of ring roads, a serpentine greenway and park parallels the river, meandering its way to the port. And just off the slender copse of green is the Metropolitan Cathedral Basilica of the Assumption of Our Lady of Valencia, or more concisely, Valencia Cathedral. Construction was completed in the 13th century, when the Sagas were being written in Iceland. The current structure sits atop what was once a Visigoth temple, then a mosque, and now is an architectural amalgam of all who've been here, a fusion of Romanesque, French Gothic, Baroque and Neoclassical. Collectively it works; arabesque geometry inlaid with stained glass, set beside sandstone arches that look like coliseum walls. This commingling of faith and time triggers feelings I've had across Scandinavia, where ancient gods and sites of pagan worship reside next to Christian cathedrals.

Inside the Valencia Basilica, both chancel and nave support towering ceilings, and you can't help but gaze upward. What should be echoey stone, however, manages to hush all who enter. Reverence pervades the aperture. The chapter house, a separate building where canons met, was joined to the nave in the 15th century, creating the current sprawling cathedral. And it's the chapter house that brings us here, now known as the Holy Grail Chapel.

The chapel's interior walls are massive stone bricks in warm sandstone hues. Dark hardwood floor has a thick runner of patterned red carpet. The hall is flanked in stepped benches and pews, creating the look of a government house, a place where elected officials might squabble. The back wall's adorned in intricate carvings, apostles and biblical scenes topped in sharp spires. Tidily aligned blocks, rows and columns of people and snippets of history, at a glance, resemble what could be the most elaborate set ever for *Hollywood Squares*. In the centre of this is a three-tiered, peaked arch, wrapped in gold. And set on an elevated stand within the arch is the Holy Chalice, known in these parts as the Valencia Chalice. Some call it the Holy Grail.

Set under glass and lit from above, the chalice is a cup made of blood-red agate. It's mounted onto a bulging stem like an onion dome with two heavy handles that make it look like a trophy. The base of the vessel is a large, inverted cup made of polished chalcedony, gem-quality stone made of silica, a type of quartz. The entire item is about 17 centimetres high and looks exceedingly heavy. Arabic writing's inscribed around the bottom. The base, stem and handles were added to the chalice well after it was originally made. It's the red agate cup, crafted in Palestine or Egypt, that we can date, made sometime between the fourth century BCE and the moment Jesus was crucified.

Along with this chalice is an ancient notice on vellum, in fact an inventory, claimed to have been found with a letter detailing the spoils gathered by Romans during Christian persecution, when churches scrambled to divide riches for hiding amongst the secretly pious. This is one of those treasures. Another reference to cataloguing Christian relics is an inventory list dated December 14, 1134, written by Don Carreras Ramírez of the San Juan de la Peña monastery, detailing this chalice and describing it as the cup in which "Christ consecrated his blood." In other words, this is the grail. The monastery gave the cup to the king at that time, Martin I of Aragon, apparently in a trade for a cup made of gold. (No doubt both thought they were getting the better end of the deal.)

In the 1980s, Pope John Paul II was here and used the chalice for mass, describing it as proof of "Christ's passage on earth." Pope Benedict XVI did much the same thing in 2006, calling the cup "this most famous chalice," the exact words used by Popes from the earliest days of Roman Catholicism, generally accepted terminology when referring to the Holy Grail.

Its authenticity has been questioned, as you can imagine. Researcher Janice Bennett traces the provenance of this chalice to third-century Pope Sixtus II and his treasurer Saint Lawrence of Valencia, with the grail supposedly making its way here to Lawrence's hometown as he and the Pope fled Rome's persecution of Christians. The journey, one of flight and passage by night, is reminiscent of Joseph and others, secretly transporting the grail. Or the subterfuge of Cathars, Crusaders and Jomsvikings, hiding the grail progressively further from Rome.

The story of this chalice leaps frustratingly from the third to sixth century, then picks up again with our inventory-keeping Don at the Monastery of San Juan de la Peña, prior to the cup swap with Spanish King Martin. Bennett's research is exhaustive, and while this particular grail has a fascinating history, the story breaks down in a spotty account of its transfer to Spain, our only worthwhile source being a sixth-century translated note written by an Augustinian monk named Donato. Perhaps Popes who've alluded to this being the grail are of a mind that if you say it enough, it's bound to be considered the truth.

Then again, they may've just been considerate, treading cautiously for the sake of those who long for it to be true.

Leaving a couple of would-be grails behind, we've returned to Barcelona, where we board an open-top bus to loop past the towering statue of Christopher Columbus. The positioning of the statue, however, is about a quarter-turn off, so the explorer now points with chest-puffed confidence to North Africa. From here we visit Barcelona's Maritime Museum, a medieval stone and brick building where Chris's fleet was assembled. Now it only seems fitting to head to that last bastion of Moorish power in these parts, Alhambra palace, where Queen Isabella met the Genoese explorer, bankrolling the epic voyage and aimless "discovery" of the Americas. According to Bugs Bunny, "The good Queen Isabella / gave her jewels to her fella / so Columbus he could sail the ocean blue!" And while we're on the topic, it may interest you to know my third-grade teacher's name was Nina. Funnily enough she drove a Pinto, and in her class I sat next to a girl named Maria. True story.

But before we follow the tributary tale of Columbus here in Spain, let's go back momentarily to where the explorer was born, the port town of Genoa, that northwestern bight of Italy due south of Milan. On its neatly scalloped Mediterranean harbour, now next to an aquarium, is Genoa Cathedral. The cathedral's dedicated to Saint Lawrence, the martyred Spaniard and Roman treasurer who brought the red agate grail to Valencia.

The cathedral's next to the water where Columbus supposedly watched ship masts grow on the horizon as they came into port and deduced, "Hey, the world must be round, like an apple, not flat like a pancake!" (At least that's what he said on *Looney Tunes*). Fact is, quite a few folks by that time were already doubting the flat earth premise, getting on board with the Pythagorean notion that our planet's a sphere.

In this particular maritime hub, the Genoa Cathedral is home to yet another purported Holy Grail, known as the Genoa Chalice. Going back to our broader definition of what a grail can be, this one's a six-sided dish of emerald-green coloured glass. The glass is Egyptian, its date of fabrication early Roman, making dates and locales coincide with our timeline. It was brought here by a Genoese merchant, Guglielmo Embriaco, and is said to be part of the booty hauled out of Caesarea, what's now Palestinian Israel, at the start of the 12th century. The grail was thought to exhibit otherworldly properties and induce miracles, many of which were attributed to its being mistaken for pure emerald rather than the rich coloured glass that it is. Precious gems were believed to contain their own inert powers of healing and magic, which over time metamorphosed into attributes associated with divine holy relics.

Late in the 13th century, chronicler Jacobus de Voragine stated this dish was the Sacro Catino, the Sacred Basin, meaning Holy Grail. This premise gained momentum over ensuing years when Pedro Tafur, a travelling Spanish historian, backed up Voragine's claim, reporting the Grail was "made from a single emerald," and housed in Genoa Cathedral. This was accepted as truth for another four centuries, and in 1805 the dish was "liberated" by Napoleon's army and lugged back to Paris. But the basin, having been hastily packed, chipped en route, indicating it wasn't solid emerald after all, leaving the authenticity of this particular grail in question.

I'm compelled to put a pin in this part of our storyline, that satisfying feeling of accomplishment you can only get upon finishing a good book. That final flipping motion to close the cover, something I tend to do slowly, like savouring the last bite of really good pie. And to do that we need to head south here in Spain to where our 15th-century viking-esque explorer Chris Columbus was laid to rest, in the town of Seville. For us it's a sortie more than anything, another figurative touchstone on this particular detour. But while we're here, allow me to share a Seville side-note. This Andalusian city is hot and dry much of the year. People liken it to a North African climate. It's where Seville oranges come from, which the British hauled home by the boatload, figuring they had a new alternative to limes for keeping scurvy at bay. But this thick-skinned variety are intensely bitter and sour. However, by cooking them and adding sugar, the English invented marmalade, managing to turn awful fruit into awful jam.

In this southern part of the country we explored the overdeveloped Costa del Sol and unending resorts of Málaga and Marbella. It reminded me of hyperinflated Florida – excessively leveraged construction and speculative finance, destined to collapse at the first market hiccup. When there's nothing but cranes on the horizon and your money's all come from elsewhere, beware. It doesn't take a prescient cambion like Merlin to see where this was headed. Mind you, not only did no one ask, no one wanted to know.

We hid for a day in the air-conditioned comfort of a touring sedan, on a private tour to Ronda, which our driver–guide pronounced with three syllables and an R that rolled forever. I kept asking the name of the place, delighting in the drum roll sound when it was properly pronounced. Our driver, Jorge, explained he was taking us to "the world's largest bull fighting ring," leaving me to wonder just how big the bull was. Maybe like Paul Bunyan's ox. But the world's biggest bull (maybe I misunderstood) was nowhere to be seen, just a huge empty ring painted the colours of a tequila sunrise. In the centre of Ronda we explored medieval streets in twists and crimps, and steep stone walkways that left us huffing under intense sun. From a high access point we peered down at Roman bath ruins, then gawked at the neck-craning arches of the oddly named Roman Bridge, in fact Muslim architecture from the ninth century.

Now to Alhambra, centre of Moorish Spain and home to Columbus's high-leverage financing. We hop a bus, with Gibraltar's Pillars of Hercules to the southwest, guarding the Mediterranean and Alboran seas. Our coach climbs, bearing east, and as we distance ourselves from the sea the temperature creeps up as well. It's late spring, and we're expecting highs of 30 degrees Celsius. Approaching Alhambra fortress and palace, the complex takes on a reddish-gold glow, ensconced in a copse of deep green. This high piece of land was originally a Roman fort (or possibly farmhouse), but the royal palace we're approaching was constructed in the 13th century by the Emir of Granada, Mohammed Ibn al-Ahmar of the Nasrid Dynasty.

In the 14th century it became a royal palace when Yusuf I, Sultan of Granada, moved in, also part of the Nasrid reign, the last Muslim dynasty on the Iberian Peninsula. Following the Christian Reconquista in 1492, this was home to Isabella and Ferdinand, where the queen famously "gave her jewels to her fella," and Columbus set off to the land mass Freydis Eriksdóttir and her brother Leif settled 500 years earlier, a place already inhabited for 33,000 years.

Columbus Day became an American tradition, with malls putting crap on sale the moment Chris landed in 1492 (I suspect). It's celebrated on the second Monday in October, a particularly prideful occasion for many. But in 1964, President Lyndon Johnson created Leif Erikson Day, celebrating "the original discovery" of America. The date chosen, October ninth, tidily preceded Columbus Day, ensuring Johnson would never again get the Italian-American vote. (Mind you, polling amongst Scandinavian-Americans soared.)

But I digress. Outside the sprawl of Alhambra palace, we've swapped the damp heat of the bus for the intensely dry Andalusian heat here in Granada. Alhambra is now a UNESCO World Heritage Site, and I feel oddly refreshed as we enter the grounds, no doubt part of its original design with cool, still pools in loggia-bordered courtyards. The name roughly translates to "The Red One," no surprise given the vermilion gleam that greeted us on the drive up. Arab poets call it "a pearl set in emeralds," a lovely description of this iridescent castle plunked in leafy surrounds.

Sauntering about in a rather organized circuit, I take in the blend of clean lines melding with intricate geometries and symmetrical patterns of Moorish design. Centring a cobbled courtyard, a dozen concrete lions hoist a burbling fountain on their backs. And I think of the lions on so many coats of arms we've seen on flags crossing Europe to get here, timeless symbols of royalty, spanning geography and religion.

Neatly trimmed shrubs frame the castle courtyard, reminiscent of a Zen garden. Outside the building a line of tall cypress and hemlock peer over a roofline, as though curious as to what it is we little folk down here find so interesting. A colonnade in sandstone borders the shrubbery, each pillar carved in what must be thousands of hours of artisanal craftsmanship. Beyond the palace wall, grounds fall away in deep, gouging steps, the look of the world's driest rice terraces.

I'm surprised how much I've enjoyed this structured excursion, an example of a geopolitically significant area attracting successive rulers, each stamping the land and building a home in a manner to make it their own. Not unlike Istanbul's Hagia Sophia, where Viking runes are carved into marble, a place of worship for Muslim, Christian and pagan. When a structure is simply too beautiful to destroy, the result, it seems, is a unique form of tolerance, and inclusivity.

Another excursion brings us in from the coast, but you'd never know it. The day has a decidedly maritime vibe, gusts of salt mizzle and a sodden cloud cover in grey. Uncertain weather. We have an array of attire: jackets, umbrellas and short-sleeved shirts. Our Basque guide Irene's once more at the wheel, Deb's riding shotgun and I'm in the back, waving at strangers, pretending to be a celebrity. No one waves back.

The town we're driving into is Guernica, Basque cultural capital. It's a beautiful setting marred by a nasty bit of history. Guernica represents another strategic crossroads, here on the north edge of Spain. Bilbao is a short distance west while Guernica town centre fronts an estuary, a confluence of the Oca and Ebro rivers, with water access to ports and the coast.

We start our visit at the city's parliament building in a sombre old room of dark wooden seats, elevated in plush red velvet. It feels like we've snuck into the House of Lords. The civic council's not sitting and it's just the three of us, whispering as though misbehaving. Paintings and stained glass adorn the foyer, Basque history and pride in huge single frames, showcasing fishers, farmers and miners. It's a softer, more colourful version of propaganda you'd expect to see from the past in a communist country: healthy proletarians happily working the land and manufacturing heavy machinery.

The compound is perched on a hillock, distinct in this flat stretch of countryside. And outside the council building is an ancient oak, the Tree of Guernica, where general assemblies have been held for hundreds of years to discuss and debate city affairs. There's an older Guernica Tree, now just a thick husk of trunk, like a massive cinnamon stick, hollow and mostly exposed to the air. It leans to one side like a wizened old man, the type that shuffles offstage as the New Year's baby is introduced. It has the same aura of weighty decisions that cling to the red seats inside. This space, like other oak trees placed in ancient town centres, are functioning reminders, testament to democracy. Both Jean-Jacques Rousseau and William Wordsworth recorded proceedings from here, their accounts positioning this as a model for elsewhere.

A short stroll down the street and we come to the work of Picasso. The painting is (also) called *Guernica*, and is as much a news story as it is a historical snapshot and outcry of rage and dismay. It's the painter's interpretation of what took place here on April 26, 1937. The Spanish Civil War was raging, with a politically diverse mishmash of Spaniards fighting the Nationalist regime of General Franco. Guernica, hub of Basque independence, was a thorn in the dictator's side, something he intended to overthrow along with the rest of Spain's Republican government. Meanwhile, Franco's small-moustached ally in Germany was looking to demonstrate his Luftwaffe, the aerial fleet that came to be associated with terror-style bombings of civilian targets. Whether Otto Rahn and his grail team were involved, we can't be certain.

What made the attack particularly horrific was the fact that local troops were known to be elsewhere. The front line was a distance away. So Guernica that day was occupied solely by civilians. It was market day. What ensued was firstly the destruction of roadways and bridges, eliminating means of escape. And for three unimaginable hours Guernica was bombed, followed by strafing fighter plane gunfire. German reports put the civilian death toll at 300. Locals said the actual number was 1,654.

The *Guernica* painting is Picasso's response to the attack. The original's on display in Madrid. What we're looking at now, on an outdoor wall in the centre of town, is a replica, identical in every way. Two other tourists are here, doing the same thing, standing back and solemnly taking it in. It's a massive piece, over three metres by seven in a landscape format. There's an absence of colour, everything grey, black and white. The scene is one of chaos and disturbing, extreme violence. A bull screams, a horse is gored, people are wailing, and a child lies dead. Flames surround the scene while something explodes overhead. Body parts litter the ground. As we contemplate this unnerving yet imperative scene, drizzle abates but ashen cloud clings determinedly overhead. And I can't help but wonder if it's always this way, right here, the weather a dark armband, worn in commemoration.

Back on the north edge of Spain, we're still in the car with Irene. The next stop we make is unplanned, one of those wonderful "Oh, yeah, right" moments of serendipity. We've now spent most of a week together: learning, sharing, walking and eating, the seeds of a proper friendship. Yes, there's commerce involved – this is a paid tour after all – but with enough of a relaxed, interpersonal vibe throughout that it feels as though we've simply come to spend time with someone from our past. Someone we want to catch up with, the stories they're sharing all new.

We pull off the main road, a winding stretch of worn, undivided asphalt, onto a dirt and rock trail, pulling to a stop in a slight widening of the path. Now we're climbing a curved track with the feel of an overgrown drive approaching a haunted manse. Wildly overgrown greenery closes in from both sides and thick, bushy palm trees tower from unkempt hedgerows.

"This is where we played when we were children," Irene says. "My grandmother's house was just over there," she adds, pointing into the thickets.

And with magician-esque flair (ta-dah!) a castle reveals itself: tall, solid, yet oddly compact, the look of a top-heavy doll's house. It could be from a fairy tale, straight off the pages of Rapunzel – crenellated parapets, neo-medieval – but I suspect it's only a couple of hundred years old, built to look much older. It was abandoned. Now it's for sale, we're told. A lone entryway's boarded and locked. Glancing up, I find myself distrusting the stony gargoyles, certain one or two may drop at any moment, or take flight.

I shake my head. "This was your playhouse?!"

Irene smiles. "It does seem grand, doesn't it? It was abandoned then, too."

"Was it safe?"

"Hmm. Probably not," she laughs. And I imagine her hair tumbling from a window high overhead, horse-mounted knights assembling for the joust.

The weather's a swirl, steel wool cloud, drizzle and muted sun, the feel of a gritty steam room. Amongst a few hundred pilgrims, we're perspiring and snaking our way on foot down a series of paved switchbacks on the side of a mountain that drops to the ocean. Sea froths on rough, rocky shore where a finger of stone joins an outcrop of land to create a quasi-island, buttressing the beach. And atop the almost-island, surrounded in fist-fighting breakers, is an isolated castle, a plummeting access of narrow, vertiginous stairs creeping through rock as though accessing a lone jedi's hut.

This is San Juan de Gaztelugatxe, just north of Bilbao. And the pilgrims? Well, most of them are here to see the site of a castle used in *Game of Thrones*, a recurring experience throughout our *Gone Viking* expeditions. Plunk us anywhere that ought to be remote, another land's end, and sure enough one of the later seasons of GOT has already been there, filming, spawning tourism and creating more pilgrimage sites for fans of George Martin.

The stony hermitage-retreat atop this wave-whipped islet is called Gaztelugatxeko Doniene in Basque, meaning "castle of rock." Find a locale here in Basque country with an "atx" in its name and you know it's a craggy summit, the language using toponyms to describe places and geography. The structure has been here since the ninth or tenth century. Records vary. But despite the venerability of the place, it's the anchoring feel of the land that gives it timelessness, while the unending bash of waves adds a sense of impermanence.

The retreat is dedicated to John the Baptist, and it's evident now that most people here aren't necessarily GOT fans. There's a sombre feeling of piousness amongst others making the descent and subsequent climb in this endless queue. Not everyone's taking selfies and I decide I was too quick to judge. It's a spiritual place for a great many pilgrims.

The white noise of sea dampens much of the chatter and I find myself easing into that meditative state of excursion in the midst of rugged terrain. The coast's a jagged line of inlets, arches and sea caves. A short distance offshore is the islet of Aketx, a seabird sanctuary, and along with the sounds of ocean there's a constant push and pull of wind. I can't imagine being aboard a ship off this shore, but the strategic outcrop of land has attracted mariners for millennia. The site still has votive offerings to bring sailors home safely.

A brass bell hangs from a heavy wood lintel, a weathered rope dangling to flagstones. And a few of us take turns, turning our backs to the water and ringing the bell three times, which is said to ensure safe passage when crossing the sea. With the echo of bell reverberating in my ears, I'm now 80 metres over the breakers. Some people count steps as they climb, but official documents still disagree on how many stairs there are. It's about 230, but each step is steep, slightly crooked, and with the yank and shove of the wind it feels like a momentous summit. An expansive view from the top accentuates a sense of being at the prow of a towering ship, heaving through open water.

This castle was built at a time when Vikings were here. Perhaps for that reason. Trace a finger down a map, following Europe's west coast from Scandinavia to here, and you see why. Pass low-lying Netherlands and Belgium, around France's jut of Brittany, along the curve of the Bay of Biscay, and you're here, where coastline pushes into Atlantic. Just west of our bell-ringing promontory lies Galicia, the extreme northwest corner of Spain.

It's another distinctive part of the country, language reminiscent of both Castilian Spanish and Portuguese. A place of hills, coasts and mariners. And like a surprisingly large swath of west Europe, this is also a place of Celts. When Romans arrived, they named the place for the Celtic tribe that lived here. Some scholars say the name Galicia is derived from the Gauls, a Greek term referring to milk, indicating the locals' fair skin. Other linguists argue Galicia comes straight from the Celtic tongue, meaning hill people. Go back far enough to a pre- or proto-Celtic time, and it can also mean people of forest. With Lisbon sitting south of this convex coast and the mouth of the Mediterranean just beyond that, it's another strategic piece of real estate. And a key to unlocking grail secrets.

Unlike most of the Iberian Peninsula, which became a Muslim stronghold in the eighth century, this pocket of cliffs and forested coasts remained staunchly Christian. When the first cornerstones were being hammered into the rock at Gaztelugatxe, this uppermost Atlantic corner of Spain became home to Saint James, or at least his remains, in Galicia's capital of Santiago de Compostela.

James, along with his younger brother John, were sons of Salome and Zebedee. Both brothers were apostles, primary disciples of Jesus. According to the Bible's New Testament, both siblings had seats at that Last Supper table, the one Leonardo felt should've happened in Tuscany. Salome (James's and John's mom) was sisters with Mary of Nazareth, mother to Jesus. Which makes Jesus Salome's nephew (and James's and John's cousin). What's key to our saga is that Aunt Salome was there, at the crucifixion, in the crowd with Joseph of Arimathea. Later, Salome was part of a small group who went to her nephew's tomb to care for the body, not unlike what Joseph did in preparation for the interment. Here we see an intriguing overlap in both Salome and Joseph's access to the body of Jesus, and potentially the grail, or its contents.

Subsequent gospels refer to Salome in differing terms, blurring her with other Marys close to Jesus. The *Secret Gospel of Mark* is one of these, muddying the waters as to Salome's part in the proceedings around the time of the crucifixion. She's referred to as a minister, which could be a pious follower as in a clergy member, or instead could be one who tends to the sick and the dead. Again, she's at the scene, along with Joseph, potentially the deceased's aunt and uncle. Where Joseph claims Jesus gave him the grail. But could Joseph's subsequent travels to England with his own set of disciples be an elaborate ruse, allowing Salome to secrete away the actual relic, hidden at some other land's end?

We're now between two pivotal landmarks in our quest. This clifftop, dedicated to John the Baptist, will lead us due west to where Saint James is interred. Two key players, both close to Jesus, who along with that extended family were present at the most significant moments the chalice appears. Between the sheen of the bell I've just rung and a dim glint of sun on the sea, I can't help but catch glimpses of grail all around.

But back to our Viking connections. Late in the first millennium, fortifications were being built along this north coast of Spain specifically to thwart Scandinavian attacks. Around here they were known as Lordomanes or Normanni, the Northmen. Santiago de Compostela was already a holy site, the end of the line for pilgrims seeking indulgence where James is buried. By this time – the ninth and tenth centuries – Scandinavian raiders were well aware that places of Christian significance tended to be well stocked with booty. Which resulted in this Iberian promontory being another highly sought prize amongst seafaring rowers from the north.

A 12th-century Spanish manuscript, citing the *Annales Castellani Recentiores*, states that in the year 970, "Northmen arrived in the country." And tenth-century chronicler Dudo of Saint-Quentin (located between Paris and Brussels) picks up the telling with accounts of Vikings bound for this coast, where they "conquered eighteen cities, attacked Spain and began to afflict it with fire and plunder severely."

Through translations of manuscripts in Latin and Arabic, with their differing calendars, dates vary, but we can be certain all of this was happening right around the turn of the first millennium. *Historia Silense*, a medieval history of the Iberian Peninsula, refers to a raid in 968, in which Northmen sailed here with a hundred ships and "plundered all of Galicia." It's the first time we learn (in these parts) of Gunnrauðr, so-called King of Scandinavia, and that these assaults from the north lasted three years. Given the distance covered to get here, we can be certain Norse camps were constructed, no doubt with moorage and longphorts for ship repair. Other historical tidbits refer to 10,000 Vikings being here, with semi-permanent Scandinavian settlements dotting this Spanish coast. Other theories speculate these wintering camps were what allowed for frequent tenth-century raids around Al-Andalus, the Iberian Peninsula. Arabic records confirm these numbers and dates.

Another note of significance is that these campaigns in Spain were the first to be written about in Scandinavian literature, specifically *Historia Norvegiæ* and the Old Norse Ágrip *af Nóregskonungasögum* (*History of the Kings of Norway*), written in the late 12th and early 13th centuries. These texts refer to Eiríkr Blóðøx (Erik Bloodaxe) dying in the tenth century while fighting in Spain. But to add a tasty morsel to the mystery, unsubstantiated sources place Eiríkr in England when he died, having sailed from Spain, his final resting place a burial mound between King Arthur's Hall and Glastonbury.

Following a sultry but windswept day of exploration and quasi-pilgrimage, we're now in San Sebastián, capital of the Basque province of Gipuzkoa. We're facing the Bay of Biscay, with the North Atlantic beyond that, while the French Pyrenees are just east of us. We arrived by bus, its signage indicating Donostia, Basque for San Sebastián. A destination for beachgoers, trekkers and foodies. The wide, deep beaches of Playa de la Concha and Playa de Ondarreta create a continuous curve of gold sand, fronting a goblet shaped bay. Isla de Santa Clara floats like an olive in the midst of the inlet, a natural breakwater, calming the sea even in offshore breeze. Steep hillsides rise from the beach and combine with the ensconcing bay to create an optical illusion of water rising to horizon, as though this huge seaside wineglass is about to spill over.

Our accommodation for now is walking distance to museums, hikes and historical sites, but tonight, as clouds roll in off the bay, we're meeting a small group for a pintxos tour on foot. A guide arrives, looking like one of the villains from *Money Heist*, the Spanish action drama, and I realize it just might be, as they killed off his character early in the series. He's dressed in a rakish fedora, angled jauntily, and despite wearing the nicest clothes from my pack I feel underdressed. With a dozen of us assembled, we head out, our group babble sounding like a mix of languages, until I realize it's just couples from Australia and Scotland, all speaking English but creating a rich array of accents.

Pintxos are Basque tapas, small, snack-like hors d'oeuvres people tend to eat while standing or leaning at high tables or bars. It's about socializing. Usually with a glass of wine, most often rioja in these parts. I do my best to tap my memory for cocktail banter, chatting with strangers, doing our best to make it feel familiar. The rioja helps. Along with the food. Soon most of our mouths are full, making smiling and nodding acceptable. Our first stop looks a bit like an abattoir, an open room with subway tiles on counters, walls and floor. A few share-plates of mussels in broth and crusty bread are passed around. One half of the dark oval shell becomes a spoon, the other a tiny bowl, and managing to eat three separate things with one hand becomes a good icebreaker. The seafood is good, the bread fresh and tasty, but the nectar of garlic, tomato and broth is the star of the show. Bread becomes napkins and flavour-soaking utensils all in one. And with fingers smelling of sea brine and shoreline, we move on to our next destination.

Sky darkens, there's a grumble overhead like a disgruntled god, then cloud cover explodes in a torrent of rain. Umbrellas become more of a deterrent than protection, and wind makes them pretty much useless. We dart between awnings and, despite swirling rain, huddle at tables with a narrow patio overhang, making our next course feel like a sit-down dinner in a perforated marquee. Dishes get more substantial: beef cheeks in wine, fish in cream sauce, and lamb with gravy. More rioja is served, and before long, splashes of rain become welcome guests at the table.

We've moved on to new accommodation, now a short distance from the mouth of the Ría de Bilbao, the Bilbao Estuary. A wide, flat river meanders through the heart of the city, inviting access and longphort potential for incoming dragon-prow ships. Our rental apartment is a walk-up with a compact kitchen, and we stock the small fridge with rice-stuffed morcilla, jamón and manchego (sheep's milk cheese). Strong instant coffee, a bottle of rioja and Alhambra beer round out our rations. There's a little grocery store a few blocks from the unit, and our time here in the city is shaping up nicely. But first, another round of evening pintxos: olives and cheese, along with roasted peppers and cured ham.

Bilbao's always been a hub of commerce, and Basque pride pervades the region. An example being the local football (soccer) squad, AC (Athletic Club) Bilbao, which only promotes Basque players (and the team's a successful one), while the city's coat of arms features a fortified church on a bridge, with a fierce pair of wolves sporting blood-red claws and fire-like tongues. The bridge is double-arched, resembling eyes staring out at the water, the look one of watchful, impenetrable strength, and the message relayed is clear.

The city's also home to one of the world's five Guggenheim Museums (along with New York, Venice, Abu Dhabi and Berlin). A stroll toward the museum brings us to Poppy, a popular tourist attraction and symbol of civic pride in the museum's sprawling outdoor concourse. Poppy, or Puppy, is a floral sculpture by American artist Jeff Koons. It's a massive highland terrier made of flowers, held together by steel. The only things visible are brilliant blooms in the shape of a seated, towering dog. It's stunning and endearing and appears in millions of Instagram feeds. I admit it's hard not to click a few frames; irrespective of angle and light, the piece is a thing of beauty.

Of all the museums I've visited this may be the most iconic. The building itself is a work of visionary art and design. I spend time outside long before I go in, walking its perimeter, doing my best to see it all through the eyes of Frank Gehry, the Canadian-American architect who designed it. The exterior's made up of shiny steel tiles, all tidily aligned, not alternating like bricks. Walls curve and hug the banks of the River Nervión, as though a flexible ship were plying its way to the city, or perhaps to the rest of the world. It's a fascinating blend of sharp angles with continuous, silky flow. And a high, skinny spider seems to be approaching. It's known as *Maman* and is nine metres high, made of bronze, steel and marble. It's a bit creepy, a far cry from the puppy of flowers, but does attract a crowd. What makes it *Maman* is the offspring-filled sac hanging beneath its thorax and abdomen, filled with large marble "eggs."

Inside the museum, the artisanal design keeps me gawking and craning my neck. There's a high, bright atrium with views of the river and surrounding hills, as though we're set in a dish. A grail, perhaps. Gehry called this space The Flower, and it serves as orientation from what's considered the museum's heart. Which draws my mind back to the heart of Saint James, concluding the Camino. Where we are now's not far from the pilgrimage route and Santiago de Compostela, the city a university town, vibrant with celebration year-round. Grand plazas, medieval walls and carvings in stone give it an ancient feel, but the unending line of trekkers with packs and walking poles can undermine the sense of introspection one might associate with pilgrimage. In Santiago Cathedral, the Botafumeiro gets lit and swung for special ceremonies, a massive thurible that smudges heady incense through the nave. The visual is mesmerizing and manages to shut up most of the tourists. Not only does it represent a spiritual cleanse like smoke rituals the world over, but it effectively freshens the room against clusters of sweat-soiled pilgrims.

While we're on this mental tributary, consider this. The number of people walking the Camino grows each year, with recent tallies approaching half a million pilgrims. Despite what individuals may or may not believe, most who complete the trek admit they can't help but feel religious, particularly in the cathedral, one of just three built at the tomb of one of the 12 apostles. Saint Peter's in Vatican City, Saint Thomas in Chennai, India, and here in Spain for Saint James. Perhaps the feeling is one of spirituality more than Christian faith. But a telltale sign ensues among many who finish the quest.

Santiago de Compostela's not quite the end of the line. It's another hundred kilometres to Cape Finisterre on the Atlantic, Spain's last finger of land, like Finistère in France, meaning "end of the earth." Roughly due north of these dots on the map lies the Land's End that started our journey, by the crumble of King Arthur's castle.

Many Camino walkers, once they visit the cathedral, simply carry on, trudging their way to the Atlantic and the Land's End of Spain. Then, with the extended pilgrimage nearly complete, they burn what was used to get there. Sometimes it's the burden of something intangible, perhaps memories written on paper. It could be a journal. Others set their worn hiking boots ablaze. (Imagine the stink!) What I find fascinating is that these rites occur only after travellers have been to the cathedral, paying homage at church before completing the most pagan of rituals, setting things alight, purification by smoke and fire.

But there's another promontory we need to explore before we move on from Spain. One that's seen more than its share of burning and fire. For much of the world it was the end of the known universe, two crags of rock named for a god, now a terminus that reveals a remarkable connection through each place we've been, and where we're bound to go next.

If it feels like we've hopped around Spain, it's because we have. I picked up trails and clues over multiple trips to the country. But I'm sparing you the uninteresting details of, as they say, how the sausage got made. Or in this case how the morcilla got made. So in the same way a tapestry consists of numerous threads, I'm simply sharing the end result, woven into a panorama as though it's been one expedition. And, I suppose, these bite-sized excursions are indeed part of our single, ongoing quest.

From the shade of a terracotta balcony bordered in orange trees, I'm back for a spell on the south coast of Spain, watching slow-moving caterers lay out mayonnaise-based food in stiflingly hot afternoon sun. Even flies meandering over the dishes look lethargic in the heat. I realize the banquet is for the function I'll be forced to attend, and I glance at my watch. The event will *start* in four hours, then continue for another four hours or so – more than enough time for the buffet to become poison. And I make a mental note to be kind to the people I visit with as it may be the last time I see them alive, or continent. Then again it couldn't possibly create any more discomfort than what I attended the previous night – a cocktail reception at one of the most inappropriate venues imaginable. It was arranged by an employee of the corporate sponsor who'd be fired as a result.

A group of us had been shuttled to the sprawling compound retreat of a billionaire international arms dealer. Who it is isn't important, plus I'm afraid to tell you his name. For a while he was the richest person anywhere. Apparently the place (which he rarely used) was rented out to the public a few times a year for tax purposes. We learned this after the fact. Which made me wonder: Why is it we only ever hear about *international* arms dealers? Do they have any regional, or municipal arms dealers? Are *their* places open to the public as well? Questions that'll likely remain unanswered. Anyhoo. As a coach hauled us into dry Spanish hills, once more I felt cast into a Hemingway story, this time reminiscent of *For Whom the Bell Tolls*.

I was dropped by a gate leading onto the property, along with some others, and just like Alhambra, it was a stark contrast to surrounding countryside, an oasis amid arid topography. It overlooked a lush emerald golf course, and we were told there were only nine members. I suspect each has an open file at C I A, M I 6 and Mossad. Part of the estate was covered in camouflage netting, obscuring it, I presume, from air strikes.

This time, believe it or not, I felt suitably dressed. We entered the mansion into a reception area, a sunken room filled with exotic animals – all dead and stuffed, along with a disturbing collection of elephant tusks. I took in the grisly décor, placed amongst artifacts that could only have come from museums, no doubt purchased or re-stolen from grave robbers. For all I know, wine was being decanted in the grail itself. I was passed a gin and tonic, which I inadvertently placed on what might've been the Ark of the Covenant, and nervously tried to blot up a wet ring with my sleeve. People moved around uncomfortably and no one mentioned the elephant in the room. Its foot was a table in the corner.

I had another G & T, which I believe is the best means of keeping both malaria and social discomfort at bay. But I was afraid of what we'd be served for dinner, possibly a soufflé of panda. So I dawdled on an open terrace overlooking the Pillars of Hercules, the north coast of Africa somewhere through a thin band of fog, a body of water sailed by a great many Vikings. Somewhere in indigo depths their treasure and comrades still lie, part of the ocean floor where Gibraltar was born. Some believe their spirits reside in the rock, part of the land and the sea, narrows and strait that could pass for the mouth of a chalice.

Now, at the entrance to the Mediterranean, where we are represents not only an interim conclusion within our saga but the starting point of another, a spur track with less deviation, a new and straight line to follow. Will this direct route lead us straight to the grail? The *actual* grail? I like to think so. We'll just have to head out and see.

PART II:
VIKING HOLY LAND

5

SOLAR PATHS

Before we leave the southwest corner of Europe, let's delve a bit deeper into Gibraltar. You can trace a great deal of western history through this hunk of Jurassic limestone, a cement crust of old ocean floor and compacted seashell. It's a British Overseas Territory and has been since the 1713 Treaty of Utrecht, when it was ceded to the UK following an Anglo-Dutch capture of this terrain from Spain, part of the Hapsburgs taking over the Spanish throne.

It remains rigidly British, stuck like a patch onto Spain. The Rock of Gibraltar is pretty much all you can see from the centre of town. Locals are known as Gibraltarians, and its flag and coat of arms are quite simple: a fortified castle with a big golden key, plunked on a slab of red. It's known as the Badge of the Rock of Gibraltar, and here they sing "God Save the King."

If you're looking out to the water, the geographic, military and economic significance of the place is obvious. The Strait of Gibraltar is considered a naval choke point, controlling access to the Mediterranean Sea. It's only 14 kilometres wide, and half the world's seagoing trade passes through here. Gibraltar's sovereignty remains a sore point in Spanish–British relations. Spain feels the land should belong to them. A cartographer would agree. But despite referendums and Spanish proposals for Britain to release this real estate, the notion continues to fall on deaf ears.

History here is extensive. There's evidence of human habitation around Gibraltar dating back 50,000 years, specifically in a place called Gorham's Cave. It was a space where Neanderthals passed the baton, so to speak (or possibly a femur), to Homo Sapiens. And it's one of the last places Neanderthals lived before being replaced (more or less) by our smaller, marginally smarter ancestors. Archaeologists have unearthed stone tools, fire pits and animal bones from 40,000 years ago in the cave, which was used until the early Bronze Age, around 3000 BCE. Then for some reason, following a staggering 400 centuries of continuous use, Gibraltar's caves were abandoned.

This transition through more modern times, Bronze and Iron Ages, may coincide with the locale becoming a place of religious significance. Phoenicians (from what is now called Lebanon) treated the cave as a shrine to protective spirits, referred to as *genii locorum* (singular, *genius loci*). Carthaginians (from what is now Tunisia) followed, then Romans did the same, worshipping and acknowledging the spiritual energy of these subterranean chambers. And I'm reminded of the vast range of spirits appearing and accompanying us on our viking pursuits: Icelandic huldufólk, Norse dísir and nymphs from ancient Greece.

Gibraltar is an anglicized version of its Arabic name, Jabal Tariq, or Mount Tariq, named for eighth-century military commander Tariq ibn Ziyad. The Moroccan peak that bookends the Strait is Jabal Musa. Together, the peaks of Tariq and Musa are known as the Pillars of Hercules.

Before Tariq and his forces were here, a few other nations came through. Soon after the Romans, Goths arrived (no doubt in dark eyeliner, listening to post-punk rock). Germanic Ostrogoths went to Italy while Visigoths came to Spain, ruling for a while before the peninsula became Al-Andalusian Caliphates. It was this group of North Africans, following the arrival of Tariq, that gave the Lothbrok boys a proper thumping as they sailed north toward home, their longships loaded with treasure.

You may recall from previous *Gone Viking* travels that the seafaring soldiers of Al-Andalus had invented cutting-edge weaponry, creating a version of Greek or Byzantine Fire, an incendiary weapon that's effectively an ancient version of napalm. It actually burns hotter on water, more lethal to ships than cannonballs. Moorish forces lobbed these projectiles from catapults onto the Vikings' retreating fleet, the strait itself becoming part of Spain's defences. As the Lothbroks sailed through the narrows, fireballs flew from the shore and Iberian missile-boats, snapping pitch-soaked timber, engulfing sails and smashing armour-clad rowers into the sea.

Despite the carnage, two-thirds of the Lothbrok fleet survived, bursting through Herculean Pillars into Atlantic to make their way north, where Björn Ironside would rule Sweden's Old Dynasty, known as the House of Uppsala. But before we track down Ironside's kingdom in Sweden, let's get to know Hercules. It was, after all, the jagged pillars of stone named for this Greek–Roman god that stood watch as the Vikings sailed home.

In Rome he was Hercules. In Greece, Herakles. Son of the woman named Alcmene and her one-time lover Zeus, god of thunder and king of the gods of Olympus. If you lived around Rome, Hercules's dad was Jupiter. Same gods, different versions. All too familiar. But we're going to follow the Greek version, where our hero spells his name Herakles, and his biological dad is Zeus. With her husband Amphitryon, Alcmene raised the boy with their daughter and son, half-sister and half-brother to Herakles.

Herakles is referred to as *heros theos*, both hero and god. A demi-god. Child of a mixed marriage, you might say. And our hero–god may be best known for his labours, the Twelve Labours of Herakles. Basically the labours were laid out as penance in the service of Eurystheus, king of Tiryns, part of south Greece. It was written about by a poet named Peisander around 600 BCE. Homer then added his own embellishments, beefing up the tale the way Shakespeare improved on the classics 2,000 years later.

Basically, Herakles was on pilgrimage, a proto-Christian trail of indulgence. He'd slaughtered his family but apparently it wasn't his fault, as he'd been consumed by madness. Not a great defence, but there you go. Wracked with guilt when he "realized what he'd done," he trekked to what was considered the navel of the world at Delphi, a short distance northwest of Athens.

This theoretical *axis mundi* is the mythological centre of the universe, and depending on where you are, it could be one of many locales. Ask an Easter Islander and they'll tell you it's the site of Ahu Te Pito Kura. To the Tohono O'odham Nation it's Baboquivari Peak, Arizona. Many feel the Earth's heart is Jerusalem's Foundation Stone, or the Hagia Sophia in Istanbul, our old Viking bastion of Miklagard. But for Herakles, the centre of it all was Delphi, a spherical stone where he spoke to the oracle Pythia, and was told to serve King Eurystheus for ten years, doing the king's bidding. His reward for completing all this would be absolution, but as a parting gift he'd also become immortal. If that ain't a proper quest, I don't know what is. In a nutshell, the king laid out these labours for Herakles's grail-like quest:

1. Slay the Nemean Lion, a vicious gold beast from Nemea, in Corinthia (where car seat leather comes from, I believe).

2. Defeat the Lernaean Hydra, a nine-headed water serpent from Lerna, entrance to the underworld.

3. Capture the Ceryneian Hind, an enormous deer with gold antlers and hooves of bronze. The king wanted this for his court at Mycenae. Oh yes, and the deer could also snort fire.

4. Capture the Erymanthian Boar. This was a shape-shifting beast, said to be "shaggy, wild, tameless, of vast weight and foaming jaws." Why the king wanted the boar is unclear. It might've just been for a pig roast.

5. Clean the Augean stables in a single day. Which sounds like the king was running out of chores. Then again, he may've simply wanted the stables cleaned, a task akin to scrubbing the coliseum toilets after the match. The stables, by the way, were for cattle. A lot of them. And the ranch belonged to Augeas, one of the Argonauts.

6. Slay the Stymphalian Birds. These were the original Angry Birds, but rather than animated pigs the birds would attack and eat people. Their feathers were made of metal and shot from their wings like bullets. And to make these creatures even more loathsome, their dung was known to be poisonous. Don't ask me who figured this out, or how.

7. Capture the Cretan Bull. This was the Minotaur's biological father.

8. Steal the Mares of Diomedes. These were monstrous horses with a taste for human flesh, and belonged to Diomedes of Thrace.

9. Obtain the Girdle of Hippolyta, Queen of the Amazon. Although this sounds like a fraternity prank, this particular "girdle" was the military belt Hippolyta inherited from her dad, Ares, god of courage and war.

10. Rustle the giant Geryon's cattle. Here we link once more to our saga. Grandson to Medusa, Geryon was a particularly vicious giant (with a great herd of cattle). His home was the mythic isle Erytheia, "far to the west in the Mediterranean." Greek scholars pinpoint this place as the south tip of Iberia, next to Gibraltar.

11. Steal three golden apples from the Hesperides. Again we're on track with our quest, as the Hesperides were spirits known as "nymphs of the gold light of sunsets," or "nymphs of the west." Daughters of Atlas (the guy with the world on his back), these maritime sprites have also been called the Atlantides, and lived just beyond Gibraltar.

12. And, finally, capture and bring back Cerberus. This was the Hound of Hades, the multi-headed, dragon-tailed dog that guarded the underworld gates. Cerberus's job was to keep the dead in their place, to prevent them from getting out and no

doubt plaguing the world with another wave of unwatchable zombie movies.

Herakles's travails represent another epic saga, one beginning at the centre of the universe and ending at the edge of the world, with our hero (yet again) concluding the quest by defeating a fresh iteration of dragon. If we plot on a map the swath of Eurasia that Herakles traversed to accomplish his labours, we'd find not only familiar geography but also some fascinating folks we already know. We haven't focused on them specifically but they've always been close, near us every step of the way. At times mysterious, blending into the land, the people I'm referring to are the mystical, Viking-esque Celts.

For the longest time I thought Celts were exclusively tribes concentrated around the British Isles and a few pockets of coast in western Europe, specifically Britons and Gaels, like those of Arthur's Welsh–Cornish lineage. But rather than a distinct ethnicity, Celts are actually an amalgam of nations sharing similar language and culture.

Celts appear around the entire Mediterranean, comprising most of Gaul and the Germanic countries across central Europe, commingling with Greeks and inhabiting parts of Asia. The vibrancy and geographical expanse of Arthurian-like Celts place these sophisticated people directly on our grail timeline, preceding the Roman Empire, carrying on through the time of Jomsvikings and grail-hiding crusaders and continuing to thrive today. Now, as we search place and time to unearth the chalice, who better to guide us on the next leg of our journey than the people who inhabit each pivotal point on our path?

The geographic diversity and cultural resiliency of Celts is astonishing. They're present at each juncture on our trek across Europe and, yes, they appear in the homeland of the Vikings. The largest historical groupings of Celtic nations are Gauls (across France, Germany, Switzerland, Austria, Luxembourg, Belgium, the Netherlands and Denmark), Celtiberians and Gallaecians (in Spain and Portugal),

Britons and Gaels (around the British Isles) and Galatians (throughout Italy, Greece and Turkey).

Interestingly, we can plot the rise of Celts from the Bronze Age, that moment in time when the caves of Gibraltar were abandoned and left to the hidden spirits, as though this growing collective rose from the earth to inhabit the rest of Eurasia. So how does Herakles fit into this, and what's the connection with Celts? Well, it's called the Via Heraklea, or Heraklean Way.

You may know of Celtic history and lore from Druids, stone circles and stories of sacrifice. As with the religious transition taking root across Scandinavia, Celts too had to adapt, reinterpreting beliefs. Invariably Celts were put to the test as Romans advanced across Europe. In Britain and Germany the Romans simply put up a wall, keeping Celts at bay. Elsewhere, we've seen Celts coexist with the legions from Rome and eventually early Christians. Through it all Celts were there, shifting the nature of worship, toeing reinforced lines when essential. But the basis of faith of these people predates most known deities. Instead, prayer in its way was no different than science, knowledge of the celestial universe. And that's where the Celts and our labouring hero from Greece link up in spectacular fashion, pointing us on our way.

The Heraklean Way is a magical path. And a very real one. It runs from the southwest corner of the Iberian Peninsula, just past the Pillars of Hercules, where the "nymphs of the gold light of sunsets" tended their apple trees, and follows an arrow-straight trajectory across the Celtic lands of western Europe. It's also the path of the sun, precisely at the summer solstice. And it allows for the tilt of the earth's axis, maintaining precise alignment between the planet's surface and the sun at its zenith. With the length of northern hemisphere summer days, the near-perfect alignment lasts for almost a week. If you thought Stonehenge was something, think of the math behind this.

Remarkably, the ground tends to be an efficient transport route, following walkable terrain. And while Romans were later known for building straight roads, they weren't averse to skirting a mountain or village if it made miles accumulate quickly. But not the Heraklean Way. Author Graham Robb describes it comprehensively in *The Ancient Paths*. Through extensive research and aerial photography, this direct ancient road of the Celts and theoretical footsteps of Herakles reveals itself, passing through fields, mountain passes, cities and towns and even a few modern motorways. This is the path we'll pick up, as we turn from the end of the earth in Spain to head east. Our grail quest hasn't changed. Yes, I'm impressed with the various Spanish chalices, not to mention the Genoese dish, but I'm in no way convinced that we've yet found our grail.

If you envision the Iberian Peninsula on a map, it almost resembles a square. Now, imagine a line running diagonally across Spain from the lower left (known as the Sacred Promontory) to the country's upper right corner. This is the route Hannibal took as he marched his vast army (90,000 troops and a few dozen elephants) from North Africa into Spain. He specifically chose the sacred route of the Celts as he made his way north and east, aligned with a rising sun and the path taken by Herakles. Yes, there was a great deal of political pageantry as he marched through Iberia, but it was a tactical route as well: spiritual, historically significant and mostly efficient.

This took place in the third century BCE. Carthage (Hannibal's turf) was at war with Rome and had been for generations, in what is known as the Punic Wars. Alexander the Great had been dead for a hundred years and the great powers of the western Mediterranean were Romans and Carthaginians, almost a North–South rivalry across the Med. Spain was allied with Rome at the time, so by starting his campaign with a quick trouncing of Iberia, Hannibal sent a clear message: he was gunning for Rome. Jesus was still, you might say, nothing more than a twinkle in somebody's eye, and ancient gods were very much in charge. Combine this with the heroic nature of Herakles's conquests, and it's no stretch to assume Hannibal fancied himself a renewed personification of the demigod.

As we say goodbye to the bullfighting rings, Iberian ham and Hemingway memories, not to mention our encounters with saints John and James, we find ourselves once more heading into the Pyrenees. Looking back I can't help but imagine the forces of Hannibal making their way here, clouds of dust and thundering earth as an endless expanse of armoured military marched this way, trumpeting elephants, the whinny of cavalry horses and bugles punctuating the shouts of commanders. Think of the logistics, feeding a mobile city of soldiers: fires and tents, clerics, healers and strategists. Quite the opposite of the sortie approach of our northern rowers, speeding through in their dragon-prowed ships.

At this juncture we're no longer in Spain, but we're not quite in France yet either. Where we are is the minuscule principality of Andorra, sandwiched between France and Spain in the steeply treed Pyrenees. It's a place for skiing and duty-free shopping, a tax haven of chic boutiques and custom-made jewellery. In the centre of town is the high, steely spire of the Church of Santa Coloma. From a distance the spired valley town resembles a sundial in a forested bowl.

Even here, following Celts and Herakles, rising sun and Hannibal too for a stretch, we're still never far from the grail. At any high point around here we can find a direct line of sight to the Château de Montségur, where grail researchers feel the cup may've last gone to ground. If we were to deviate from our Heraklean Way and go there (from here) by car, the road forms a perfect S, the exact thing grail writers Thomas Malory and John Hardyng said to never dismiss. Clues like this and secrets buried in etymology made up much of their work. An S, they'd insist, is the symbol for *san-gréal*, meaning Holy Grail, or *sang réal*, as in the bloodline of Jesus. Which seems like a stretch, but both were adamant regarding these kinds of details. No different, I suppose, than us seeking signposted scallop shells to find our way from Saint Michael's to Saint James's Camino, from one land's end to another.

Only we're not taking that S-shaped road. With a plane and a train we'll leapfrog these Celtic Gaul hills, staying true to our Heraklean

Way, on the path of a high summer sun. From the wooded greens of the Pyrenees our solstice road will take us over the Rhône, slicing into Switzerland and Etruscan Italy, where Hannibal marched his army of elephants into the snowy Alps. Some consider this region, from the Swiss border to Austria, the Celtic homeland. But before we get there, with Andorra and Spain now in our rear-view mirror, let's spend time once again in France, where intriguing new clues to the grail have surfaced.

It's no secret that relics, in part, became a means to an end for Christian places of worship, and a great source of revenue. Churches, temples and basilicas prosper from pilgrimage. Pilgrims mean donations, donations mean expansion, and in theory more souls can be saved. Relics in particular have always brought in the pilgrims. So it comes as no surprise that nearly 200 grail-like bowls and cups "vie for the title." The cliché of a quest for the Holy Grail has been an incentive to trekkers and pilgrims for a very long time.

In Spain we pilgrims are called peregrinas or peregrinos. In Italy, pellegrini. Here in France we're pèlerines or pèlerins. Two thousand years of trekking toward sites of significance as newly "discovered" relics continue to surface. It's been estimated that if every "piece of the true cross" were gathered and reassembled, we'd have enough lumber to crucify most of the cast from the Old Testament. However, one of the most notable relics that's managed to remain elusive is the holy lance, also known as the Spear of Destiny or Lance of Longinus.

According to the Bible, as in most crucifixions, Jesus wasn't dead when he was put on the cross. Death by crucifixion tended to be slow and miserable, an example to others. Whether out of impatience, cruelty or possibly compassion, as Jesus hung on the cross, blood seeping from wounds inflicted by nails and a thorny crown, an "unnamed Roman soldier" gave him a stab with a spear (the lance). This was likely the wound that Aunt Salome and Uncle Joseph did their best to clean up, perhaps resulting in the contents of the grail. If we follow the story of the mysterious soldier, it's said that he fled the army, converted to Christianity and in his own Heraklean manner of pilgrimage went on to repent for his sins, save souls and eventually become Saint Longinus.

Here in France (where we're now pèlerines et pèlerins), our grail-thread weaves like wool on a loom. The French telling of the Arthurian cycle began with 12th-century writer Chrétien de Troyes and his unfinished verse *Perceval, le Conte du Graal*. It was the first literary appearance of the grail, picked up by other French authors and subsequent Germans and Britons. However, 600 years earlier, a Frankish bishop named Arculf was on pilgrimage in the Holy Land when he saw what he said was the Last Supper chalice on display outside of Jerusalem. Could this be the equivalent of another true cross or was it the actual grail?

After Chrétien's Arthurian writings, Bavarian poet Albrecht von Scharfenberg penned *Der Jüngere Titurel* and a piece titled *Merlin*, referencing the grail and Parzival. But what brings these things back to our path here in France is that it's the city of Troyes where the grail, it seems, reappeared. The chalice von Scharfenberg wrote about was seen by multiple pilgrims in Constantinople, consistent with Arculf's account. This reputed grail was housed next to the Black Sea, the same spot where Herakles stole Diomedes's horses, and the place Vikings knew as Miklagard. And it's this grail from what's now Turkey that was said to have been brought to France. Allegedly it came to the place where Chrétien first wrote of it, in Troyes. So is this the same grail that Arculf saw "near Jerusalem"? Might he have actually seen it in Turkey, but generalized his geography? Or fudged a bit to embellish the extent of his pilgrimage?

Troyes, home to Gallic Celts, is situated in the heart of Champagne, between our Heraklean Way and Paris. In the village centre stands Cathédrale Saint-Pierre Saint-Paul, dedicated to both Peter and Paul, a chunky Gothic structure tucked in a loop of the Seine. The current church replaced what stood when Chrétien was here, as he no doubt fussed with his poetic notes, deciding what best rhymes with *grail*. Although it's been rebuilt multiple times, each chapel has its own remarkable history. One of the most notable being from the fifth century when Attila came through, his own Caliburn longsword raised in a show of conquest. But the Bishop of Troyes met the Hun at the gates, and in a rare showing of empathy, Attila left the cathedral intact, allowing the bishop and his clerics to carry on undisturbed. A story consistent with what Arthur endeavoured to do with Excalibur, in the words of the king, "a blade for healing, not hacking."

A few centuries after that brave bishop's time, Troyes Cathedral was damaged during Norman invasions and rebuilt in the tenth century. This is the church where an aging Chrétien went to pray and work on his poems (*assail? impale? dragon-tail?*). A matter of days before his passing the church suffered a terrible fire. The poet would've smelled the charred wood and watched as the cleanup began. Now, bits of that thousand-year-old structure are preserved and displayed in the current Cathedral of Troyes.

The grail that made its way here from Miklagard (or possibly nearer Jerusalem) would've crossed 3000 kilometres that neatly mirror our Heraklean Way. It reportedly remained in the protection of Troyes for half a millennium, until late in the 18th century, the height of the French Revolution, when a fascinating unwinding of accounts ensues. As the fight for liberté, égalité and fraternité raged, the grail simply vanished. Some said it was lost. Others claimed it was only ever a duplicate. (How anyone could verify *that* makes you scratch your head.) But what stands out is the explosion of contradictory explanations. "Verified" conflicting stories. Which shows rather convincingly that anyone and everyone close to the grail was lying, throwing up smokescreens or planting red herrings. Which smacks of that last time around, when crusaders and our chivalrous Vikings from Poland stole away with what they called the Gallic trésor, their mysterious holy treasure.

Back to our Heraklean Way. We're now on the south coast of France. The Côte d'Azur. Apart from the Sacred Promontory in the far corner of Spain, this is the closest we'll be to the sea on our Celtic path of the solstice. Our diagonal line across Europe hugs the coast between Agde and Montpellier at a bight in the Med called the Gulf of Lion which leads us into Marseille. Here the Rhône incorporates the Druentia, a linguistic derivative of Druids if there ever was one. (Word symbologists Malory and Hardyng high-five.) It's also a vibrant, global hub, brimming with history. So let's stop for a good look around.

The port of Marseille has been integral to Mediterranean culture and trade since 600 BCE. Greeks from the city of Phocaea in Asia Minor are credited with founding this French town, and it represents what might be the most significant point in the coming together of Celts and Greeks. Around markets and piers, new concepts changed hands along with textiles, produce and seafood. Ideas and language were shared, and we see a blending of philosophy and science from this era. Celts got here mostly by land, often by chariot, great wagon-like vehicles hauled by stout ponies. A carved circle with spokes, a miniature version of those chariot wheels, would often be found on a Celt's person, symbol of movement and science, the interconnectivity of nature with the universe of humans and gods. It's a pattern we see in the swirls of Celtic crosses and knots, designs reminiscent of whorl growths in wood and inked tattoo art.

Romans copied Celtic chariot design, over time improving their speed, and we're left to wonder just how much modern science and philosophy came from the Greeks or in fact was adapted through learning from druidic Celts. Many Greeks and travellers from the Celtic heartland were multilingual, fluent in the primary languages of Europe. It brings to mind the British–Arabic dinars of King Offa, currency for the Mediterranean and aspirations of global trade.

Following the mouth of the Rhône into Marseille, the first impression is one of a cosmopolitan centre. Past the marina with its rock breakwater and pristine white sailboats, it looks as though nothing's changed since the time Vikings were here and perhaps the grail appeared. Buildings in stone with splashing high fountains could be straight out of Athens. Greek gods and mythical beasts are carved into sandstone, and open-walled columns look like a setting for toga-clad orators, strolling about and debating new laws from the senate. And this *was* a centre of early democracy, with a legislative assembly of 600 elected officials. Cathedrals too resemble basilicas and mosques from across the Mediterranean. High fortified walls, designed to withstand catapult siege, surround ornate chapels with onion dome spires. It feels as though we could be anywhere from the south of Spain to the shores of Byzantium.

Marseille is the oldest city in France and one of the oldest in Europe. When Greeks arrived they called it Massalia, and now it's best known for soap, the savon de Marseille. Following 30 years of urban investment and economic development, it's been named European Capital of Culture by the EU, and next to Paris has more museums than anywhere else in the country. Inlets along the coast, connecting fishing communities, have a decidedly fjord-like look, and you can see the appeal for Ragnar's sons, choosing these shores to winter their longships. No doubt the sunshine appealed as well. And a proliferation of grape vines.

Marseille, or Massalia, has always been an enclave of independence. As with wealthy ports the world over, economic affluence tends to create its own fortification. We still see this at the narrows of Gibraltar with lucrative refuelling stations. The same way mighty Venice commanded the Dalmatian coast for centuries. Marseille's sea-hugging corniche with buildings in red-tile roofs in fact reminds me of that part of the world.

Marseille's power ensured the port remained politically independent, even as Hannibal made his way through. But the city was forced to take sides during Caesar's civil war in 49 BCE. Marseille bet against Caesar, and in the words of the grail-knight from *Indiana Jones and the Last Crusade*, "They chose...poorly." Caesar was victorious, and Marseilles was taken over by Rome. The town again played a pivotal role during the French revolution, when what's now the national anthem was sung for the first time, right here. Although written in the north at Strasbourg, the song's still known as "La Marseillaise."

Now, let me introduce you to Pytheas, a true explorer and in a way, one of the very first Vikings. Born in Massalia (Marseille) in 350 BCE, he was also one of the earliest Celtic Greeks. He's considered a geographer, explorer and astronomer, but I like to think of him as a student of the world, wide-eyed with an open mind. At the age of 25 he set off. His trip wasn't clearly defined, but we can assume he wanted to see it all, to go as far as humanly possible and perhaps that little bit further. Despite taking place three-and-a-half centuries before the Last Supper, the voyage of Pytheas was indeed a grail-like quest, one in search of wisdom, enlightenment and a taste of immortality. But like our Scandinavian explorers, while experiences were extensive, records of those adventures are sparse. Most accounts of Pytheas's travels, like the Sagas, were written years later, compiling oral legend and snippets that survived through memory and repetition of tales.

We can be fairly certain Pytheas set sail from his hometown of Massalia, one of the ancient world's great ports (along with Ephesus, Alexandria and Athens). He would've sailed from the gulf through the Balearic Sea, then on through the Pillars of Hercules, a route roughly the same as Hannibal, Herakles and the Greek sun-god Helios late in the day. His ship rounded Spain's Sacred Promontory, possibly skirting the gold apple orchards of nymphs. Then he followed the coasts and the tides heading north, the path of homeward-bound Danes.

Ships at the time tended to stay close to shore, keeping land within sight, only veering to open water to avoid rocky headlands or the roil of shifting shoals. Because of this, Pytheas and his shipmates would've spotted each subsequent point of land's end: Finisterre in

Spain, Brittany's Finistère, and the westernmost point of England. He would eventually circumnavigate the British Isles from the Celtic to the North Sea, cross Scandinavian waters and beyond, sailing further north, he believed, than anyone had before.

Pytheas was the first scientific explorer to experience the Arctic by sea. He described polar ice, what Saint Brendan would later compare to crystal cathedrals and floating castles of silver. As he went, Pytheas continued to meet and communicate with Celts and Germanic tribes, fishing from coracles and hollowed canoes, their Iron Age settlements, called oppida, built on high ground, facing the sea and the path of the sun. As he went further north, he spoke of the magnificence of sunshine at midnight. No doubt he would question whether or not he'd outsailed the gods themselves, or if this was where Helios came to rest. Imagine his wonder on his Celtic travails, arriving at a place on the globe in a moment of time when the solstice would hang, suspended, refusing to change the world's course.

But the gods did return, the world carried on, and Helios seemed to vanish. Pytheas spoke of a place of perpetual darkness and snow. Remarkably, accounts of this far northern land were already known, not from Mediterranean travellers but by Arctic nomads wandering south. The Greeks called this place Hyperborea, meaning "above the north wind." There were rumours of Hyperborean people living in a "paradise of perpetual sun, beyond the reach of the wind." So those previous travellers had experienced northern summer, while the accounts of Pytheas correspond not only to a similar season but to winter solstice as well.

In another first for geographers, Pytheas spoke of the land known as Thule, a place where he realized tides respond to the path of the moon. Insightful, cutting-edge stuff. You can't help but admire this proto-Viking explorer, possibly doing more for science than personal gain. Accounts place him northwest of the Orkneys, and although anthropologists believe Pytheas may've been in the Faroes, it's more likely he sailed to Iceland. A wonderfully illuminated map, the *Carta*

Marina, created by Swedish cartographer Olaus Magnus in the 16th century, places the Isle of Thule (which Magnus spells *Tile*) in a pod of surfacing sea monsters. A spout of water emanating from the top of one's head, and a reference to the beasts as balena, indicate they were likely just fierce-looking whales.

When I found myself beyond the islands of Orkney, bound for what might be Thule, I didn't spot any monsters. No kraken or even a passing walrus. Although I *had* just made my way from some carved bits of walrus ivory. No, not in the creepy reception room of our blacklisted arms-dealing host in Spain. These ones were set under glass, raised on a well-lit dais in the British Museum. They were Lewis Chessmen, a few pieces of one set of players in the weather-worn colour of cream. As their name indicates, the chessmen, believed to have been carved by a woman from Norway, were discovered on the Island of Lewis, in Scotland's Outer Hebrides, one of the last bits of land you encounter before arriving at the black shores of Thule.

Whoever it was that first located this island – Celts, Scandinavians, possibly Sami or Inuit hunters – Thule was named by the Greeks, and notations appear from roughly that time, written on scrolls in Rome. What I love about references to exotic and "new" distant lands is that elements of science, philosophy and art converge, as voyagers trek toward the unknown, hoping to unmask the gods.

It raises the question, how did Pytheas get here? Which route did he take? Sailing around the Iberian Peninsula into the Bay of Biscay, he'd have been at sea quite some time, possibly weeks, before reaching the same latitude as where he began, back in the Mediterranean. As he passed through the scatter of islets that comprise the end of the land in France, he was due west of Troyes, possible home of the grail.

Reaching the southwest of England, known as Belerion, he'd have passed the Lizard Peninsula, Britain's most southerly point. It's the place where 2,500 years later I'd do the very same thing as I followed the Vikings, with seven other sailors, racing to outrun a tempest. The engine on our cutter had died, leaving us reliant on current and wind,

and the front half of the boat was submerged with each smash of increasing waves. There was a splintering *crack* like a gunshot as wind
shattered the top third of our mast, the topsail flapping and useless.
We were tethered to the deck with lifelines, zipped snug into bulky
survival suits, but our radio worked and we were only a few hours from
shelter. What I remember is the aroma of sheep on the cliffs, blowing
out from the land to the sea.

If Pytheas did as we'd done, bearing east toward the narrows of the
Channel, he'd pass the spot where William would eventually cross
and then conquer, offspring of Norman Viking lord Rollo. In addition to the land's end of Belerion, England's southeast region of Kent
was another key geographical point, along with its northerly tip at
Orkney. These were known as the three corners of Britain: Belerion,
Kantion and Orkas.

On a map you can see how Great Britain resembles a tall, slender
triangle, and was used, quite literally, as a means of triangulation, creating navigational rhumb lines. Road builders, architects and astron-
omers were already using theodolites called dioptra, surveyors' rods
with dual sight points. In conjunction with spirals and whorls, triads
and three-sided angles were the most frequent methods of demarcation
in Celtic science, art and design. The secrets of triangles could follow
the sun and the stars, predict seasons, and measure weight, distance
and time. Which in part is why they appeared in the segmented spokes
of small wheels so many Celts carried as talismans.

As Pytheas made his way toward the North Sea, he was cutting
through watery roads of the Danes, future paths of east–west invasion,
migration and trade. With the Danish homeland due east, on Britain's
Northumberland shores were the moors of York, and a fortified town
that would centre the Danelaw, Viking capital of Britain. It's where
another Lothbrok would rule, Ivar Ragnarsson, Ivar the Boneless, son
of Ragnar and brother to Hastein and Björn. While two other boys
from the brood, Ubba and Halfdan Ragnarsson, led the mass immigration, or invasion, of the "Great Heathen Army" that would occupy

the Kentish corner of England in 865. Had Pytheas arrived 11 centuries later, he could almost have plotted his course from the Med to the north of England by triangulating sites run by the Lothbroks.

At this juncture we can pinpoint where Pytheas was on his journey. It's been recorded in three separate sources: the *Bibliotheca Historica* written by the Sicilian Greek Diodorus, the 17-volume *Geographica* written by Strabo in Anatolia, and the *Naturalis Historia* by Pliny the Elder, who lived and wrote in Rome. Using the height or elevation of midwinter sun, Pytheas was able to calculate his latitude with admirable precision, giving us an exact place and time as he passed the neck of Great Britain, where Hadrian would build his wall. The next latitudinal reading we have places Pytheas outside Inverness, just south of Orkney. Which is where we gain wonderful insight and detail as to the people Pytheas met and the manner in which they lived in north Scotland.

He describes homes built of timber and reeds, where grains were brought indoors to avoid the damp of sea air. He referenced the diet being made up of tubers, roots and herbs, with little in the way of fresh fruit or meat. Porridge was already a staple, made from a type of millet that grew in thin soil. Coming from a wine growing region, Pytheas went on to note his fascination with the locals' manner of fermentation, and their ability to distill liquor from honey and grain.

According to Pytheas he traversed the "whole" of Britain, referring specifically to travelling the land's "perimeter." But despite the relative precision of latitude, distances remained approximate. Stadia were the units of measure, a stade being about 180 strides, or metres. These measurements related to Roman miles, generally used to determine how long it would take an army to move between places. Pytheas measured Great Britain at 40,000 stadia, a bit under 5,000 miles, and said it took about a month and a half to circumnavigate.

Using these descriptions and his own calculations, Claudius Ptolemy, an Egyptian Roman from Alexandria, mapped it out, and did a fine job of it too. Working from Ptolemy's *Geographia*, 15th-century mapmaker Johannes Schnitzer created an illuminated chart of the entire Mediterranean, including Asia Minor and North Africa. It looks pretty much the same as in the *National Geographic* world atlas I had as a kid.

But when the same manner of map reconstruction was done for Great Britain using descriptions Pytheas made, reinterpreted by Ptolemy, the resulting map is intriguingly flawed. England and Ireland look more or less spot on, and so too does Scotland, except that the country is flopped over to one side, as though someone left the cake out in the rain (the cake in this case being what's north of the Firth of Forth). The coast is accurate, so are offshore islands, but everything's laid out on the same latitude. Which tells us at some point in that dim winter light Pytheas cocked up his celestial readings. But it verifies that he knew the lay of the land (and the sea), with an accuracy that could only be attained by being there.

Now on to Thule. Like a game of "whisper" going round the room, with each new telling of the tale details increasingly vary. That's the case with respect to where exactly this island's located. Pytheas said that he sailed six days north from the top end of Britain. Frustratingly, he failed to mention if he bore east or west. Given the tides and the season we know it was right around midsummer. Some scholars believe that he travelled to Norway. Other calculations plot Pytheas veering into the Baltic, across north Germany and the future site of Jomsborg, which would place Thule near the coast of Estonia.

To bring it back to etymology, a great deal's revealed by the choice and use of place names. In classical literature, Ultima Thule was used to denote the farthest reaches of Thule, or "beyond the borders of the known world." Consensus through the Middle Ages, backed up by standardized distances, tended to agree that Pytheas's Thule was indeed Iceland, and that Ultima Thule was Greenland.

Twentieth-century Greenlandic–Dane anthropologist and explorer Knud Rasmussen was born there, at Ultima Thule, in the northwest of Greenland. In 1910 he travelled up the frozen west side of the world's biggest island to establish a missionary and trading post at a place he too called Thule. Now it's properly called Qaanaaq, a community of about 650 people, all multilingual, speaking a mixture of Inuktun, Kalaallisut (Greenlandic Inuit) and Danish. Rasmussen would go on to complete the first crossing of the Northwest Passage by dogsled, and remains one of the best-known modern-day Vikings.

When I arrived at Ultima Thule, I was dropped at the southwestern toe of the island. I'd flown in from the Thule of Pytheas, the plane taking off over Reykjavik harbour, the place living up to its translated moniker of "smoky bay." Sea fret and a frosty comingle of vog (volcanic fog) spilled over the tundra to hide most of the coast. I shivered in my seat, watching as "the borders of the known world" vanished. Three hours later, over the Arctic Circle and what Pytheas called "solidified sea," the plane I was on with two dozen Greenlanders began its descent. The coast's the most rugged I've seen, fjords like the edges of Norway but packed in ice with barely a sliver of arable land. There wasn't a tree to be seen.

Pytheas must've felt much the same when he navigated these waters. He spoke of the sea around Thule and "places where land properly speaking no longer exists, nor sea nor air, but a mixture of things, like a marine lung, where earth and water and all things are suspended, as if a link between all elements, on which one can neither walk nor sail."

My travels across Thule and Ultima Thule concentrated on Viking-themed sites, from a place where Sagas sprang to life, a gruesome statue museum in Reykjavik, to the piers of the Old Port. We sailed into lumps of a haar-covered sea the colour of slate and tar to watch eider ducks bob and rainbow-beaked puffins dive for smelt and sardines. At the port town of Njardvik I spent time aboard the *Íslendingur*, a longship displayed in the glass-walled atrium of Reykjanesbær's Viking World Museum.

Íslendingur is a replica of the *Gokstad*, a ship now in Oslo. And at the turn of the current millennium *Íslendingur* set sail, crossing the Atlantic to commemorate Leif Erikson making the same journey a thousand years earlier. Some time later, while giving a presentation at a

Scandinavian Cultural Centre, I met Norwegian boatbuilder Kristian Frostad, the man who designed and constructed the *Munin*, another *Gokstad* replica, only this version plied the Pacific.

From the ice-covered fjords in south Greenland, by way of small boat and a half-day's climb over mountains, I came to the place where Thorhild and Erik built their own modest craft and a homestead to raise their four children: Freydís Eiríksdóttir and her brothers, Thorvald, Thorstein and Leif Erikson. Just past the Norse farm was the subterranean home of a Bronze Age family of Greenlandic Inuit. On icy wet ground I crawled on all fours to peer into the space and saw nothing but black. The place smelled of peat, a slight whiff of iron-rich soil. I could've sworn I caught aromas of old fire and a family in skins, but after 3,500 years I'm sure it was all in my mind.

That night I ate hearty stew made from fin whale, the flavour and texture of strip loin beef in a gravy that tasted like goulash. I trekked a low ridge of hills to a minuscule village tucked in a valley of rock. Exposed earth was the colour of stone from Sedona, and blankets of tinder-dry moss added splashes of copper and black. The sound of sheep echoed from somewhere, ricocheting through sheer stony cliffs. An inlet of the iceberg-clogged fjord remained mostly liquid, splashing with salmon and char.

The next day, after a meal of reindeer, I made my way back, another climb and descent. But unlike Pytheas, I was picked up by motorboat, where I carried on to a tiny museum in the community of Narsarsuaq. I learned more of the seafarers who settled here, those who wouldn't return to their homeland. Which was not Pytheas's destiny. From these farthest reaches, with his unnamed crew, Pytheas set sail for warm waters.

Currents tend to move east to west in this region, and when combined with prevailing Gulf Stream southwesterlies, this meant that Pytheas and his shipmates must've continuously tacked and gybed, zigzagging back to the south. With pack ice and icebergs behind them, they made for the west edge of Britain, no doubt passing again what became Norse Shetland and Orkney.

In his book *Sixty Degrees North*, Scottish author Malachy Tallack tells of leaving his Shetland home and meeting new people from Norway.

"Where are you from?" he was asked, in singsong-accented English.

"Shetland," he replied.

"So, you're one of us!" the Norseman said with a warm and familiar smile.

When Deb and I trekked through the area and spent time on Orkney, our geographical timeline remained a blur. Land still spits up Stone Age communities and barrows, dotted with Bronze Age standing stones and druidic places of worship. Celt and Norse influence create a cultural roux, the language alone a hybrid of territory and history.

For 600 years through the Golden Age of Vikings, these islands were part of Norway. Early in the 13th century Norwegian King Haakon IV sailed here, past Ronaldsay, Burray and Scapa. He came to Kirkwall on the island of Mainland, the exact spot where we started our 21st-century Orcadian exploration. The king died here in 1263, just before Yule celebrations, and was interred at St Magnus Cathedral. Now you're just as likely to find a cruise ship's worth of tourists filling the medieval building of red and gold sandstone, doubling the town's population every few weeks in the summer. But with a moderate stroll or a very short drive you can have a good stretch of time-bending archipelago all to yourself.

Before we depart from these northerly isles, let's take a quick look at the king, a perfect example of an Arthurian, grail-chasing, crusader Viking. King Haakon IV was raised devoutly Christian. Despite power, influence and mostly contented subjects, all that seemed to matter to the Norse king was approval from Rome. But the Pope at the time, Gregory IX, refused to acknowledge Haakon's claim to the throne, stating that Haakon was an illegitimate son. So Haakon took it upon himself to gain favour with the Holy See in the only way he knew how. By converting pagans.

At this time, the middle of the 13th century, Mongolian armies were pushing their way into Europe, forcing the Karelian people (Russian Finns) further west. Christianity wasn't yet the pre-eminent faith in the region, and so in a somewhat well-intentioned but clearly tactical move, Haakon opened his borders, welcoming Finnish refugees, provided they converted to the king's religion.

The Pope still wasn't swayed, but perhaps Haakon's prayers were answered when Pope Gregory died, replaced by Pope Innocent IV, who felt Haakon's work was not only admirable but exemplary. The new Pope got himself a new fan and powerful ally in the north, and Haakon finally got his papal blessing and royal recognition as he filled the Malangen region of Norway with shiny new Christians from Finland.

At this point in his journey, Pytheas would've had a decision to make. He could go back the way he came, in the relative shelter of the Channel, in which case he'd again pass lowland coasts where Flemish farmers would migrate to Wales. Or he could continue down the west side of Britain. By this time, however, his mind seemed made up, the odyssey becoming more focused with each passing stade. What began as a somewhat ambiguous trek now had a stated directive, that being to sail around Britain's entire perimeter.

From Orkney we can assume Pytheas sailed south through the Hebrides, past the beach where the Lewis Chessmen were found. He'd no doubt weave through myriad coves of the Isle of Skye, a place I'd come to know well. It was here I believe I saw selkies, seal folk from Celtic and Norse mythology, beings capable of therianthropy – shape-shifting – not unlike Merlin or our mermaid from Zennor. Selkies, however, are seals in water, humans when on dry land. Not so much hybrids as two distinct creatures, living in one embodiment. Selkies were known to keep company with swan maidens, creatures who metamorphosed from humans to swans. Perhaps it was these humanoid swans that pulled the boat steered by the grail knight Lohengrin.

It was a spectacular cove on the west side of Skye, a short hike from the end of a road. The beach was made up entirely of shells in every conceivable colour. There was a short but steep slope, a platform ideal for picnics. And when I looked back at the water I was watched by a hundred eyes. Fifty seals bobbed in the shallows, staring directly at me. I took a few steps to the right and 50 heads swivelled to follow. Then I moved to the left, again followed by swivelling stares. For a moment I felt I ought to perform, maybe a song or a soft-shoe shuffle. There was no mistaking the human-like traits in their warm and liquid brown eyes. How easy it would be, when magic was real and fairies still lived in the hills, to see these questioning faces gazing up from the sea and know they might join you one day.

From the beach we went to the hills, the lunar landscape of Black and Red Cuillins. A slow and serpentine drive took us into their peaks. Severe cliffs in moss-coloured green fell away to the coast and the sea. What look like colossal stalagmites rise from the ground next to ancient volcanic cones, some of the oldest rock in existence, the look of Herakles's underworld. We followed a jagged thin track that felt like navigating a windowsill on the lip of the earth, and I fought a vertiginous urge to drop to the ground and never get up. We finished the night at a pub, where a cèilidh kicked into gear. A bodhrán kept beat and two fiddles had every toe tapping. Our accommodation was a tiny cottage on a sheep farm, where we slept by a hardwood fire and ate eggs from red hens twice a day.

Carrying on through the Hebrides by ferry, bus and car, and on foot, Deb and I arrived at Mull and the bright painted port of Tobermory. Fish and chips with creamy chowder in a seaside pub by a fire had life looking close to perfect. We visited the holy island of Iona. Vikings called this area the Southern Isles, part of the Norse Kingdom of Isles from the ninth century to the time of King Haakon IV. Iona Abbey sits like a captain's bridge at the helm of the vessel-like island. It's the site of the monastery founded in 563 by Ireland's Saint Columba, a crusader in his own way, sharing traits with Saint Michael, his sword used not only to heal but also to hack. Which in part is why he sailed to Iona, another pilgrim with 12 companions.

This small lump of real estate represents a pivotal point in the shifting of Great Britain's Celts from the teachings of Druids to beliefs that were based on a Bible. The new faith became known as Celtic Christianity. Yet, in a fascinatingly druidic way, these Celtic Christians used celestial systems to determine their own holy dates. A new calculation for Easter deviated from what Christians in Rome believed it should be, creating an unmendable rift we still see in these branches of common faith. According to Anglo-Saxon chronicler Bede, Iona eventually bent to the rules set down by Rome in the eighth century, a few generations before Norsemen began to arrive. It's also when the *Book of Columba* was first written in the monastery that bore his name. And it's here they first carved ornate crosses in druidic swirls sculpted with rings, what would come to be known as Celtic crosses.

Columba's book, a marvel of calligraphy and illumination, was moved to the Abbey of Kells in the northeast of Ireland, and for that reason is also known as the *Book of Kells*. With Vikings starting to make a habit of raiding abbeys, treasure throughout these Southern Isles was systematically hauled further west, hidden beneath Irish churches.

When I saw Columba's *Book of Kells*, it felt like the world briefly folded, the slightest hitch in time. It was raised under glass, a spotlight glinting off gold leaf and hand-painted pigment that made the entire thing glow. There were spirits in there to be sure, a thousand years of faith, and just beneath that, the wisdom of Druids. The book had been moved to Dublin by this time, and was on display at the library of Trinity College. The space resembles a nave, two towering storeys of deep, stained wood, arching ceiling supports and shelves housing over six million volumes of content. Knowledge pulsed in the air, a heady tincture of worldly secrets.

And yes, Pytheas could have gone there, veering west from the Hebrides to circle the isle of Éire. But he'd first have to pass the neck of Scotland once more, where we find yet another key tangent. The Firth of Clyde snakes into Glasgow, a deep fjord at the foot of Loch Lomond. The city's a place of voyagers, shipbuilding still prevalent, a space of history, architecture and grit. Never before have I been out on a Friday night and seen every establishment, *every* establishment, with muscle-bound bouncers out front. Not only clubs and bars but even small shops and McDonald's. I made a point of not starting a fight. Across the narrow of land sits Edinburgh, home to a few more Norse chessmen from Lewis, while just south of that, on the way to Lindisfarne's holy isle, we find Rosslyn Chapel, placed on a powerful ley line.

So what exactly is a ley line? These are straight tracks or landlines thought to possess waves of energy. Some claim they were discovered a hundred years ago, identified by recreational archaeologist Alfred Watkins in 1921 as he hiked a rise in the Herefordshire countryside on the English–Welsh border. The area's part of the Welsh Marches (King Offa's domain) and follows the Wye River valley. It's where Tolkien and Lewis were said to have walked, inspiration for Middle Earth and Narnian hills.

It was a clear and bright afternoon when Watkins had his eureka moment. With a bit of elevation he was able to see for miles. And he noticed distinct lines in the landscape. Not like chalk on playing fields, but in the way that centuries of humanity had not only designed their lives but in fact responded to the will of the land. More than simply topography. He saw it in Stone Age fencing, forests, pastures and the organization of towns. Through clearings of woods he noted placement of early Anglo-Saxon settlements such as Weobley and Leysters, places with "ley" in their names. Thus the ley lines. Tibetan monks have come to these places as well, and those with the skill of dowsing.

All agree. Like the architectural flow of feng shui, there's something decidedly present in these ancient linear spaces.

Of course Alfred hadn't "discovered" anything. He'd simply noticed what the land was coaxing from those who lived here. Ancient Celts and Druids knew this all along. Trace the path of the sun, the spin of the earth, our place in it all, and you can't help but sense an alignment. You can use it to plan and plant crops, build stables and homes, and even to travel the world.

Then the notion of ley lines was embraced by New Age spiritualists and anti-establishment activists. Before long, these energy lines, which indeed span the globe, were said to be road maps for aliens, and pseudo-scientists gave the whole thing a bad name. Until Dan Brown came along, and *The Da Vinci Code*, became its own form of truth. Despite his work being a novel, it draws together much of the history we have of the grail and the Bible. And together he weaves a deliciously plausible concept that Jesus perhaps had offspring.

Here's where a version of the Rose Line comes into play, another term for *sang réal*, or the notion of a royal bloodline from Jesus. Now we can see a heightened appeal of getting our hands on the grail, if there is in fact DNA on the cup or the gauze that blotted a wound. And with this Rosslyn or Rose Line chapel placed directly on a critical ley line, we see another blurring of Marys, from the Virgin Mary to Mary Magdalene, one being the mother of Jesus, the other perhaps his lover.

A writer whose work I enjoy recounts the time he went on a quasi-researching trip to Rosslyn. He'd arranged to be shown the chapel by a local and knowledgeable dowser. If you've ever experienced this fascinating type of "mining" you know it can turn skeptics into believers. Whether it's searching for metal or water, burial chambers or the earth's core vibrations, there's no denying the presence of magnetic powers. Some dowsers use divining rods of iron, others prefer branches of willow, witch hazel or peach, while some use nothing more than their senses, finding flows in invisible lines. The dowser in Rosslyn passed the writer a jaguar tooth (three centuries old) and told him to concentrate on the small fang. Once his initial embarrassment wore off (the chapel still buzzed with tourists and fans of Dan Brown), he was indeed aware of a warmth penetrating his hand, with a slight sense of vibration.

"My god!" he said to the dowser. "What kind of magic is in this tooth?!"

The dowser smiled. "Oh, there's nothin' in the tooth. It just keeps ya' from gettin' distracted."

Not unlike meditation. So much of the power of tapping into heightened awareness is about muting the clutter and chatter.

If you've seen the film *The Da Vinci Code*, with Audrey Tautou, Tom Hanks and Gandalf, you already know what Rosslyn Chapel looks like. Built in the 15th century, it reminds me of King Haakon IV's resting place at the cathedral in Kirkwall. Incredible blocks of sandstone take on the colours of beachside at sunrise, hues of amber, honey and rose. Inside Rosslyn are a staggering number of carvings, hundreds of intricate faces. An intriguing tidbit of history is the fact that there's no building design, as though those who erected this structure were simply guided by powers emanating from the land.

There are more than a hundred carvings of Green Men faces, peering from lintels and keystones, a decidedly druidic presence in the house of a new-world god. Freemason researcher Henning Klovekorn believes the chapel's design emanates from the Viking world. He points to the prominent architectural feature known as the Apprentice Pillar. This, Klovekorn states, is fashioned after the ash tree Yggdrasil, hub of Norse mythology, centre of the nine worlds of gods and humanity. He points out the dragon design carved near the base of the pillar, gnawing at the roots of the ash, while subtly carved foliage is again a symbol of druidic nature, a Teutonic blur where Germanic Celts and Norse intertwine like the limbs of the sacred tree.

The story of the Apprentice Pillar is another darkly intriguing one. Apparently the lead mason involved in the chapel's construction was unable to be on site for a spell. But with no blueprints or design, he felt things couldn't go too far wrong in his absence. (Clearly he'd never had a contractor redo his kitchen while he was away on vacation.) When the master mason returned, he learned that his apprentice had gone ahead and finished carving the beautiful central feature, not only doing a bang-up job but doing it much better than the master mason was capable of.

Rather than giving the skilled upstart a pat on the back or a raise, the master mason gave the young carver a skull-splitting whack on the head with a hammer. Needless to say, the apprentice wouldn't be showing up again for work, or anything else for that matter. The legend further claims that there was no corpse. The body had vanished. Leaving us to wonder if the story's a cautionary tale to not show up your boss, or it's been fabricated. Or perhaps it's the same as the chapel in Kirkwall, where the corpse of a murder victim was found 800 years later, entombed in a beautiful carving of stone set in the heart of the nave.

Back to our proto-crusader and grail guide Pytheas, still travelling south to the lower left corner of Britain. We know at this point he had his sights set on one other island, a place that was already ancient, a destination for every seagoing dynasty. And now it's where we'll head as well. To the elusive tin island of Ictis. Although we're well into Pytheas's odyssey (he'd been at sea for no less than three seasons), it's only at this point in his journey, which we learn from the writing of Pliny, that in addition to seeing the world and furthering science our explorer had been looking for amber and tin. Combined with copper to make bronze, tin was the backbone of commerce and industry, no different than oil today. It even fuelled the arts, finding its way into sculptures and symbols of dynastic prominence over the next two millennia.

The southwest of England was blessed with deep veins of this soft, shiny metal. Which in part was what drew Mediterranean sailors to the shores of Britannia. One island in particular was known to be perhaps the greatest source of this precious commodity. According to Pytheas, "There is an island named Ictis lying inwards six days' sail from Britain, where tin is found, and to which the Britons cross in boats of wickerwork covered with stitched hides."

As with his time in north Scotland, again we learn details of the locals that Pytheas met on his travels. The above being a perfect description of Celtic coracles, same as the boat made of ox-hide Saint Brendan sailed across the Arctic, quite possibly to the shores of Vinland. And from the accounts of Pytheas written by Diodorus, we learn of Cornish tin mining and the welcoming people who lived at the land's end of England.

"The inhabitants of that part of Britain which is called Belerion are very fond of strangers and from their dealings with foreign merchants are civilized in their manner of life. They prepare the tin, working very carefully the earth in which it is produced. The ground is rocky but it contains earthy veins, the produce of which is ground down, smelted and purified. They beat the metal into masses shaped like knuckle-bones and carry it off to a certain island off Britain called Ictis. During the ebb of the tide the intervening space is left dry and they carry over to the island the tin in abundance in their wagons. Here the merchants buy tin from the natives and carry it over to Gaul, and after travelling overland for about thirty days they finally bring their loads on horses to the mouth of the Rhone."

This indicates we have Cornish miners hammering out ingots of tin and trading with Celts from the south coast of France. And apparently they're awfully friendly. So where does that leave us with Ictis? Where exactly is this island of tin? Some researchers say it must be St Michael's Mount, start of our transcontinental Camino and another hub of Celtic Christianity. Other historians argue it's the Isle of Wight, overlooking burial mounds of the Viking Kings' Graves in the South Downs. Then again, "six days' sail from Britain" could put us back into France. But before we sail on from the south side of England we have to consider one other candidate. Ictis could be hidden amongst Belerion's Isles of Scilly.

Which takes us back to earlier druidic encounters, when I traipsed my way around these shores in the footsteps of Vikings. On one of the first of these I was on my own, spindrift strafing my face, blown from somewhere in Wales. Typical maritime weather, each season buffeting headlands, all in the span of a morning. I'd flown across the Atlantic the previous day, then travelled a few hours by train in a jagged Celtic-like swirl, west to east, a bit north, then south by southwest. At the end of the line I slung a small pack on my back and made my way to a room with a view of the water, a mingle of Celtic Sea in peridot blue with indigo waves of Atlantic.

Beneath my sloped-ceiling room through an open window, I could make out a crumble of concrete, what was once a fishing dock. Since that time the pier has been rebuilt and shifted to a better-protected curve of the shore, a bay that always looks turquoise. It could be South Pacific, apart from the climate. But it *was* the edge of the Gulf Stream, evident in flora and fauna, naturally occurring palm trees and colourful songbirds blown in from Africa and the Azores. To the north and the east was the source of those Vikings, Norse and Danes who made this place their own. A few days of hiking would take me to where Arthur was king, at the cliffs on the end of the land. Due south I'd stumble aboard a boat of mahogany and teak, one mast and four prominent sails. And from the southern extreme of Britannia, I'd head to the North Atlantic. My destination? That place where the daughters of Atlas, those "nymphs of the west," reside. I had come to explore the Isles of Scilly, where Percival might be interred, a spot nearest to setting sun, where Helios parked his chariot at night and Druids drew ley lines over the world.

To get there I started my trek on foot before sun even rose. My body believed it was Pacific Time, but the rest of the region knew better. I was sleepy but wakeful and made my way across a soft sand beach, finding a trail and climbing through seaside hills. A pod of bottlenose dolphins made the trek by my side for a while, their breath an ambient score like the rasp of clearing snorkels. Sun gradually came and then went in the clouds but the scene felt vibrant as the dolphins swam past, slowly leaving me in their wake.

The lack of sleep and a constant upwards trudge was taking its toll, and a part of me (okay, all of me) wanted to simply stop or turn back. But I recalled a Jack Kerouac line, stated as only an American can, "In the end, you won't remember the time you spent working in the office or mowing your lawn. Climb that goddamn mountain." So, if only to get Jack off my back, I kept climbing, following a well-worn footpath, occasional mud, sand and rock, until I came to a circle of stone. Set back from the path, it was easily missed, but its presence still boggles the mind. Anywhere else in the world this would have tour bus access, ticket booths and a souvenir shop. Maybe an interpretive centre and café that serves cream teas. But here, there was none of that. No signage and no easy access. You either stumble upon this compact window onto prehistory or you miss it, to carry on in an internet world.

The next time I had an encounter like this, Deb and I were together, trekking our way around the top of Britain's triangle at Orkney. Seaside cliffs were high, reminiscent of the Cliffs of Moher, where Ireland sheers into Atlantic. The colours of shale and limestone and granite turn black with the bashing of waves. Helios was there, unsurprisingly, peeking in sundogs of light, some turning to bolts of rainbow. A spot of horizon stood out from low cloud and I believed I could almost see Shetland. Directly offshore from the path we were on was an impossible crag of islet. It's where Vikings arrived, managing to assail the cliffs and build a whole village, like a monastery set in Tibet. The locale made no architectural sense, apart from being utterly impregnable, with spectacular ocean views. It was already here when the Lothbroks set sail, some to rule chunks of this land, while the rest made their way through the Pillars of Hercules with an eye to finance a dynasty.

The path over Orkney was a mushy blend of moor and seeping groundwater. I slipped and fell hard more than once, and the slope of the land left me feeling as though I was always at risk of plummeting into the sea, past cliff-hugging nests and the scream of petrels and kittiwakes. But we persevered, clocking up distance, history and photos of wide-angle vistas. Ironically, back where we started, we saw what amazed us most. Another series of standing stone columns, the likes of which dotted Arthurian coasts. Here in the North Sea, the stones raised by Druids, and perhaps Stone Age clerics before them, stood in isolation, lone sentries left to guard who knows what. Perhaps they too had been part of circles and rounds, the rest of which fell back to earth or, as so often happens, got removed so that farmers could farm.

Two more experiences come to mind, witnessing work of the elders. One near Lamorna, where pirates still lurk and two Bronze Age stones stand akimbo. Unlike most circles of stone, these mythical Piper's Stones are enormous, hidden from hikers and roads, the occasional hum of a car damped by yew trees and maple. We had to work just to glimpse them through ground cover and over two fences. But their permanence was reassuring, as though righteous things never change, and it made me feel linked to the land.

The other encounter was on our way back from a long coastal walk, over dunes on a seaside salt path. We traipsed through foxgloves and gorse, on a mix of sand-soil and dirt. A golf course bisected some fields. Between us and the water was where Saint Anta's chapel was said to be buried in sand, driven by wind or maybe a shifting of faith. Across from where we walked, a solid stone church now stands, built in the Middle Ages. And just past the church, off the 14th fairway, hidden in a hedge of blackthorn, is a stone in the shape of a T-like cross, a cross that could be Thor's hammer. It's one of the oldest relics of the Christian era on the Penwith Peninsula, from transitional days of Druids doing what had to be done. Perhaps embracing new concepts, placating the powers that be, or keeping an open mind. Like the fluidic nature of Celtic cross carvings, where geometric design akin to celestial whorls became doors onto new beliefs.

So let's see if we can locate Pytheas's elusive island of Ictis. In Falmouth I boarded the four-sailed, solid-wood cutter moored at one of the long harbour docks. Chunky container ships sat at anchor in the mouth of the River Fal, the Carrick Roads running north like a fjord making its way toward London. The term Roads in these parts relates to the water, as this stretch of river is, in a manner, a highway. It's been busy through here since the time of King Henry VIII, and his castle defences still guard the headlands at St Mawes and Pendennis.

As we sailed from Falmouth, crenellated parapets loomed, recollections of cannon fire, and I admit I felt uneasy. Then again it may've just been my stomach as I got my sea legs. Along with the fact that I was put at the helm, steering us out of the bustling harbour like some cruel driver's exam without an instructor. At the start of our journey, we still had an engine, and all of our mast was intact. We passed Land's End as a summer sun set and a sickle of Moorish moon rose in orange sky. It felt as though we'd been thrust into art, the sky shifting from pastel to oil.

Supper was boiled ham and boiled potatoes, with a side of boiled cabbage. It seemed our skipper's culinary secrets were hot water and salt. But I suppose we were keeping scurvy at bay (my teeth remained firmly in place). We sailed through the night. I was back at the helm as the skipper sipped tea and we heaved through the black into increasing waves. It only reached gale force five, which a seasoned sailor might scoff at, but it was sufficient for each of the crew to spew eaten food to the fishes. The skipper, mind you, retained full ownership of his meal.

The only previous time I recall staying up through the night I was a teen on the last night of school. My hometown designated a countryside field where we could party, play music and say stupid things very loudly. It was a rifle range, and the more I think about it, the more I wonder if the venue choice wasn't a bit diabolical. I presume the members of the gun club knew we were there. Surprisingly, I remember the next day's sunrise quite clearly. Same time of year, right around summer solstice. Perhaps that's why the old memory flashed in my mind as we spotted our Belerion destination ease from horizon. Behind us, rising from the sea, the sun was enormous, liquid and amber gold. All of us aboard the cutter were silent. It felt like we'd entered a temple, or more accurately a temple had swallowed us whole, a ragtag collection of Jonahs. It was the same feeling I had when I marched from the sand through the circle of stone, fatigued yet oddly refreshed, rejuvenated in a way more impactful than coffee or sleep. What it's like, I believe, after long meditation or particularly passionate prayer.

We sailed toward the garrisoned walls of St Mary's. And it was then that our engine died, forcing us to tack into northerlies, where we managed to make the last bit of land before Spain, easing into the lee of St Agnes. Prior to Pytheas, Phoenicians were here. A few Greeks as well. But it's been the realm of the Celts since before anyone wrote of it. In fact, where we were was midway between two other Celtic land's ends. From the Gallic region where Pytheas set sail we were now in Gaelic terrain. Due north by the plummeting cliffs of Éire is the town of Galway, while south is the Galician corner of Spain, all derived from our globetrotting Celts. Only now I've learned that these Isles were never great sources of tin. Maybe I was trying too hard to unravel new clues in the wake of Pytheas. Then again, maybe this was where he came to find amber.

He wouldn't be the first person sailing here looking for something that no longer exists. Early inhabitants were Celtic Britons known as the Brythonic, who inhabited these British coasts, relations of Celts in Brittany. Each of these far western lands has a story of Arthur, each offering hints at the grail. The water we crossed to get here, past England's Land's End, is the purported location of Arthur's lost city of Lyonesse. Where Tristan was due to be prince before truncating his career by falling in love with the king's bride Isolde. Brittany Celts have their own version, the legend of Ys, another sunken island off the land's end of Finistère. While the Welsh tell the story of Cantref Gwaelod, or the

Lowland One Hundred, a sunken site beyond Cardigan Bay in west Wales, thought to be the Welsh Atlantis.

Countless Vikings came through as well, perhaps the most notable being Olaf Crowbone, Olaf Tryggvason, in the tenth century. We have record of Crowbone's travels through the Isles of Scilly from the *Heimskringla*, written by Snorri Sturluson. Scilly had been home to exiled monks since the fifth century, some thought to possess the gift of prescience. And Crowbone sailed to the Isles looking not only for treasure but for answers as well, a pagan pilgrimage. There'd be no indulgence for one who prayed to old gods, but what he sought was enlightenment, his very own grail-like quest. The journey continued, Crowbone covering the same distance as Pytheas, but his warriors had grown impatient. We can imagine a *Bounty*-esque crew on the longship, rowing against their will. They all knew the stories of Lothbroks, who'd not only gathered vast wealth but did so in warmth with good food and wine. So, with a mutinous edge aboard Crowbone's boat, he found the seer of Scilly, a seafaring cleric from Spain. The two met in a hut of wattle and daub by the bay where we anchored our cutter. And in a fug of smudge smoke the seer told Crowbone his fortune.

"Thou wilt become a renowned king and do celebrated deeds. But when thou comest to thy ships many of thy people will conspire against thee, and a battle will follow in which many of thy men will fall, and thou wilt be wounded almost to death, yet after seven days thou shalt be well of thy wounds, and immediately thou shalt be baptised."

It played out just as the seer predicted. Crowbone returned to his ships, half his crew mutinied, a lethal fight broke out (which Crowbone's side won), and sure enough he was injured. But upon his recovery he was only too happy to be baptised. You have to think if the lotto was a thing back then, Crowbone would've had the seer help him pick numbers as well.

Crowbone lived a few years in the Danelaw, moving from Ireland to England, but returned to Norway in 995, where Norse elder Haakon Sigurdsson's leadership was being challenged, insurgents doing their best to topple the current government. Crowbone managed to band rebel factions and that same year overthrew Haakon, assumed Norway's throne, and became King Olaf Tryggvason, his reign lasting to the year 1000.

Two hundred years later, the Scillies were called Syllingar, the Hebrides Suðreyar, and our next record of Norse being here comes from the *Orkneyinga Saga*, stating that "Sweyn Asleifsson went south, under Ireland, and seized a barge belonging to some monks in Syllingar." The Saga goes on to say, "Three chiefs – Swein, Þorbjörn and Eirik – went out on a plundering expedition. They went first to the Suðreyar, and all along the west to the Syllingar, where they gained a great victory in Maríuhöfn on Columba's-mass, and took much booty. Then they returned to the Orkneys."

Columba's-mass took place on June ninth, and Maríuhöfn is St Mary's harbour, where we intended to land until a dead engine and wind pushed us south. Which was where I first set foot on the Scillies, in fact the islet of Gugh, which attaches to St Agnes at low tide, a quick paddle from the old cleric's hut.

That remarkable sun seemed to leap in the sky, eager to reach its zenith. The skipper had boiled some sausage he served with a tin of tomatoes (boiled by somebody else). And with that as my breakfast, I set off to explore two islands. What struck me was a feeling of remoteness. Our crew of seven scattered and vanished. It would be hours before I'd see anyone else. There was windswept rock, wild thistle and marram grass. I heard peacocks and gulls and a cuckoo. I scrambled through crumbling medieval castles and hunks of basalt reminiscent of the Cuillins, all of it close to the sea.

On the island of Tresco are the ruins of a Benedictine abbey, part of the brotherhood we encountered at St Michael's Mount. A huge tropical garden grows next to the abbey. The Isles of Scilly are known for flowers, one of the region's primary exports, and it felt as though I'd strolled into a colouring book (a completed one), like my hike on the path next to dolphins, every nuance of colour aglow.

Past the abbey and gardens is the Valhalla Museum, as though placed at this dot on the map from one of the worlds beneath Yggdrasil. Three thousand years of maritime history are captured here, with a view of the garden, red abbey brick and a field of gorse by the water. Countless ships have sunk in these shallows, exposed to the blast of Atlantic. But most of the figureheads on display are from the past two centuries: bright-painted monks sporting tonsures and crosses next to buxom and windblown women.

The Isles are also a mecca for ornithologists. It's the first bit of landfall for migrating birds, and they come from as far as Siberia. I saw more species than I'd ever seen, whizzing by before I could even identify breeds or scribble notes in a journal. It's also a place of gigs, slender heavy rowboats, not unlike longships. Most are sculled by a team of six rowers, each pulling a single long oar. The races are international, highly sponsored and fiercely competitive. While the sailboat I was aboard was a pilot cutter, gigs served as pilot boats too. Historically they'd bolt from harbours to guide ships through unfamiliar water. Speed was essential for safety as well as the competition of commerce. First out, first hired. First back, first paid.

By the time I was due to return to the mainland, I'd seen sun rise from the sea no less than seven spectacular times. With each entry into my journal I'd try to describe it anew, but found myself coming back to the same colour palette, the honey hues of amber. No doubt you'd have figured this out much sooner than me, but I got there eventually. From somewhere in the east along Herakles's path, near the source of a solstice sun, someone was signalling me.

No, it wasn't ore steering me here like Pytheas, who sought both tin and amber. Seven brilliant clues, rising in amber tones, were telling me exactly where I should be, or at least the direction to go. And yes, although I saw the colour of amber starting each day on the sea, the *source* of that stone in its physical form must be back in the direction of Rome. And as much as I hate to rely on clichés, perhaps when things are said a great many times they in fact contain nuggets of truth. Maybe all roads *do* lead to Rome. If we retrace the Via Heraklea over Celtic lands toward that amber sun we'll get there, or least to the heart of Tuscany.

We didn't yet know what was in store on our homeward journey at sail. Sure, we knew a big storm was blowing our way. Which was why we left in a hurry, shoving off from St Martin's by the spot where Swein, Þorbjörn and Eirik filled their longships on Columba's-mass. We just didn't know the extent of the urgency with which we'd be forced to sail.

Long story short, we survived, which you already knew. But the conclusion of Pytheas's globe-spanning journey ends with a bit of a question mark. We know he got home safely as well, back to Marseilles, where we're left to decide for ourselves how his shipmates fared. Which puts us back, quite tidily I might add, onto our druidic sun-line, leading us east to the Alps. Along this line we keep finding clues, seemingly spilled from the grail. On the solstice path from Spain over France into Italy lie a series of Templar chapels; some are strongholds, others discreet, nearly retreats. Overgrown tracks lead toward Troyes, and still have place names like Champ Merlin. Neatly enough, a great many points coincide with the Compostela, our Camino Way.

Most of these forgotten locales are positioned like relay stations, a sort of telegraph line without wires or poles. Long-distance signalling has been a means of communication for as long as people have conversed. Whether with hunters or armies, the manner in which information travelled evolved to increase efficiency. Fire beacons were common, often on high points of land, and messengers like Pheidippides, the original marathon runner. Another fascinating precursor to phones and email was known as the shouting lines. This likely originated amongst farmers or oppida villagers as a means of defence. Utilizing the land: cliff walls, valleys, bodies of water and riverbeds, strategically located individuals with a decent set of lungs can holler with clarity over remarkable distances. A few well-placed people can create a rapid news channel spanning a country. Sure, you run the risk of that game of "whisper" breaking down content, but in the same way that semaphore eliminates error, so too can carefully chosen word-bites and code. Like the whistle of shepherds with well-trained dogs. Carrier pigeons, falcons and hawks worked as well, but required time and resources, and still left much to chance.

The beauty of these communication channels is that more often than not they followed terrain like ley lines. Think of the songlines, or dream tracks of Australia's Indigenous Nations. This was a means not only of learning and retaining lineage and cultural history but of literally knowing the lay of the land, paths between water, food and shelter. In a similar manner, geographical mapping songs have been passed on and sung for generations across Asia's "–stan" countries east of the Caspian, same as early Celtic topographical text called dindshenchas, meaning "the lore of places." Just like the singing of legends and family trees amongst Polynesians, Indigenous North Americans, and Scandinavians before Sagas were penned.

A great migratory side-note, consistent with every tale of transhumance and exodus, coincides with the path we're on. It was during the time of Pytheas that a vast group of Celts (multiple tribes) travelled the route of Herakles, under a solstice sun, to relocate in the west near the end of the Earth, past Gibraltar's pillars at the Sacred Promontory. There's an Iron Age accounting of this, scratched in neat script on a sheet of metal, found in an ancient Swiss village. You'll recall Austria and Switzerland were considered by some to be the Celtic homeland. Apparently Ambicatus, king of the Celts, said it was time to find greener pastures, and split the tribes in two, one half led by Prince Segovesus, the other by a prince named Bellovesus. And with something akin to a coin toss, Bellovesus led his group south into Tuscany, while Segovesus headed to Spain.

There's an interesting cross-hatch line, perpendicular to our Heraklean Way, like a road map for Celts who went south into Italy. We'll soon catch up with these migrants, their path critical to our grail quest. After all, the world was divided as to where people felt the holy chalice could or should be, with one group saying it had to be Rome, the other determined to keep it anywhere else. For now, we'll track those Celts into Italy, while the rest of Austria's druidic offspring followed Herakles out from the Alps, no doubt harmonizing their way to the chorus of "Climb Ev'ry Mountain."

The cartographic cross-hatch, pointing Bellovesus and company to Italy, is in fact another druidic celestial route, the line of the *winter* solstice. While Herakles followed the lengthiest day, these Celts made their way toward a new home on the path of the world's longest night. This intersection of summer and winter solstices occurs near the Italian town of Arona on Lake Maggiore. In the same way Lake Geneva separates France from Switzerland, Lake Maggiore is the regional boundary between Piedmont and Lombardy, what Vikings called Langbarðaland, land of the Lombards. If we follow Bellovesus and the winter solstice line, bearing southeast, we find ourselves on the E62 motorway. Perhaps unsurprisingly it's the exact route, a beeline, to what the ancients knew as Mediolanum. A few ancient centres are known as such, but in north Italy, near the meeting of solstice and equinox lines, lies the most significant Mediolanum of all. Now we call it Milan.

On a tangential note, when I was a kid I had a collection of Italianate gemstones, semi-precious bits of rock, jewels and shiny bric-a-brac. It included cut pieces of garnet that powered mechanical watches, a slice of lapis lazuli, a marbled malachite elephant and a shard of rose-coloured quartz. But perhaps the pride of my small collection was a nugget of amber, the same tone as each of those early mornings, when sun rose from the sea to ignite the Heraklean Way. Inside the smooth piece of petrified pitch was a tiny black ant, encased long before ice covered the world. When you think of the age of that ant and the amber, it makes the timeline of our conjoined quests, Vikings and Pytheas, seem not only concurrent but current. Perhaps *that's* the magic inherent in gems, and the emerald grail of Italy.

It's the sensation I felt when I returned to Falmouth and spent an evening with archaeologists from Exeter University. Together we studied and handled Bronze and Stone Age tools, generously loaned for an evening of relaxed study at a pub overlooking the harbour. The remarkable finds were all local, the oldest in fact having popped from the earth just over the river where swans swam and I spent a day hiking through muck for new views. The experience was a remarkable one, prodding the poet in me to put pen to paper, a piece I call "Falmouth in Bronze," a version of which appears in *Forever Cast in Endless Time*. That electric touch of ancient artifacts, even through soft gloves, eliminated the concept of separate places or times.

A yawn from gaping Carrack Roads, Falmouth gleaming proud
in Penryn town, cloud swirls wink sun in slow and pulsing strobes
slate nimbus eager, fat with rain, a dampened glitter ball
a rippled river morphs to dance floor, swans in pairs set sail
turn beak to beak, touch tails, and drift, in alabaster hearts

I find the courage, cross the floor, hike mud around a headland
where a hoard submerged itself in sog and peaty bog
until it coughed and gagged, then spat out Bronze Age history
patina gristle left in loam and roots to rot for centuries
but now, unearthed, it's passed to me, in delicate white gloves

four thousand years suspended in this moment, in my palms
an adze in malachite, a shade of Asian jade
alchemy from artisans, knapped DNA and time
I'm there, both here, and now, time swaddled into velvet
which I cradle like a firstborn, reverie I can't articulate
knowing I have held this once before

ITALY

If you wondered where we left off with Indiana Jones and his dad with respect to *their* search for the grail, let me catch you up. That thick red line making its way to the sound of a roaring prop-plane left from New York, and like most flights from that era stopped to refuel in Vinland. My mom-in-law tells the story of having to make that same stop on her first transatlantic flight, then once more for fuel in Greenland. Which I'm certain was Narsarsuaq, at one time an army base with an airfield, where I'd be a few decades later trekking hills capped in ice to the home of Thorhild and Erik the Red. What Mom remembers about that flight is being served a glass of goat's milk, something she'd never had before. Sixty years later she can still describe the taste.

On the other side of the Atlantic, at this point on his own, Indiana made his way toward Italy, convinced it would lead him not only to his father but ultimately to the grail. What I love about Italy (aside from the food) is the fact that we're seemingly so far from where we began yet right in the thick of it all. A place where all our tangents collide, like beams from a seasonal sun. Each radiant path converges: Herakles and the Celts, Viking crusaders, Arthurian knights and the grail. And they meet up right here, at a boot-shaped peninsula, kicking the ribs of the Med.

When I first came here I was a teenager, not far removed from that all-nighter camped on the rifle range. I had no idea the cuisine of this rather small nation was so fabulously diverse. In the Etruscan north I went nearly a month without seeing a fish. Sure, there was anchovy paste in most everything, but dishes are based more on meat. Pizzas are thin with minimal toppings, each ingredient exceptional. Nothing like the Pizza Hut deep-dish Hawaiian I grew up with. Part of me thought these Italians hadn't quite figured it out, that pizza was *meant* to have pineapple. But I got on board rather quickly, discovering "real" carbonara, served on spaghetti with thick cubes of lardon, which I ate three times a day. I had a closet-sized room in a chic new hotel, décor as minimalist as the pizza. And as I explored, rather than taking pictures I chose to buy souvenir books with professional photos, each weighing half a kilo. Twenty books in I realized I was in trouble when I could no longer lift my pack.

After Rome, this is Italy's largest city, centre of high fashion, an alpha city to the economy. Remember our bustling gamma city in Spain? Imagine that, only supercharged, with haute couture. Milan. Mediolanum. Middle of the line. Where Leonardo painted his version of *The Last Supper.* If we believe the branch of research Dan Brown opted to follow, the Renaissance painter was trying to send us a message. That the grail wasn't a vessel at all. Not a bowl, dish or cup. But in fact the holy chalice represented femininity and the receptive channel of a womb.

That story concludes things at Rosslyn, sort of, but also follows the other Rose Line, not only the notion of a royal blood line but the original line of the rose. A pre-eminent ley line bisecting the world, the original prime meridian. It runs by Troyes into Paris. For navigational purposes, this was the starting point, absolute zero, as longitude couldn't yet be effectively measured at sea. Triangulation through planets and stars, dream lines and song could only place voyagers on shifting water with geographic approximation at best.

These Rose Lines bring us back, in a way, to Mary. Or more accurately, the Marys. We have Mary Magdalene, mislabelled a sex worker as part of a smear campaign, almost certainly a spouse-like companion to Jesus. And we have Virgin Mary, his mom. But just to throw another wrinkle of ambiguity into the mix we have biblical references to Aunt Salome going by Mary as well. Three Marys, all close to Jesus and what may be the grail, assuming we return to the notion that the grail's what we first envision when we imagine a cup or a chalice.

In the mid-19th century, that original prime meridian line was "moved" out of France into England, from Paris to Greenwich. Having made a point of standing on both, I wasn't aware of any difference at all, apart from an hour on my watch. An easy meridian access point in Paris is next to the Louvre, just up from the Île de la Cité, where Ragnar shook down the church on Easter in 845. In Greenwich the setting's equally impressive, an octagonal observatory in glass on a hill with a view of Gravesend at the mouth of the Thames.

Having arrived in Milan, the first thing I did was go to the Duomo. They started building this place, Milan Cathedral, 600 years earlier, finishing it a mere generation ago. It could be the world's most elaborate, intricate wedding cake puzzle, one taking a lifetime to complete, or in this case six *centuries* worth of lifetimes. It's considered the Church of Lombardy, dedicated to the Virgin Mary. Ring roads radiate from this structure like druidic spirals with a decidedly Roman stamp. The cathedral gleams white, a beacon, and when sun shines as it did when I got here, you need to wear shades to admire the exterior. A hundred designers are credited with being "lead architect" on this colossal enterprise. Timeline and materials aside, the politics alone associated with construction are staggering. Dozens of Popes, thousands of financiers and a parade of royals and emperors, all wanting to have a say. Napoleon weighed in too, naturally, in 1805, demanding someone new finish the nave for his inauguration (he intended to be king of Italy as well). Despite all this, the whole works remarkably well, overly ornate but solid and handsome in its intricacies.

Every writer through here, it seems, wanted to have a say. Oscar Wilde simply said it was vile. Too busy. While Henry James was much kinder, describing it as "a structure not supremely interesting, not logical, not commandingly beautiful, but grandly curious and supremely rich." A hundred years before its completion, Mark Twain commented as well, as he toured the world writing *Innocents Abroad*. "What a wonder!" he wrote. "So grand, so solemn, so vast! And yet so delicate, so airy, so graceful! A very world of solid weight, and yet it seems a delusion of frostwork that might vanish with a breath!"

Granted, an excess of exclamation, but that's exactly what you feel when you first spot this monolith, Italy's largest church.

We've talked about relics, their appeal and allure to the pious and pilgrims, and this place has a whopper. The Holy Nail, one of three iron spikes supposedly pulled from the true cross. It's displayed once a year, but now, as on most days, there's just a tiny red light high in the dome over the apse where the crucifixion nail's said to be kept. The rare occasions when it's brought out are known as the Rite of the Nivola, another agonizing glimpse from a distance at the treasure for DNA hunters who believe in a royal blood line.

I find more historical nuggets scattered about the cathedral, subtle brushstrokes of paint to add to our grail quest canvas. One of these being a magnificent sundial by the entrance, the work of artists from Milan's prestigious Brera Academy. A slender strip of brass is embedded in the stone floor, and at noon a ray of light strikes the line and the gnomon precisely, casting its shadow on a south wall. (A gnomon is the vertical, pointy part on the dial, like the Alps that directed us here.) Both summer and winter solstices are marked out, as well as the signs of the zodiac. As with the Green Men at Roslyn, we see science, nature and myth all getting seats at the table. Zodiac signs served as unfailing road maps, whether crossing land or sea. Pytheas wrote of reaching the top of Britain under the Crab (Cancer, sign of water), while the Great Bear (Ursa Major, sign of Callisto the nymph) led him north toward Thule.

Meanwhile, underneath the cathedral, excavations have revealed the crumbling remains of places of worship from the earliest days of Christianity. Archaeologists call it a hypogeum, which is a posh word for underground chamber. (I suspect in undergrad studies they're underground chambers, then at some point in master's or doctoral work they become hypogea.) Regardless, these subterranean chapels were dedicated to Santa Tecla and Santa Maria Maggiore (like the lake) and are now incorporated into the apse of the current Duomo. It's what we've seen throughout our travels, new places of worship built over old, not simply a show of progress or power, not merely high points of land, but perhaps something more, vibrational lines like the leys or the path of the stars, the stuff that gets dowsers vibrating and even the rest of us sense on those blissful moments when our minds are uncluttered.

There's one more item of particular interest to us here, and it's actually hard to find. Not quite two-dimensional, not quite three. It looks like a sculpture that's been placed on a wall and then squashed, but not entirely. It has a bas-relief look, deeply etched outlines carved into simple grey stone. It could easily be overlooked or dismissed as masonry folly, the way you might put up an old picture to cover a hole in the wall. It's referred to as the Duomo's interpretation, or representation, of the Holy Grail. This unassuming carving is on a slightly recessed wall. The only thing that gives it an impression of grandeur is that this "grail" radiates beams of light. Carved stone has the look of light refracting within the chalice, with beams flowing out to each point on the compass, every conceivable path of a star. But something more makes this grail representation stand out, giving it an almost otherworldly dimension. And that's the vessel itself, which isn't a cup or a goblet, nor is it a dish or a plate. It's a funerary urn, with a lid, something to store the ashes of loved ones, or someone revered.

Cremation has been part of human ritual for a very long time. The oldest and best examples are from 17,000 years ago, found near Australia's Lake Mungo in the midst of a triad of capitals: Sydney, Melbourne and Adelaide, in the interior of New South Wales. Along with votive offerings and a metallic container, the cremated human remains were buried with ritualistic and ceremonial care. Which opens a whole other line of questions. Could the grail be its own little mausoleum? A compact, transportable tomb? Funeral pyres and cremation tend to destroy DNA evidence, which deflates the balloon for royal bloodline believers. But there are so many references to post-crucifixion preparations for the *burial* of Jesus. Cremation wasn't as prevalent in this part of the world as it was elsewhere, south and east Asia being good examples. And despite the stunning visual associated with

Viking burials at sea, a longship engulfed in flame, the vast majority of northern funerals were about the deceased being buried in earth, as we see at countless barrows, burial mounds and cemeteries across Scandinavian Europe.

I've now joined a small group with a guide to ramble our way through Milan (within the main ring road) for about a kilometre and a half, from the white sprawl of the cathedral to something nearly the opposite, the comparatively humble Basilica di Sant'Ambrogio. The structure's fairly close to the ground, save for a bell tower, and made of simple red brick. Ochre roof tiles give it a look like we're back in the centre of Spain. Inside is elaborate stonework but heavy and simple design, not ornate like the labyrinthine Duomo. Wood pews have a single small aisle, each row rigidly uninviting.

What brings us here are the chessboards. And as much as I'd love to suss out a thread to our Lewis Chessmen, these boards have their own unusual provenance, most of which is speculation. The boards are a bit of a mystery. Four of them decorate the chapel, placed on the façade and interior walls. They're actually vertical stone inlays in the pattern (exact size and dimensions) of a standard chessboard. But squares are white and red rather than black. Several theories exist as to why they're here. Folklore suggests the pattern confuses the devil, sending him scurrying from hallowed ground, or maybe he just dislikes the game. Others believe it's another nod to a pagan past, geometrics associated with planets, stars and druidic augurs. But the theory that intrigues me most is a link to our Knights Templar. The symbolism of the chessboard has been said to possess the ability to recall or summon protectors of the grail. Whether that's symbolic phraseology or literal remains unclear. The tie-in to the Templars is that these chessboards were added to the church in 1133, when the basilica became Cistercian, run by Benedictine monks led by Bernard of Clairvaux.

Born in the 11th century, Bernard hailed from the French side of Lake Geneva, where he became an abbot and later a saint. He was politically active and powerful, founding Clairvaux Abbey in the region known as Val d'Absinthe. Yes, the French-Swiss region where the spirit absinthe comes from. What stands out on Bernard's resume is the fact that he went to Troyes, attended secret meetings and took a leadership role in what's called the Council of Troyes. It was here that he outlined Knights Templar rules, Arthurian codes of conduct that became a template for chivalry, military honour and religious nobility. The same lofty standards Jomsvikings exemplified a century earlier.

One wall-mounted chessboard in particular grabs my attention. It's visibly deteriorated. Our guide explains that the brick composition here is inferior and material breakdown is accelerating. It's part of a mosaic in the primary apse, with an impression of Jesus seated on a throne. Our guide further explains that the nature of chess, traditionally white and black but here with white and blood red, denotes the age-old clash of good versus evil.

I can't be the only one seeing the symbolism in this deteriorating picture of Jesus, the match being currently played, a planet of lives on the line. The devil here doesn't seem particularly scared or confused. If these two are indeed opponents, the game board at this stage looks like the result could be a draw. As Michael and George fought their dragons, that serpent in Rosslyn gnawing the roots of Yggdrasil is another version of the very same thing. It was known as Jörmungandr, the Midgard Serpent, and it was Thor's job to fight *that* particular embodiment of evil on earth. And I wonder if, given the choice, these hackers and healers might also prefer settling scores on a board in lieu of a battlefield.

With my fill of cathedrals, basilicas and unending matches of chess, it's time to move on. I have an approximate plan for our route but not much more than that, leaving space for side trips and distractions as they arise. For now let's pick up once more with our Celtic guides, those time-bending travellers leading us under the sun.

Roman historian Titus Livius, known as Livy, wrote most of what we know of this area from the time of Pytheas to the birth of Jesus, a time proto-Vikings were discovering much of the world. It's Livy who wrote of the split of the Gallic Celts, with their migrations to Spain and to Italy. Interestingly, each account seems to start in the Alps, once more the high peaks acting as a sundial gnomon, pivotal history radiating from needle-like points.

Let's jump ahead on our timeline. After Herakles, Hannibal was here, then Attila. Goths were in charge for a while, until Milan became part of the Charlemagne Empire, which ran most of central west Europe through the Golden Age of Vikings. It was a Carolingian king who made Norseman Rollo a lord in France, establishing the bloodline of William, conqueror of England. By the 11th century, just ahead of the Renaissance, city states like Milan were flexing their economic muscle and distancing themselves from Rome. This was followed by the emergence of other powerful centres like Genoa, Naples, Florence, Sienna and Venice. Like so many places we've been, this was never a homogeneous nation.

I'm aboard an immaculate bus with comfy seats that even recline a little. The morning was overcast as we looped Milan's big white cathedral, passed the basilica with its red and white chessboards, and veered away from our solstice line. In a rather neat twist, it happens to be spring equinox. Our destination for now is Venice, a fairly straight line due east from Milan, on the north coast of the Adriatic, which takes us through a few more intriguing locales.

It's been a couple of hours on the bus and we're about halfway to the sea. The road skirts Lago di Garda (Lake Garda), which, like Lake Maggiore, serves as a regional border. We're now leaving Langbarðaland, Scandinavian land of the Lombards. But before we do, let's take a moment to remember, as this was a significant place in the annals of Viking history.

Nearly three dozen runestones exist in south Sweden, commemorating Vikings who travelled, fought and perished here, in Italy and

Greece. They're known, rather unimaginatively, as the Italy and Greece Runestones. Most are from the 11th century, referred to collectively as the Varangian Runestones. The runic lines, engraved onto stone, are a written version of Old Norse. Some of the stones are located in Uppland while others are in Södermanland, coastal provinces on either side of the Stockholm fjord.

Most of these stones are memorials to members of the Byzantine Emperor's Varangian Guard who fought Lombard princes in Italy. Others fell defending the territory from invading Normans, descendants of Rollo, Scandinavian relations from a few generations earlier. Which makes these commemorative stones that much more tragic, like civil war memorials, when families found themselves across trench lines from one another. I find myself thinking of cenotaphs and remembrance, mourning those who gave their lives to something they felt was worth fighting for, or simply had no choice. People laid to rest far from home, now a line on a stone or in concrete.

As our bus pulls into Verona, I'll be joining another tour to see what else I can learn. In the city centre we're dropped by a symmetrical oxbow S-curve in the Adige River. Not quite as tidy as the S-road pointing us from Andorra to Montségur, but I suppose it could still be a sign. Verona's often deemed Shakespearean (although it's unlikely the bard ever visited), as two of his most famous plays are set here, *The Two Gentlemen of Verona* and good old *Romeo and Juliet*.

The city's another UNESCO World Heritage Site, in part for its culture but mostly for its urban architecture, medieval and well preserved. Strolling from the bus, I find myself in a clump of Shakespeare fans itching to shout, "Wherefore art thou?!" Which I admit is rather appealing. So we go to "the balcony," known as Juliet's House, or Casa di Giulietta, by the second crook of the S in the river. It's a large courtyard-building in blushing brick with lush ivy growing like drapery from the second storey. Each storey has over-height ceilings, so although the structure doesn't have many floors, it feels like it reaches the sky. And poking out from one wall, facing the courtyard, is perhaps the most famous balcony of all. It's the only one on the building and the stone-work looks rather new. Perhaps it's just well maintained. There's a life-size statue of Juliet nearby, and tours will take you through her bed-chamber, where an elegant gown's on display. The fabric is heavy, par-tially pleated in hanging folds, and radiates medieval nouveau riche, the same amber tones as Heraklean sunrise. Like many places, this is considered a Roman city, and the massive Verona Arena amphithe-atre adds to the Romanesque vibe. (The arena's a few winding blocks from Juliet's House.) But the town was actually founded by Celts, six centuries before the Last Supper.

After a snack at a stand-up espresso kiosk (crustless egg sandwich), I follow the south bank of the Adige to two more places of interest. One of these has drawn a few tourists but nothing compared to Juliet's place. It's the Basilica of San Zeno Maggiore, built in the year Bernard of Clairvaux was in Troyes, writing the Templar's rules. For me it's a simple literary touchpoint, a checkmark on the agenda. What I'm look-ing at is the third structure built on this site, church over church over church. The bottom slab of this architectural layer cake was a shrine to Saint Zeno, patron saint of Verona from the fourth century. Now the top of the cake is a Romanesque façade with a 70-metre-high bell tower. Its significance? Dante mentions this spot in his *Divine Comedy*. Not unlike Juliet's balcony, one of those nifty bits of literary content that muddle the waters of historical fiction with fact.

Another kilometre downriver is my last stop on this Verona sojourn, the compact Basilica of San Lorenzo. In another bookend of sorts, this particular church was completed as our Benedictine Bernard lay on his deathbed, his life's work complete. Inside the San Lorenzo church are magnificent columns of sandstone, striped like huge barber poles. They look like candy canes, or cylindrical versions of the Milanese red and white chessboards. The primary altar piece is a likeness of Madonna. Not the one that vogued but one of our Marys, cradling baby Jesus. This place is another stacking of chapels, and what lies beneath the current foundation are remnants of what's considered paleo-Christian relics. Not quite the transitional proto-Christian ruins we passed in the sand dunes of Cornwall, but still some of the earliest archaeological remains of a Christian place of worship.

Back on the bus, still heading east, an hour on the road takes us to another World Heritage Site, the ancient city of Padua. Padua calls itself the oldest city in northern Italy. It's sufficiently old that historians can't agree on how it got named. Some say the root word means plain, while others insist it comes from the Po, Italy's longest river, which runs from the Alps to the Adriatic. Now the town name's associated with Saint Anthony of Padua, the Portuguese Franciscan friar who made this place home. In part, the city's gotten its UNESCO designation for the basilica frescoes painted by Giotto di Bondone, a Florentine artist and architect. Born in the 13th century, Giotto is considered "the most sovereign master of painting in his time, who drew all his figures and their postures according to nature." In other words, Leonardo two centuries sooner.

Scrovegni Chapel, here in Padua, contains Giotto's most famous pieces. His work's considered early Renaissance, but I'd argue the Renaissance started right here, with Giotto. The chapel too was ahead of its time, intended not only as a place of inclusive worship and interment, but an annual mystery play as well. Mystery plays were the earliest form of medieval theatre in Europe. They varied from ancient Greek productions in that performances focused on biblical stories: the world's creation, garden of Eden and so on, with accompanying music in the form of hymnal song. The term *mystery* was often used synonymously with miracle. Later, mystery simply meant craft, as in the craft of acting and singing. Mystery plays would be put on in cycles, with a single performance happening over multiple days. You may recall from previous *Gone Viking* adventures when I went to Yorkminster for *The Greatest Story Ever Told*, a seemingly unending mystery play. Two hours in, when we broke for *first* intermission, I realized I was in over my head, renaming the show *The* Longest *Story Ever Told*. I snuck out for a kebab and a starlit walk home.

The same way we touched on Shakespearean work in Verona, here in the birthplace of mystery plays, *actual* mystery follows Giotto as it seems to have done with Shakespeare. No one seems certain as to when Giotto was born, or where exactly, although Florentines claim he's one of their own. As with any great collection of art, theories abound as to authenticity and original authorship, or, in this case, who put brushes in paint and daubed it on walls and ceilings. And here at Scrovegni Chapel, Giotto's work covers *every* wall, *plus* the ceiling. Frescoes wrap around surfaces, divided in panels of biblical history, each episode like a frame from an outsized graphic novel. There are scenes from the life of Jesus, and others of the Virgin Mary. There's the salvation story and a less common depiction of God telling the archangel Gabriel to let Mary know she's expecting. Despite the church financing Giotto's work, there's a lovely softness to his artistic interpretations, as though the scenes we're witnessing just may've come from any or all of the Abrahamic faiths: Christianity, Judaism or Islam.

It's now late in the day but we have a bit further to go. From the frescoes of Padua, the bus joins fast-moving highway and for another brief blip of time we're back on our solstice line, bearing northeast into Venice. It's a city I've been to a few times. One stay was in a high-ceil-inged room, once part of a massive palazzo. Chubby cherubs on the ceiling mooned us for the duration of our layover. Tall-paned windows opened onto a canal, and every so often we'd hear the strong baritone of a gondolier serenading passengers as they'd glide past on red pillows.

"Ahh, Venice!" was what Indy said when he got here. Mind you, he was in the throes of a passionate affair. Turns out his love interest was a Nazi. (Muted trumpet, *wah-wahh*.)

This was where Hastein and Björn Lothbrok *intended* to go. This and the centre of Rome. But we're led to believe their navigational skills let them down. After capturing Pisa they bypassed Florence, and as they made their way north they missed the turnoff to Venice, wind-ing up instead at the walled city of Luni. Fortunately our bus hasn't made that mistake, and I haul a bag from the station onto a vaporetto.

These water buses are the mass transit version of gondolas, without the glamour or singing. And in a knot of locals and tourists, we burble our way to the centre of Venice.

Indy came here searching for grail clues at the Campo San Barnaba, so I feel an obligation to go there as well. His destination was a fictitious library, while mine is the actual church. It has a solid façade the colour of sun-bleached stone and looks like it belongs in ancient Greece. Behind the thick frontal wall is a building in brick, with a bell tower set behind that.

Satisfied with the touchstone, I cross the Ponte dell'Accademia over the Grand Canal and veer toward Piazza San Marco. The previous time I was here the whole square was flooded, several centimetres of water. People still strolled and danced while stringed trios played from the corners. They sloshed through seawater and sewage, occasional bits of detritus, and despite the cringe factor, when sun set and lights shone on the piazza, it *did* look romantic.

Fish here is more plentiful than meat and game, and I dined on grilled sardines with fried onions, served in a nest of polenta. I used John Berendt's memoir *The City of Falling Angels* to navigate the city, a dreamy blend of poetic prose. The title alludes to the fact that Venice is crumbling, finding its way back to the sea, like the Celtic legend of Ys at Finistère, this place a future Atlantis. The angels that fall refer to winged gargoyles and spirits in stone, decorations on building exteriors that erode and literally fall to the ground. Maintaining them all is impossible, and locals know to watch for these "falling angels."

Now, with Berendt's direction and an openness to getting lost, I track down another nugget on our quest for the grail, akin to the radiant urn in Milan. Across two minor canals is the Venetian opera house Teatro La Fenice. Like the chapels we saw in Verona, Padua and elsewhere, La Fenice is composed of three layers, or more accurately three iterations. Fenice, by the way, is a phoenix, the mythical bird that immortally rises from ashes. Aptly enough, each previous iteration of this grand opera house burned to the ground. Once in the 18th century, once in the 19th, and most recently in 1996. But after a few years of coordination and fundraising, with a colossal burst of community effort (and 90 million euros) this lavish space was completely reconstructed in under two years.

Just beyond that we come to what I've been looking for, known as the *Holy Grail Between Angels*. Its provenance is unknown, the moniker fairly recent. It's another bas-relief carving in stone, same as the wall at the Milanese Duomo. This too is clearly a depiction of the grail. It's held aloft by two angels in flight, their wings wide, knees bent as though bearing a heavy burden. It resembles a wreath, a coat of arms like countless crests and regional flags we've passed getting here. But what's striking about this "grail between angels" is its similarity to the one in Milan. This too looks like a funerary urn, a chalice topped with a lid like a trophy. Of course it could be a coincidence, but I can't dismiss it as such. There might be something to this new notion of what exactly the grail might be. And wouldn't you know it? The moment I use Google to get my bearings (Berendt's writing is lovely but it can't take the place of a map), I see once again where we are is a topographical S (Malory and Hardyng can barely contain themselves), as the Grand Canal here meanders in a backwards S-curve through the centre of Venice – how an S will appear in Latin.

I've made my way to the docks, and the medieval Venetian skyline has me feeling I'm boarding a boat like Pytheas, or even Columbus, off to the sill of the world, where balena hunt and a trench-dwelling kraken resides. There's a mist rolling in, making its way past Murano, artisan island of crystal and glass. It's almost a sea fret or haar, what we've tramped through on shorelines and sliced through by sail throughout our excursions. Only this has an earthy aroma, more than just salt and sea, in fact lingering woodsmoke blowing from mainland and islands. It's a kind of sfumato, the fragrant fog that clings to Etruscan hills, a blend of low, heavy air that mingles with olivewood smoke. The same term's used to describe a style of Renaissance painting, wispy brushstrokes like breeze, so subtle it's almost imperceptible. It's the root of vanishing points on canvas and earthen-toned eyes that follow wherever you go.

The first time I witnessed real sfumato, in the hills outside Florence, I watched it creep down an embankment like an opal-hued serpent, formless and hypnotizing, consuming the land as it moved. There, the scent of olivewood smoke was strong and I peered from a second floor window, the shutter and glass open wide. The scene unfolded through goalposts of green, in fact two towering cypresses. The methodical advance of the mist plunked me once more into scenes of *Excalibur*, Merlin casting the land in a fog, enabling Uther Pendragon (Arthur's dad) to change shape, a pseudo-cambion, and ride through his enemy's camp undetected. An all-encompassing magic, swallowing time. Like the smudge in the shack of the seer on Scilly, where Olaf first learned he'd be king.

The boat that I'll board here in Venice, however, isn't carved out of olive or cypress. Nor the oak that was used for the flexible hulls of the longships that crossed the Atlantic. This monster's made of steel, a small floating town painted white, a ship to house 3,000 people. But before we set sail down the Dalmatian coast we've two more stops here in Italy, another two touchstones I hope will reveal further clues on our quest.

Back to Florence for a moment, heart of Langbarðaland, where candle-like cypress dot the banks of the Arno, evergreens adding height to ground-hugging vineyards and olive groves. Along with the land's khaki palette, the earth itself pervades every building. Mary McCarthy describes it well in *The Stones of Florence*: "White, black, grey, dun and bronze are the colours of Florence – the colours of stone and metal, the primitive elements of Nature out of which the first civilizations were hammered."

In the 13th century, Templars too hammered and carved out a claim on this region, with Florence becoming a critical outpost. It was a time when the knights and the city alike were reaching their heights of power. While Italian city states grew as centres of commerce, so too had Templars become pioneers, in the burgeoning business of banking.

Originally, it was the job of Knights Templar to provide safe passage for pilgrims, ensuring the well-being of long distance travellers for their treks of indulgence. Whether the routes had been built by Romans or Celts, surveyors or Heraklean sun, road journeys could be made with peace of mind knowing the Templars were on patrol. Ensuring pilgrims made it safely to relic sites, where they could fill pews and donation boxes, became a top church priority. Which made Templars primary players. So much so that Rome made the Knights an organized charity.

The Templar organization increased rapidly in size and financial clout, and is considered by some to have been the world's first multinational corporation. Money collection and management soon became a vast business enterprise. Before long, "Templar Inc." was a mere 10 per cent knights, and 90 per cent administration and money managers. High finance became its own art form. Endorsed promissory notes and certified cheques were invented by Templars. The Knights financed royalty, and with the blessing of the church Templar coffers underwrote much of Europe. For a time it seemed they'd surpass the church in power and influence. Which of course got alarm bells ringing. And as we know, nothing's too big to fail.

The undoing of the Knights Templar began in a clandestine manner. King Philip IV of France was deeply in debt to the Templars, but rather than pay what he owed he decided it would be simpler (and more cost effective) to fabricate cultist rumours about the cross-wearing knights, and encouraged Rome to side with him, labelling the Templars as outlaws. Which the church got on board with. Thus began the inquisition of Templars and the eventual disappearance of our medieval grail protectors.

But before the nastiness of this particular Inquisition, when the Templar financial organization was still taking off, Florence was key. It was here the Knights owned a particular church, San Jacopo in Campo Corbolini, as much a bank as a chapel. From the unit where Deb and I stayed on the south side of the Arno, it was a two-kilometre stroll across a choice of four bridges past Florence Cathedral, best known for its dome by Brunelleschi and campanile (bell tower) by Giotto, our painter of biblical scenes in Padua.

We've spoken of the Knights' distinctive attire, the red cross on white background worn on mantles (tunic-like vests) over suits of armour. The cross insignia, in the colours of Sant'Ambrogio chessboards, is known as the Maltese or Solar Cross, depending on the order of the colours, which strikes me as another nod to paths of nature and ancient gods. Coming here, past the near-neon magnitude of Florence Cathedral, the discretion of the church of San Jacopo makes the unassuming building virtually disappear. Which was perhaps the intention. It doesn't even look like a church from the outside. At least not around here, where cathedrals tend to be statements of power and wealth.

The Templar church exterior actually *resembles* a bank, with metal bars under low, curved arches. The entryway could pass for outsized tellers' windows from a century ago, with the whole thing resembling a government building. But above a pair of simple wood doors, set beneath a Roman arch lintel, is a colour-inverted Solar Cross, this one white against red. It's faded from age but still looks as though it's maintained, attractive and understated. Columns supporting exterior arches are carved at the top with coats of arms from grail protectors. Each crest has the look of a stamp to seal letters with wax, and they feel somehow familiar, comforting almost, like a mat at the door of a welcoming home.

Somewhat jarringly, the chapel interior is starkly white. There's a high arching nave, an odd contrast to the exterior, as though entering an illusion. And I'm struck by another mild shock. The apse is set up with state-of-the-art AV (audiovisual) equipment. Of course I shouldn't be surprised. I've been in plenty of churches with great sound systems, projectors and screens, but something about that initial feeling of amorphous space and time catapulted me into the past, more so than usual. Maybe it was the ensigns of knights, signatures in their way. The perimeter of the interior does nothing to quell the sensation. A tombstone stands out, inscribed to the Lion of Florence, Luigi Tornabuoni, who looks like Columba or Saint Michael, leaning with casual confidence on a longsword, a rosary draped over that, with a bible tucked under his arm. He's wearing religious robes but there's no mistaking this is a soldier you don't want to mess with.

Templar history almost comes to a head in this space: some fact, some speculation, all contributing to rumour-mongering and the Knights' eventual dissolution by the church. Templars were known to be secretive. Rites of initiation were guarded, symbols and prayers kept private. It was a closely held order, intended for good more so than propaganda.

John the Baptist in particular was a sticking point associated with the Templars, something the church could hang on to. John was revered by the Templars. Too much so, according to Rome. When someone other than Jesus was being held in particularly high regard it was seen as encroaching on idolatry or false worship. It was claimed, although never verified, that Knights Templar worshipped John above all, and the grail they kept was the plate for his head. (In case you were unaware, John was beheaded.) Other accounts claim the Templars still had the head, and used it as an altar.

Although timelines don't quite align, another branch of research introduces the Shroud of Turin to the debate. Along with the true cross, holy nails, holy lance and Holy Grail, the shroud is considered amongst the most precious of relics. It's a swath of linen with the likeness of a man's face imposed onto it like a photo film negative. Some believe this was the cloth used to wrap the body of Jesus for burial, and the facial imprint is his. The shroud re-emerged in popular literature and conspiracy theories when the 2006 Winter Olympics were held in Turin, a small town nestled in Italian Alps. Another nugget is the fact that Turin lies on our Via Heraklea, the last major west-to-east stop before hitting Milan.

With respect to the Templars, some theorists claim the image on the shroud is not that of Jesus but rather the face of John the Baptist. This may've given the church more fodder against the Knights, but the shroud first appeared in the mid-14th century, well after most Templars were gone, disbanded, killed off or absorbed into other knightly orders. Many researchers discredit the shroud altogether, claiming it's been manufactured, an authentic-looking fake. And despite *my* head still being attached (unlike John's), it's starting to swim with the influx of info. Which oozes from arches and walls in the Templars' bank-like church, or perhaps it's a church-like bank.

I alluded to it earlier, now let's make it so, and follow the road to Rome. In theory we could choose any of them (if they *all* in fact lead there), but I'm on a bus heading south by southeast on the E35, following the equinox line from Florence to Rome. I haven't forgotten about our ship leaving Venice. We'll be back soon enough. But this side trip had to take place right now, to put us into the Vatican in time for Palm Sunday. This Florentine-Roman detour actually took place on a separate trip, but it melds with our narrative so I'm sharing it with you here now. We could probably place our story in Rome at any time and it would always fit, as this was the starting point for much of Europe's written history, church politics and timeless cautionary tales of ego and overexpansion.

Through a squiggle of ring roads, I enter Rome on a bus that swings into a two-lane roundabout where five lanes of traffic race in a circular scrum. I'm sitting by a window and to my delight and horror we sheer off the side mirror of a Renault. It actually went *shing!* Neither vehicle slowed in the least. I felt a bit like Jason Bourne on a Tilt-A-Whirl. And vowed to never, ever drive here.

The bus eventually parks and I check into a nondescript hotel, walking distance to places I find appealing, and methodically check things off my sightseeing list: Spanish Steps, Sistine Chapel, Trevi Fountain, the Forum, Pantheon and Coliseum. If the Lothbrok boys *had* made it here they'd have had a heyday. The city's half the size of London but somehow feels four times busier. Everything's vibrant, hot and boisterous in an agreeable way, but I'm glad I can hide in air conditioning whenever I feel the need.

The Tiber snakes its way through town, paralleling ring roads and offering up more S-curves than I can count. Rome's one of the oldest settlement sites in Europe, and given the city's timeline, each imperial monolith here is a relative new-build. I find the Coliseum perhaps the most time-bending structure. Maybe it's that childhood part of me that can almost hear the rumble of centurion chariots, roar of lions, clash of gladiatorial swords and howl of toga-clad spectators. But with the grail in mind we've an agenda to keep, and there's a specific locale here to find. From the Coliseum, it's a three-kilometre walk past a park and around the train station to the sixth-century Basilica of Saint Lawrence, one of the first Christian pilgrimage sites. And here, deep underground in the basilica catacombs, we can find the Holy Grail, according to archaeologist Alfredo Barbagallo.

The church looks like a villa: outbuildings with heavy stone walls and arches, red tile roof, a campanile and towering plinth in red marble, capped in the namesake saint. According to Barbagallo there's an actual guide to the catacombs written by friar Giuseppe da Bra, in which he describes a vaulted room under the church, 20 metres square, and where "in the corner of a wall-seat there can be seen a terracotta funnel whose lower part opens out over the face of a skeleton." This represents the funeral rite in which the deceased are offered food and drink. In other words, it's a grail, one used to serve wine at a formal gathering.

Barbagallo goes on with further details from the friar's account, describing the catacomb funnel room. "In excavations under the paving of this chapel four skeletons were found in a line. They had in their mouths coin from the imperial age and from the last days of the republic." This is what tips the scales for Barbagallo, giving us an approximate timeline, along with the positioning of the corpses, the coins in their mouths, and one other skeleton placed directly in front of the chalice-like vessel.

"I'm convinced this is the object called the Holy Grail," Barbagallo has said.

Well, if *he's* convinced...

You'll recall Saint Lawrence was the treasurer who's believed to have shuttled the grail from here to his hometown in Spain. But not according to Barbagallo, who claims Lawrence was martyred right here, so he couldn't possibly have smuggled the grail from the city. I decide there's only one way to find out.

"Can I see the grail?" I ask.

"No."

"Ah, mi scusi," I try again. "Per favore, *may* I see the grail?"

"Ah," a smile from the attendant. "No."

I do a quick online search of the facility to see if I can't find a clue, maybe a doorway marked "Grail." But it turns out the archaeologist who says that it's here wasn't allowed in either. And he certainly didn't make it downstairs. So it's one of those research jobs more in keeping with historical speculation rather than fact finding. But he's gotten his article published in a couple of places, so that's something. I'm glad I didn't come here just for this. In fact the main reason I'm here is to see some Swiss Guards, and perhaps shake the hand of the Pope.

Early the next morning, I make my way from the hotel to the centre of Rome, and disappear in the midst of the country. It's one of those nifty tricks like boarding the Hogwarts Express at Platform 9¾. Only this isn't King's Cross. It's Vatican City. On Palm Sunday.

This is the Sunday before Easter. No more quibbling about the day, it's the one most people agree on, even though the date changes constantly. I'm shuffling forward in a crush of 300,000 people, slowly pressing our way forward like the world's biggest concert event. We're in St. Peter's Square, fronting St. Peter's Basilica, the largest church in the world. Given the size of the crowd I realize I may not get a chance to meet his holiness after all.

"Sir! Sir! Just a few questions please, for my Viking book!"

Perhaps not.

So instead I wait alongside everyone else, and grab a slice of cold, terrible pizza from a vendor. I suspect every big gathering has drawn hawkers and punters for as long as there've been gatherings. Fêtes, fairs and, yes, people coming together to commune and for prayer. But despite the slight feel of a street market here in the square, a pious energy runs through everything. It's treacly thick, slightly intoxicating and surprisingly inviting.

I spot a couple of Swiss Guards, the more modern version of Byzantine Viking Varangians. Their ceremonial yellow and blue with tall white panache stands out, even at a distance. And after a couple of hours a hush falls. I'm still not sure how we all knew, but we did, the moment the Pope stepped onto his small, high balcony to address the crowd from a very long way away. To my naked eye he's a tiny white dot. A white dot speaking Italian. The sound system's exceptional, broadcasting his words and prayer through the square. I understand none of it but still feel oddly guilty. Perhaps I *do* understand. But the experience is a special one, same as being at any holy site or gathering of predominantly devoted believers. And I feel a great deal of respect for the faithful.

A brief blip of time has elapsed, a trifling on our quest, and we've returned to north Italy, south of the Alps and training grounds of papal guards, homeland to Celts, and where the Von Trapp family singers harmonized and trekked mountain passes, I believe. And like a baserunner rounding second going for third, we've touched once again on the Heraklean Way at Milan, where solstice and equinox lines intersect, creating a neat little X. Well, a massive one, actually. This, more or less, is the place where Indy said, "Forget any ideas you've got about lost cities, exotic travel, and digging up the world. We do *not* follow maps to buried treasure, and X never, ever marks the spot."

But Indy hadn't read Graham Robb, nor did he know the path that we're on. And although he did a fine job of traversing the world unearthing relics, he didn't have the same experience with the Ark of the Covenant I believe I had. Okay, that one's a stretch, but you should've seen this thing at the arms dealer's hacienda! I mean, seriously. But putting all that aside, it's *exactly* where we are. Where X marks the spot, between lost cities, doing our best to find buried treasure. So I'm sorry, Indy, you've got it wrong. This time our quest is true.

I shuffle up the gangway onto the giant white boat made of steel, to set sail from Venice at sunset. And I can't help but feel I've poked the fire just right, logs settling into place, the cooperation of embers and sparks all jumping in flame. We've found another corner piece to our puzzle, two or three sides now intact, and we're bound for where Herakles started his journey. The place where gods lay the groundwork for eternal paths, leaving us to determine our routes. Not only a starting point for our grail quest, but perhaps the prologue to all of it.

↑

GREECE AND TURKEY

What struck me most was the sun. Not literally, but in an oddly obverse kind of way. Because when we heaved our way west under sail in the North Atlantic, it was an easterly sun rising from sea that perpetually lit our path. But now, heading east to Herakles's home, it's the sun in the west that dominates. As our cruise ship lumbers from Venice harbour, the scatter of islets and sea are aglow, deeper than the amber of Pytheas, a rich coral hue with the pink tones of salmon, as though the ocean's offering up its very own treasure.

And unlike the cork-in-a-tub feeling of stormy Atlantic, here in the Adriatic the water's virtually calm. Combined with the tonnage of our vessel, it feels like the world's smoothest flight. A flight with extra legroom. Our little cabin's midship, a few storeys up, with a small balcony that for now faces northeast, where I have a sliding view of Trieste, a sliver of Slovenia, and a chunky Croatian peninsula. We'll sail through the night down the Dalmatian coast, past Zadar and the islands off Split. Tomorrow we arrive in Dubrovnik.

From the 9th to the 12th centuries, the Venetian navy eradicated pirates from these waters, allowing trade goods and money to flow from the east into Europe. Much of that business came from Muslim traders and the Byzantine Empire. Although ocean-going Norse raiders from the west didn't make it this far, Scandinavian rowers, Rus traders and Varangian migrants were coming this way from the east, more examples of Vikings dotting the *mappae mundi*, medieval maps of the world.

By the 13th century, Venice was the richest city in Europe and the Templars' bank-cum-church of San Jacopo was generating staggering sums of money. Records show the city on stilts had 36,000 sailors running 3,300 ships, dominating Mediterranean commerce. Having walked the crumbling canals through old phoenix ashes as angels threatened to fall, I couldn't help but feel it's a place that used to be.

In our little stateroom I sleep well to the rumble of engine and lull of a gentle sea, and wake as we pull into port for a day on the shores of Croatia. Dubrovnik dates back, more or less, to the seventh century, when it was called Ragusa. Rome had shrunk into imperial hibernation and Celts were re-establishing themselves across Europe, referring to the four centuries of imperialism as "the Roman interlude." This stretch of coastline and sea, following the equinox line southeast from Milan, was part of the Byzantine Empire before coming under the protection of Venice. Dubrovnik is now a World Heritage Site, based mainly on the medieval architecture in the walled Old Town. From 1991 to 1995 the war of independence raged here, part of the dissolution of Yugoslavia. Despite touch-ups and preservation of building façades, bullet holes are still visible in exterior walls and plaster.

When this fortified port became part of Venice, the crusades were in full swing. Enter once more our Knights Templar, who went to the Holy Land to fight for the church of Rome. For 200 years, off and on, from the late 11th to 13th centuries, war waged for control of Jerusalem. The Holy City was run by Islamic leaders, and Christian armies from across Europe travelled east to fight for the prized real estate. Timelines are broken into what are considered eight major crusades, prolonged periods of catapult fire, siege and battlefield clashes.

Dubrovnik, or Ragusa, was ahead of the curve at this time and through the Renaissance, a liberal city state of modern law with inclusive immigration policies, one of the first places to outlaw slavery, early in the 15th century. Like any strategic locale, it appealed to every power player in the area. Despite relative autonomy, it's been part of Byzantium, Venice, Hungary, France, Italy, Yugoslavia, Austria and the Ottoman Empire. And perhaps because of this, the country retains unbendable national pride.

We spend half a day walking immaculate streets, sipping strong coffee and poking in shops. The highlight for me was accessing the town from the hills on a bus from the big modern port. It provided an almost aerial view, looking down an embankment to the red-roofed and reinforced town, with circular walls hanging on shoreline rock. Despite the shimmy of the bus, it felt like a peephole into another era.

Back aboard the ship, we dine on fish with white wine and some sort of chocolate dessert. Overnight in the blackness we pass Montenegro and Albania, and following another good sleep I wake just before sunrise. Wearing a toque for the chill of sea air, I sit on our tiny deck, feeling as though I've got the world to myself. There's a mesmeric *whoosh* of wake, feathery white, slicing away from our hull. The water is true aquamarine, which sounds unimaginative but that's the colour it is. If I had to hazard a guess I'd say where we are is the meeting point of the Adriatic and Ionian Seas. And when I lean out, over the railing and into the wind, I can catch my first glimpse of Greece. It's Corfu, with mainland a bit further southeast.

As sea froths its white noise, both calming and titillating, I'm again thrown back in time. This stretch of water's where Odysseus sailed, and the Greeks that were bound for Marseilles. The Templars who travelled by sea rather than overland came through here on their way to Jerusalem. It was a throughway for Herakles too. And no doubt the grail, or at least a few iterations of vessel, plate and chalice.

Historians say you get a snapshot of the Mediterranean Middle Ages here in Corfu, by way of a string of medieval castles that crown this long, slender island. The national government's designated the capital of Corfu City as a kastropolis, or castle city. Fortified strongholds were, for the most part, defence against pirates and Ottomans. Its position is key: the mouth of the Adriatic at the narrows by Italy's boot heel. By the 17th century this little island was one of the most heavily fortified places in Europe and is another World Heritage Site, boasting the first university, theatre and opera house of the modern Greek era.

Even in this part of the world Corfu's considered old, with written history going back 1,300 years before Jesus. It was part of Corinth, the powerful pocket of Greece to the south, a narrow of land that connects the Peloponnese peninsula to the European mainland. Where we are was called Korkyra, named for a nymph abducted by Poseidon, god of the sea, one of the gods of Olympus. Yes, by the way, there were 12 of *them*, too. The name Corfu is a phonetic, latinized version of its Byzantine name, meaning "city of peaks," referring to its hilly terrain. Now, with our cruise ship moored at a berth on the island's east side, we're again on a bus, driving up island, into those Byzantine hills.

I'm overdressed (I believe) for a grail quest, although at least I haven't had to wear a tie. It's another work-oriented function, but I don't believe we'll be dining with any international fugitives this time around. I'm one of a rather large group being recognized for something that seems quite important to the organizers. Not so much to the recipients. However, the setting's nice and the views are spectacular.

Where we are is the Achillion Palace. Built in the 19th century, it's designed to replicate the mystical site of Phaeacia, considered Utopia in Greek mythology. Homer mentions the place (the mythological one) in the *Odyssey*, and it's the last stop Odysseus makes on his decade-long journey before heading home to Ithaca. Fun fact: they filmed a Bond movie here. Naturally, I'm tempted to purse my lips ever so slightly and order a shaken martini. But instead we're hustled into assigned seating and each of us is given a sculpture, a ten-kilo hunk of granite in the shape of some guy reclined eating grapes. And I wonder where I can discreetly dump this hernia-inducing memento.

The palace ground offers a broad vista of open sea, and once more we're ensconced in cypress. I half expect the rolling green earth to conjure another snake of sfumato. This view of Ionian Sea could be a backdrop to countless Renaissance paintings, vanishing points and the hills of Etruscan towns that served as one painter's take on the Holy Land.

Our palatial banquet wraps up, allowing us to return to the ship to sail at sunset. Back on board, well fed and watered, we're still overdressed and it's terribly early. With imaginings of James Bond lingering, I feel we've no choice but to hit the casino.

I'm not much of a gambler, as you'll see. But I figure I can play slot machine blackjack, not lose too much money, and also get happily bloated on beer. There's a change machine to turn notes into coins. Without putting any thought into it I slide a 50-euro note into the machine. What hadn't occurred to me, however, is of course you're supposed to put a little catch bucket under the spout that shoots out the coins. So the contraption devours my note and then machineguns me with 50 one-euro coins. For a split second, before the humiliation set it, I actually felt like a winner, as though I'd hit the jackpot and this game was paying off big. But the fleeting sense of euphoria vanished almost immediately as I became quite the opposite of a winner, dropping to the floor, scrambling and clawing about to gather my coins. In my good suit.

Bond.

James Bond.

Overnight we've sailed to Santorini, Aegean mixing with Mediterranean, which puts us right in the thick of things. We've arrived by the equinox line, which connects to our solstice X on Herakles's path, and remnants of his labours are everywhere. Just northwest of here is where he caught the lion, hind and boar, not to mention the deadly birds from Stymphalia. Northeast is Thrace, where he stole Diomedes's horses, while directly south of us is Crete, the spot where he beat up the Minotaur's four-legged father. If we stick to our equinox line all the way from the Alps, we'd hit Delphi like a bull's eye, considered the womb of Herakles's Earth. From this spot Zeus released two crows, one flying west, the other east, to plot the breadth of the globe. It's where Herakles got his to-do list, outlining his pilgrimage path. And it was a stopping point too for crusading knights, making their way to where the grail first became holy.

While we're here let's revisit the Minotaur's dad for a moment, the belligerent bull from Crete. Our current moorage, like most of this Greek archipelago, was home to the early civilization of Minoa. Archaeological records indicate Minoans lived here at the start of the Bronze Age, from at least 3500 BCE. Their legendary king was Minos, son of Zeus, another bloodline of gods, and it's where the oldest city in Europe still stands, the town of Knossos. Beneath its colonnade walls was the labyrinth, an endless maze of corridors where the Minotaur brooded, hunted and ate. (It's no wonder the bullish family had issues.)

I'm awake early, excited as our ship drops anchor. I've recovered from last night's casino embarrassment and for the rest of the week will pay for everything with one-euro coins. As I stand on our little balcony and take in surroundings, all I can think of is water. It's striking. And somehow familiar. Maybe it's the age of the place, some primal connection, or more likely the fact that Santorini appears in countless travel magazines: blue-domed orthodox churches with blinding white limestone, hanging on indigo sea. Maybe it's the plummeting cliffs of the caldera. The whole island's a steep-sided crater, a volcanic crescent that could pass for a sharp sickle moon. And the water's the deepest shade of navy I've seen since we sailed from Venice. I remember a play I attended, the story set here. A fisherman casts his net from a skiff and gazes into the sea.

"How deep is the water?" his passenger asks.

The fisherman pauses, as though doing the math, squints into the blue and finally answers, "Maybe 1000 metres...maybe 10,000...maybe goes down forever."

The thought of which leaves me dizzy, and giddy. And I let my imagination drift there, sinking slowly into the depths. Then smile as I hear the voice of Zeus, which sounds a lot like Liam Neeson, growling from Olympus: "Release the kraken!"

Maybe it's one of the underworld portals. Herakles found two on his path, where he encountered the dragon-like hound and the hydra. An interesting twist in our tale is that Glastonbury Tor – where the Lady of the Lake changed Lancelot's diapers and Joseph might've hidden the grail – is *also* considered a portal to the underworld. Much like Avalon, where Camelot faithful believe Arthur's not dead but resting, awaiting a suitable time to wake and perhaps reawaken the world.

But for now let's explore Santorini. Buildings in white cling to the edge of the caldera but the main part of town tops the island, a somewhat flat patch with aerie views of what once was Minoa. To get up there we have a choice to make: squeeze into a creaking funicular made entirely of rust, or join a shuffle of pack animals and sweaty tourists to climb cobbled switchbacks paved in donkey shit.

We opt for the donkey shit.

Following a tiptoeing, serpentine climb, we're in the heart of Santorini town, narrow streets with mopeds, an agreeable crush of tourists and locals getting on with life. Shop windows display endless arrays of olives and oils in colourful bottles and jars. I see the locale in the art, from decorative glass to sculptures and prints, everything in emerald and sapphire hues, the colours of sea and sky.

The place name comes from Saint Irene, Santa Irini. It's been called Strongýlē ("circular") and Kallístē ("beautiful"), and while its proper name is Thēra, Santorini just seems to stick. Next to Crete, the best Minoan archaeological sites are here, 5,000-year-old buildings and streets, preserved in ash from a massive volcanic explosion that devastated the Minoan culture, like an asteroid wiping out dinosaurs. The island blew around 1600 BCE, and research here is similar to that of Pompeii, only older. It's the kind of event that enables anthropologists to pinpoint dating in crusty layers of lava and rock left behind.

In the Bronze Age this small city boomed, a commercial hub with three-storey buildings, hot and cold running water, and an established art scene, indicating a prosperous place and time. Lustrous frescoes have been unearthed here, landscapes in sunset colours with farmers in fields of spices. Apart from villagers' attire, the scenes could be taking place now. Some believe what was lost to the sea in the volcanic quake could be another Atlantis. After the Minoans seemingly ceased to be, this was Phoenician terrain, before becoming Roman, Byzantine and eventually part of Greece.

I buy a small journal, also with scenes of the sea, as well as some snacks to enjoy aboard ship: a rubbery round of Greek gouda, green olives and Mythos beer. We find a patio for late lunch and sip a small bottle of acidic white wine, which we have with fava, lamb meatballs and pita. Done with the donkeys for now, we squeeze into the rusty funicular for the steep descent to the water, where we board a tender back to the ship.

Again we set sail in sunset, and it's a good one. Not like setting sun near the equator, which I consider a light switch, bright and then instantly dark. Here we enjoy a fiery ball easing itself into the water, like a bather dipping toes, testing the temperature before committing. Colours deepen with the sun's descent, the look of an egg poaching gently in simmering sea. And I wonder if somewhere down there (maybe 1000 metres, maybe 10,000) if another Atlantis is now being lit, its own watery, inverted sunrise.

As the last of the sun shifts the water from honey to amber, we weave north through a rippling sea. That night I dream vividly; maybe it's our northerly shift, heading into the chop of katabatic winds. Also called Meltemi or Etesian gusts, these high pressure systems blow from the Balkans, challenging sailors since Homer's time, and in late summer these blasts often grow into Asian monsoons. Although I consider dream sequences lazy writing, I feel a need to share this one with you, as it may prove relevant to our search. What played in my head was a jangly, metallic sound, like slightly out-of-tune jingle bells. The sound came from riders on horseback, armoured in chain mail (which was invented by Celts, by the way). I was watching it all from a distance, and although focused it wasn't perfectly clear, as though the first breaths of sfumato had begun to swallow the land. It was a procession of sorts. No pageantry, just two lines of medieval military, travelling light, for speed. And in their midst was a wagon, a heavy Celtic chariot with wide wooden wheels, built for rough roads, although their path was straight as a lance. The container on the wagon was simple, not particularly large, wood banded in iron, reinforced for strength and security. I could make out a crest on a soldier's mantle, not the familiar cross of crusaders, but a druidic swirl, set into three solar rays. They could've been Round Table knights, Jomsvikings or possibly Byzantine Guards. The other thing that stood out was their shields: circular, oak, set with a boss and painted to match their crests. They looked like Viking shields, something you'd expect to see on the gunwales of longships, but there was no mistaking the Celtic influence.

I woke wondering who they might be, and what it was that was being transported. Maybe too much research and speculation spilling over from my waking mind, layered up like archaeology in pumice. Or it could be I'd had my imagination on lockdown too long, my subconscious mind giving those dim recesses of cerebral cortex a little off-leash time. Regardless, it felt somehow poignant, as though we're closing in on something that only now wants to be revealed. Naturally, I recall another line from *Indiana Jones*, in which Walter Donovan states with confidence, "As you can see, we are on the verge of completing a quest that began almost two thousand years ago." It's a confidence I find reassuring.

Today's a day at sea. For some that means poolside and an extra half-dozen meals. For me it's room service pizza and a second chair on the deck to create a little ottoman. Not quite an empire, but I still feel quite regal as Aegean islands slip by. The northerly wind's picking up and there's more movement through the ship, a noticeable to-and-fro. And I like to believe I know, to a degree, what Odysseus may have felt like.

As we make our way east, Greek islands dwindle and I can spot offshore rocks of Turkey. Much as in Corfu, some islets are almost entirely castle, the fortified island of Tenedos a prime example. We don't have a great distance to cover today, and like circling planes waiting for runways, I suspect we're killing time until our Turkish moorage is available. I read a bit more of crusades and rulers of the eastern Mediterranean, from Islamic Caliphates to Sultanates, and the Ayyubid Dynasty under Saladin. And as was the case in so many places we've visited, the fight for control of Jerusalem was a seemingly unending chess match, a particularly brutal one lasting centuries. These clashes, however, continued to drive advancement of siege strategies and weaponry, the type that eventually threshed the Cathars from Montségur and perhaps sent the grail northward.

Eventually we skirt the island of Samos and dock at the port of Kuşadası. To the north is Istanbul's Golden Horn, the narrows of the Bosphorus and the Black Sea, what Vikings and Rus knew as Miklagard. If you google it now on a map you'll be dropped at the Hagia Sophia, the cathedral, now mosque, where a Scandinavian guard carved his runic inscription, "Halfdan carved these runes," still visible in the mottled white marble of a top-storey gallery.

As massive ropes get looped and knotted to secure us to a pier, I'm struck by a new sensation of arrival. This patch of globe really is its own middle earth, a bridge between worlds, cartographical, cultural and spiritual. When I step off the boat I've effectively leapt from Europe to Asia. And despite this being a secular country, there's no mistaking a shift in religion. Onion-domed turrets and mosques are the norm, loudspeakers broadcast muezzins' calls, and flags sport an Islamic moon. Mecca still lies toward rising sun but it's sharply south of us here. Next to the port is a chunky headland and a long, slender beach of gold sand. We join a group, board a bus and head inland, our first stop the ancient city of Ephesus. Where we are is Anatolia, where Strabo wrote of Pytheas in his voluminous *Geographica*. At one time this was all part of Greece, the region known as Ionia.

The bus parks in a patch of tamped dust and we step into dry, intense heat. We're close to the sea but it feels like desert. This was oceanside not too long ago, water having receded over the past 3,000 years. Ephesus was a port, constructed around 1000 BCE and rivalling Alexandria, Athens and the Fertile Crescent of Mesopotamia. It was one of the 12 cities of the Ionian League, a centre for commerce and government policy, and eventually became part of the Roman Republic.

We walk for a while on a path of crumbling cobble and rock, and cresting a rise in the land we come to one of the seven wonders of the ancient world: the Temple of Artemis. It was built in the sixth century BCE, then rebuilt a few times after fire and flood, but the interesting bits are what remain from the end of the Roman Empire, around the year 400. A solitary stone column in white still stands, like a lone wedding cake ornament or a long-abandoned gnomon. Nearby is a heavy rock cairn with cut stones like a dais. Atop this is what's left of the decorative top of one column, which I learn is called the capital. Now it just looks like an anvil.

The mostly complete column seems to be the star of the show, a monument to the past. But unlike smooth-sided obelisks of Egypt, this Greco-Roman structure is a neat stack of 12 massive discs of stone, each carved with uniform ridgelines, giving the whole a striped effect. It's only upright from balance and weight, and I can't imagine it passing a building inspection. I suppose when it was fully constructed, load-bearing arches held it in place. Perhaps it's obvious why I didn't pursue the lofty career of architect, but if I learned one thing from Lego, it's that you're supposed to interlock the bricks.

Around the perimeter of the pillar are a few low rockpiles, no doubt previous plinths for other, now crumbled columns. And a series of wide, shallow steps descend to what was likely a pool or bath. There's a great quote describing this place when it was built, perhaps one of the earliest travelogues, written by the Greek poet Antipater in the second century BCE. Referring to the world's seven wonders he states, "I have set eyes on Babylon and the statue of Zeus by the Alpheus River, hanging gardens and colossus of the Sun, the huge labour of high pyramids and vast tomb of Mausolus. But when I saw the Temple of Artemis, those other marvels lost their brilliancy."

If this is in fact the best of the best I wonder what's next, and whether it's worth seeing. But I'm keeping an open mind, and carry on with the group. We pass another small clump of people going the opposite way and exchange a few smiles and nods. Some are lathering on sunscreen, others are taking photos. And one fellow's pointing out all the facts and figures the guide's gotten wrong. I wonder if this was what Antipater experienced when he came through, taking notes with a quill on papyrus.

Our next stop is the Library of Celsus, which is now just a façade. It looks like the most elaborate movie set, one of those you need to film straight on, like in an old western. The library has its own layered story of construction and reconstruction. It began early in the second century, commissioned by Gaius Julius Aquila as a monument to his dad, Asia's administrator for Rome, the Right Honourable Tiberius Julius Celsus Polemaeanus. (To his friends he probably just went by Tiberius Julius Celsus Polemaeanus, and his son no doubt called him sir.) The structure Gaius built for his dad, however, was still incomplete at the time all the family had passed. But then Hadrian came into power, the proactive builder who put up the wall between England and Scotland, and a short while later this spectacular library was finally completed.

It served as a combination reading room, lending space and community centre as well, containing 16,000 books, in fact scrolls. Containers of upright rolls of papyrus would have been placed around the central main room for browsers to peruse and to read. Taking books out of libraries wasn't yet a thing. There were extra-large windows along the east wall for natural light. Walls had recessed, closing cupboards with labels to accommodate additional titles, likely the most valuable volumes. These custom-built bookshelves are known as armaria, standard features in well-financed reading rooms from ancient times, an early precursor to armoires.

In 262 most of the library was destroyed in an earthquake and fire. Some historians suspect the fire occurred as a result of the quake, while others say it wasn't a quake at all and that the fire was started during a Gothic invasion. However it happened, the place was trashed. And remained that way for a very long time. Pieces of cornerstone, shelving and architectural bric-a-brac were hauled away by an assortment of archaeologists and light-fingered museum curators, and parts of this building are on display in Istanbul and Vienna. Then a dedicated team reassembled what they could to recreate the façade. A few key pieces of rock have been copied, replaced or simply left missing, like a friendly, gap-toothed smile. What's standing now looks a bit wonky, but its venerability remains, along with, I like to believe, the essence of 2,000 years worth of reading.

We head back to the bus, a reverse of the modest hike over cobbles through dry clumps of rat-tail grass. Our guide points out that this was part of a road of marble that led to the water, when it was a port, its dock where our bus is now parked. And it's here that Antony put on a show to welcome Cleopatra, or so the story goes. Julius Caesar had been assassinated, leaving General Mark Antony and a couple of other key players in charge of Rome. Cleopatra was Queen of Egypt following her father's passing (she and her dad had ruled as a team for a while). Then Antony and Cleopatra met, secured a political alliance between Egypt and Rome, hit it off, had adorable twins (a girl and a boy) and became the hot celebrity couple of the day. Not sure if they had a cute couples' nickname or not. Antatra? Cleotony? Not as fun as Brangelina, but maybe it works better in hieroglyphs. Regardless, upon Cleopatra's arrival here at Ephesus, the streets were lined with well-wishers pouring red wine on the white marble stones, a regal greeting and the origin, we're told, of a red carpet welcome.

Air conditioning in the bus is a welcome relief, for a moment, but now it feels like a meat locker. At least there's no risk of succumbing to heat stroke. The bus veers south and we begin to climb. There's more vegetation and trees like what we saw in the lumpy Etruscan hills, but this definitely feels as though we've got one foot in Mediterranean Europe, the other in the Mid East. There are olive groves and grapes, a few cypress trees and some vine-wrapped deciduous with waxy green leaves.

The drive is short but slow and methodical, purposeful somehow, and we park alongside a few other buses. We've clearly gained altitude.

The temperature's comfortably cool and trees are plentiful. There's a lush ground cover of bushes and greenery and the air seems richer, whether from the perfume of flowers, oxygenation of trees, or something more, I can't say.

There's a trail leading on, a bit of climbing, which seems lightly paved but it's from the tread of pilgrims' feet, compacting earth into a narrow, sunbaked walkway, its own kind of solar path. There's a tiny canal, the look of a natural creek, burbling alongside the path. Leaf-laden trees are now hanging over the trail and it's starting to look like Eden.

Up ahead is a small, dome-roofed chapel, a modest building of sandstone. We're now in a near-silent queue of travellers and pilgrims moving forward, as slow and purposeful as the bus ascending the hill to get here. The footpath serpentines a bit, up to the open entryway of the little church, known as Mother Mary's House. Yes, one of our Marys. But the one who lived here, we're told, is the one Gabriel called upon, the mother of Jesus.

There's a wishing wall (not a typo) next to a fountain. Pilgrims drink from the water fed from the creek-like canal, and treat *that* as a wishing well. Believers claim to have had illnesses cured by consuming the water, the same underground spring from which Mary supposedly drank. I take a small sip and it has a sharp but clear taste, much nicer than the Santorini beach wine.

The line of people continues to move (no stopping, please) and we shuffle our way into the chapel. A small side room is where Mary slept, a slightly raised sleeping pallet, everything simple and compact. I've never been in a group of this size that's so utterly silent. There must be a hundred of us, inching forward with a gentle reverence I find wondrous. Forget the healing spring water out front. If we could bottle *this* and serve it at gatherings, strangers becoming patient and kind, I'd invest everything just to give it away. (Okay, I might keep a little walking around money, but you get the gist.)

One interior wall has an altar that looks like a hearth set beneath an arch of brickwork. There's a vase of fresh flowers and a simple cross on a stand, quite the opposite of garish cathedrals and duomos we've visited in getting here. Outside, at the wishing wall, people are writing small prayers, notes of request or forgiveness, tucking the small folds of paper into cracks between stones. The wall looks like it's completely constructed of paper, a binding of thousands of prayers (maybe 10,000, maybe goes on forever).

A cynic might question this place, the number of times it's been rebuilt, its similarity to relics housed in so many churches, attracting pilgrims along with their purses. But the palpable sense of commitment, not so much faith as unwavering *knowing* that seems to pervade the space, leaves me feeling remarkably positive. Optimistic about everything. The church in Rome doesn't expressly acknowledge this as the home of Mary, but the place has been blessed by a number of Popes and a series of Vatican visitors. Similar to the papal references to one or more of the grails in Spain, without actually saying the item in question is the genuine article. Like we've seen so many times before. Why disbelieve anything? It could all be true.

Although we've been moving steadily as we pass through the house, I do my best to retain each detail, taking mental inventory like a memory game to recall later, imagining myself like Sherlock Holmes, believing there must be clues in here somewhere. Could there be something amongst Mary's possessions that resembles a grail? Could Dan Brown's *da Vinci* storyline be based on fact, and Mary herself was the grail?

If this space is any indicator, Mary, *this* Mary, lived a simple existence, deeply pious (no kidding), minimalist and seemingly eager to keep to herself. It exudes the simplicity of a nun's existence. There are no signs of personal items. Perhaps that was considered vanity. I think of church references to the grail, holy relics like crosses, nails and lances, and this humble home as well. The sleeping pallet could very well be the grail, as much as the vase of flowers, a shroud with a face, or a bit of bloodstained gauze from the offspring of whoever lived here. Maybe I was looking at this wrong all along, trying to unearth facts. In *Indiana Jones*, Indy's dad explains to his son, "Archaeology is the search for *fact*, not truth." In which case this place could be all about the latter. As our slow-moving line weaves from the house in an S, past the healing fountain and a prayer-plastered wall, I'm left to wonder if this slice of middle earth is its own middle ground, a path between fact and truth.

It was here, people claim, that Mary's ascension took place. Not the simple definition like getting a raise or promotion, but the meatier meaning, going directly to heaven. The term often used is assumption. Apparently there were a few attendants at her side as she passed away. There's a quote that states, "At the end of her earthly course, Mary was assumed into heavenly glory, body and soul." In other words, job well done, now off (or up) you go. But those words don't appear in the Bible. It was written and read by a Pope in the last century, but said with conviction, and now it's another truth.

As we carry on through this Eden-esque space to return to our bus, I find myself thinking the whole thing through, and what exactly ascension might be. I know people who've felt an essence pass through their body at the moment a loved one dies, irrespective of where they are. I remember when my nana passed peacefully in a hospital bed, her gaze went from clear to slightly opaque, that nebulous, middle-distance focus, and she said, "Oh! Look at all the beautiful flowers!" then passed with a Mona Lisa smile. And a friend tells of his experience when he saw angels appear at his father's funeral. "There were two of them, and they were big."

Paintings of Mary's ascension are mostly grand and artistically interpretive. Of course there wasn't anyone there at that moment with an easel, palette and brushes, so we're left with creative impressions skewed toward whoever commissioned the pieces. They tend to include a lot of swirly, portal-like cloud formations and clumps of well-dressed, welcoming saints, not like those cheeky cherubs hanging over our heads in Venice.

What's said to have taken place here is much the same as the description of Galahad's ascent into heaven when he finally found the grail. Percival and Bors were there when he passed. Each telling refers to bright light. One version has him escorted by angels, up through the clouds. Another has him fading out of existence – poof! – while an earthlier version has him simply passing away, leaving his friends to tend to the body and give him a quiet burial. Which brings the grail into question again. In the versions where Galahad physically rises to heaven, he allegedly keeps the chalice. The rationale being that no other person could ever again be so pure of heart, and thereby no one else could possess the cup. Leaving nothing for grail hunters to find.

It does open up the whole can of worms about passing on, what that means and where we go. Ascension's an uplifting term, clearly. But that's not a generally held belief. Greeks defined two distinct types of burial, often referred to as sacrifice, perhaps a throwback to ancient Celtic rites in which the dead (or not quite dead) were "sacrificed" to not only appease the gods but ensure the departed could find their way forward, in other words get into the equivalent of the Valhalla after-party.

In Greek terminology the deceased would either have a chthonic burial, meaning underground, or an Olympian one, meaning heavenly. Like an elevator: two choices, up or down. We've seen plenty of both on our travels, from crucifixion, cremation and boat burning to burial barrows, crypts and mounds. Which brings us back to the underworld. Herakles laboured at two separate gates (one of which may've been Glastonbury), while Dante describes a great deal of it, but the two so-called destinations can't be simply defined. Technically, the underworld was considered more of an interim respite (like circling planes), a waiting room for the deceased as the next stop in their journey evolved, not quite the clichés of heaven and hell, with their accompanying soundtracks of angelic harps or jazz solos on loop.

The most familiar path to the underworld was likely the river Styx, transport route for the newly departed. But there were actually half a dozen mythological rivers meandering through the worlds of both living and dead, some navigated by punt, others by rowboat. Most of the waterways sound undesirable: the Acheron, a river of pain; the Lethe, a river of forgetfulness; the Phlegethon, a river of fire; the Cocytus, a river of wailing. But there was also a body of water known as Oceanus, a broad river encircling the world, dividing things longitudinally. To the east lay the underworld, while western domains held the land of mortals. No good and bad as such, just different paths. Perhaps the original prime meridian.

Back in the bus it feels extra chilly. Maybe I'm out of adrenaline. I'm staring out a window, contemplative, as we wend down a tree-lined road through dry fields to the beach and the port. The current one, not the one that once was. If I could glean anything from Mary's house, it's that the person who made that their home wasn't one to hang on to things. It wasn't a place you'd hide treasure or mementoes that might change the world. It was a spiritual place, to be sure. I'd even call it holy. But if the three Marys (Virgin Mary, Mary Magdalene and Aunt "Mary" Salome) were at the crucifixion, and perhaps with Joseph at the burial cave, there's no way this Mary took a chalice into safekeeping.

The more I think about how treasure was stored from that time through the Middle Ages, the more I believe a physical grail would *have* to be constantly moved. Citizens in this part of the world knew that Rome was adept at sniffing out caches intended to elude taxation. Hiding or burying things won't keep them safe. (Ask any dead pharaoh.) And long before metal detectors, dowsers could suss out precious commodities deep underground. Monks across Britain knew this as well, once Columba came to Iona. Even sound investments didn't ensure security, a lesson the Templars learned rather harshly as the church pilfered their hard-earned finances. But before our grail-protecting knights established their high-risk hedge funds, they secured a base south of here, in Jerusalem, as the city became the ultimate prize in Islamic and Christian Crusades.

CITY OF SEVENTY NAMES

Yerushalayim. Al-Quds. Bayt al-Maqdis. It's been called the City of Seventy Names. And at 5,000 years of age, Jerusalem is truly an ancient centre. Not only a World Heritage Site, but a Heritage Site in Danger, listed as a site at risk of destruction by nature or humankind. A meeting place for nomadic shepherds since the Stone Age, and depending on who you ask, the capital of both Israel and Palestine, holy to each Abrahamic religion. For lovers of statistics, the city's been besieged and/or sacked 56 times, changing hands amongst warring factions an additional 48 times. If you thought every holy site was as tranquil as Mary's home, think again.

Now, if you're in England or you watch Premier League football (soccer), this is something you already know. But in case you're unfamiliar with it, the hymn, now a song, called "Jerusalem" is the unofficial English anthem. It tends to be sung prior to ceremonial games, or gets belted out by fans during a match to rally their team or gloat when their side's dominating. It's one of my most aurally vivid childhood memories, watching international soccer on TV and hearing English fans sing as though marching to the Holy Land. It was particularly moving as I'd mistakenly thought all fans from that part of the world were hooligans. Since then I've learned nearly half of them aren't.

The song comes from the poem "And Did Those Feet in Ancient Time," written by William Blake early in the 1800s. And poses a fascinating query, one that could redefine the route we're on. The opening lines go like this: "And did those feet in ancient time / Walk upon England's mountains green / And was the holy Lamb of God / on England's pleasant pastures seen?"

It's as though Blake too wants to be part of our grail quest, perhaps to take the helm and steer for a while. The poet postulates that re-risen Jesus didn't simply hand over the grail to Joseph for transport to England, but that the two made the road trip together, ultimately climbing the green pap of Glastonbury. Which would put the grail spitting distance from King Arthur's court, as though it's been there all along.

We know Uncle Joseph was a travelling businessman, but an intriguing thread of research claims he was a tin merchant, and his westerly trek was no different than that of Pytheas, heading to the land's end of Belerion in search of Cornish mines. Like a few million others, he'd be eager to flee the restrictions of Rome, particularly if he had a grail to hide and a travel companion who happened to be his previously deceased nephew.

Blake's poem plays off the biblical references (from the *Book of Revelation*) to a second coming, where Jesus is looking to establish a New Jerusalem, perhaps a more peaceful one, on the path of a setting sun. Since "Jerusalem" first became a musical hymn, it's been used by both Conservatives and Liberals as a campaign song, and somehow seems to circumvent the whole separation of church and state thing. Even today, the notion of a new Holy Land tends to instill more national pride than religious zeal. Which I suspect adds to the grail's somewhat secular, timeless appeal.

It was in the 12th century that the Templars based themselves in the Israeli/Palestinian capital, at Jerusalem's holy hub of the Temple Mount. Now, it's a walled plaza with a gold dome set in an octagon. One of these perimeter enclosures is the Western Wall, the most sacred place in the Jewish faith, and where Muhammad had his own ascension to paradise. At a glance it looks like a much grander, imposing version of the wishing wall at Ephesus, and I find myself once more overwhelmed with something I find hard to articulate, perhaps simply a desire to know more.

At this juncture, the Templars were a newly established church charity, protectors of pilgrims travelling to the Holy Land. In 1120 Baldwin 11, King of Jerusalem, granted the Templars a wing of the

Temple Mount palace to establish their headquarters. From the get-go, the knights possessed a certain mystique, as this Christian HQ was in fact a mosque, built on what was once the Temple of Solomon. They called their new base Solomon's Temple, which spawned the moniker Templars, or so the story goes. Funnily enough, the order positioned itself as a collection of "poor soldiers," intended to be as minimalist as our Mary from Ephesus. One of their emblems was a depiction of two knights riding a single horse, indicating not only teamwork but choosing an impoverished life of service and piety. They didn't yet realize their business model was a licence to print money.

When Bernard of Clairvaux was in Troyes, writing the Templars' rules, he successfully pitched the notion of allowing the order to grow financially, which it did in spades. The savvy monk's campaign for the knights was circulated in a letter under the tagline "In Praise of the New Knighthood." Church supporters and wealthy aristocrats ate it up, gifting land and money to the Templars, encouraging the best and brightest to work with the knights and to train, fight, and protect the Holy Land. Momentum was on their side. In 1139 Pope Innocent II issued a papal bull that was effectively a Templar carte blanche, enabling them to travel anywhere freely and be accountable only to the Pope. In other words the knights were, for a time, above the law.

The site of the Templars' HQ further strengthened their political and historical significance. Solomon's Temple, beneath the Temple Mount, was the place where King David brought the Ark of the Covenant (the *actual* one), his plan being to build the holiest chapel in the holiest city to accommodate the holiest relic. But according to the Hebrew Bible, or Old Testament, God disallowed it, saying David had spilled too much blood during his reign. But David's son Solomon, it seems, was less of a fighter, more of a city planner, and managed to construct the temple.

From the Temple Mount, it's a ten-minute, weaving stroll through the Christian Quarter of Jerusalem's Old City, around the Church of Saint John the Baptist to the Church of the Holy Sepulchre. And it's here we have two of Christianity's holiest sites: the place where Jesus was crucified, and the cave tomb where he spent a few days following his death, presumably the place Joseph of Arimathea had prearranged.

Hadrian (builder of walls and well-lit libraries) was here as well, and in the year 130 had the cave filled in with a new temple built on top. As you've likely deduced, he wasn't a fan of Christians. The temple he built was dedicated to Herakles's biological dad, Zeus – Jupiter to the Romans – god of thunder and a few other things (basically Thor in a toga). And somewhere deep in this architectural, mythological soup lies the spot we have to assume our Marys and Joseph tended to Jesus post crucifixion, plus that subsequent period when the body was cleansed for temporary interment, along with, perhaps, a few items for burial. We can't be sure if this is the place Joseph received the grail from phantasmal Jesus, or if it was already elsewhere in safekeeping. Then again, it may've already been packed into caravan bags with rations and water for Joseph's trans-European tin hunt. And maybe, just maybe, there was an extra bedroll for his nephew, their destination the cliffs of Tintagel.

Now, as much as I like the notion of losing myself in ambiguous time and space, like all of us, I'm never far removed from the rest of the world. In between transit and research and meals, occasionally getting some rest, I'm still checking email and corresponding with friends and family. And I've just received a fun message, although the sender doesn't yet know how fitting it is, prescient in its own way. It's from my good friend Mala Rai. She and I write together at times, sharing visual prompts to create the occasional poem or story. The intention being to have some fun and flex artistic muscle. Once we write something (we take turns providing the cue), we share and critique our work. This time it was Mala's turn to come up with the prompt, and what I've received is a photo, taken inside a chapel in Ireland. It's a place we've both visited. Only unbeknownst to her (I suspect), set inside the coastal church, at the edge of the photo, is a simple banner that features the grail. It's subtle, and no doubt eludes most parishioners. But for me it's a beacon. Another small sign, or a clue. Regardless, I love that it's here, in my inbox, and I've no choice but to run with it, and share this with you as well.

In recapping lands' ends and Celt-sailed waters that join where we've come from to here, I find it all somewhat humbling, particularly where we are, the region resonating with piety. We're still close to Herakles's home, bridging pilgrimage paths with myth and the trails of emigrants seeking new lands. And although I may not find answers to every question we have, at least I can postulate. So with a poetic pen in hand, I come up with this, what I'm calling "The Cup's Discretion."

Over rough rubble rocks at Galicia, once the towering tower of
   Herakles
a clairvoyant cleric gazed out to the waves, down a lone longitudinal
   line

the seer saw surf-riding curraghs and coracles, seeking a new Celtic
   land
through the wash of a swash glinting emerald hues, a new rock to
   raise crosses and kin

past shallow shore shoals around islets, and a land's end or two on
   the way
an inlet of land pierced a county called Cork, where the barrows and
   cairns face the sea

the peaty green turf of a town holds a chapel, the highest on all of
   the isle
where astride an arched apse, near the neck of the nave, stands a
   standard, its symbol a song

of the chalice they banned from King Solomon's sands to perpetual
   paths of the sun
the cup on the vane, cast in gold, set on green, called the grail as it's
   called the gods home

Back to our knights, who never seem too far removed from the grail.
The whole "poor soldier" thing pretty much evaporated as Templar
wealth accumulated. No more sharing of horses as far as I can tell.
Meanwhile, fighting continued in the Holy Land. At this time the
knights had perfected tightly organized assault cavalry units, or shock
troops, of heavily armoured war horses. These elite fighting groups
were a precursor to tanks, designed to break enemy lines for infantry.
The Templars' opponent at this time was Saladin, Sultan of Syria and
Egypt, the commander renowned for his army's tactical prowess, sheer
numbers, and fearlessness.

In 1177, on a dusty plain outside the walled city, the Battle of
Montgisard occurred: 26,000 of Saladin's soldiers facing Christian
forces they outnumbered four to one. It seemed Muslim victory was
imminent. But a Templar shock troop of 500 destrier-mounted knights
thundered onto the field, smashing the line, winning the battle and
retaining control of Jerusalem.

It didn't last, however. Ten years later, in 1187, Saladin captured
Jerusalem at the Battle of Hattin, re-establishing his military dom-
inance. The fighting is well documented, with medieval painters depicting much of the battle. *Chronica Majora*, a 13th-century manuscript by English Benedictine Matthew Paris, contains one of these
paintings, a graphic illumination of a cavalry clash. On one side are
the forces of Saladin, on the other Christian knights. Apart from
the colour and style, at a glance it could pass for Picasso's *Guernica*, a
great deal of blood with severed body parts scattered about, all being
trampled by horses. It's tough to make out where one sword-swinging

soldier ends and the next one begins. Everyone's wearing chain mail and mantles: Muslims in hoods, their opponents in small rounded helmets. The Christian armour is in tones of diluted blue, while the sultanate forces are adorned in green, the colour still known as Saladin. The detail's exceptional. In the eyes of each soldier you see both fierceness and fear through a tangle of horses and hooves.

This particular round of fighting marked a sharp decline of Templar strength in the Holy Land. Perhaps because of their overwhelming initial success, additional orders of knights had grown, including Teutonic Knights and the Knights Hospitaller. As Islamic forces strengthened their hold around Jerusalem, these clusters of Christian knights retreated to places like Acre (on the coast by Haifa) and into the Mediterranean itself, to the islands of Cyprus, Rhodes and Malta. Other Teutonic Knights ventured north to the Baltic, where we last saw Jomsvikings and King Harald Bluetooth.

The Templars, however, retained elements of what made them strong, that sense of historical place, like gathering atop the Temple of Solomon. Using this model, they built strongholds with features like those of the Church of the Holy Sepulchre, utilizing domes, curves and heavy round walls. From above, these structures resemble the oaken-swirl rounds of Druids and Celts, another nod to the natural world like Rosslyn's Green Men with their Nordic detail. An alternate Templar headquarters was constructed in London, at Temple Church, which King John turned into England's royal treasury in the 12th century, utilizing Templar financial expertise. The squat round chapel and surrounding garden still command a broad view of the Thames.

Now, let's step back for a moment and take another look around. I admit I don't see any hills that resemble Leonardo's *Last Supper* landscape. Less undulation, less green. But I do feel a sense of familiarity in the amber tones of the region. Maybe it's the angle of the sun on the Med, or the fact that we're close once again to the equinox line. We could follow it back to our X at Milan, where Leonardo stood at his easel, but instead of veering southwest in the solstice steps of

Herakles we could just carry on, back to that part of the globe where we started, the most likely route that Joseph would take, if indeed he trekked toward England.

Maybe those shades of amber are a whispered reminder of Pytheas, if his search for that gem pushed him further than tin or a lust for geographic discovery. We know he was influenced by roaming Celts and Greeks that travelled to Gaul. But I'm struck once again by the lure of his map, that lopsided version of Britain. Some historians suspect records derived from his misconstrued readings, with Scotland pointing to the right, indicate Pytheas actually sailed east to the Baltic, believing he was still heading north. It would fit with his hunt for amber. Although the fossilized resin is found around the world, the best gem-quality deposits are in northern Europe and it's still often called Baltic amber.

Perhaps I should've seen this sooner, but there are a number of signs, clues even, pointing us back to the north. As crusaders gradually left the Holy Land, Teutonic Knights that went to the home of Jomsvikings might warrant a closer look, where King Harald's remembered in Pomerania and, we believe, our grail at one time was hidden. It would represent a tidy continuation of our Via Heraklea if we hung a right at the Milanese X, going northeast past the Alps toward Poland. And if we want to include every thread woven into our tapestry, I'd be remiss not to mention Thor Heyerdahl's search for Odin.

One of the Norse anthropologist's most controversial theories was his hypothesis that Scandinavians began their own Celtic-like migration from this part of the globe, just beyond Miklagard by the Black and the Caspian seas. He cited the Sagas, mythology and Old Norse tales that tell of a mass movement of people relocating from a place called Asir, which Heyerdahl placed on the map in the region of Azerbaijan. We can even locate complementary ley and equinox lines that link this bit of Mid East to Sweden and Norway.

According to Heyerdahl, cave drawings and art from 8,000 years ago located here, east of the Mediterranean, depict longships, war canoes powered by oar with high prows that resemble a dragon's head. These, he explains, are proto-Viking ships, precursors to the keeled boats of oak Danes and Norse sailed west and Swedes rowed through Europe to Asia. He goes on to plot the path of northern gods, akin to our following Herakles under the line of the sun. Deities such as Odin, known across Europe as Woden, would've led that pilgrimage. Interestingly, in the same way Zeus released two crows, their objective to map the world, Odin released his own corvids, two ravens named Huginn and Muninn. These prescient, winged cartographers were the embodiment of thought and memory, what Odin deemed indicative of true strength and wisdom.

This theory could fit with our own breadcrumb trail, as the Teutonic crusaders arrived at a time when most of Europe was transitioning from pagan beliefs. King Harald navigated the change adeptly. So too did the people of Iceland, after law-speaker Thorgeir Thorkelsson announced at the Althing in the year 1000 that the country would officially be Christian.

Following this, we need to briefly examine what's known as the Wendish Crusade, when Teutonic Knights fought in northern Europe. These were early and transitional Christian Saxons and Danes, fighting pagan Slavs in the land of Baltic amber. The fighting was loosely based on faith, supported by the church of Rome, but like recent oil-based wars, these northern crusades were all about resources. The Baltic region had rich fishing grounds, fertile land and an invaluably rare trait amongst livestock. Their coats were unusually lustrous and thick, resulting in a booming fur industry. Maybe this was already common knowledge amongst traders and travellers like Pytheas, if he did in fact come to where amber's abundant and pure.

Which brings us once more to a pilgrimage interchange: on-ramps, off-ramps and a Celtic-like cloverleaf, where our primary players convene. Not yet walking onstage for a hand-holding bow, mind you, but it feels like the final act, when everything falls into place. We've come a long way to discover a great many things called the grail. Although it may seem for the moment we're going back in time and place, I'm convinced this is how we'll move forward. And I love that for now we'll link up with a Heyerdahl trail, as no one was better at coaxing history from hearsay and lore. So let's follow a bit more mythology and a celestial path to another sacred site the gods call their home. Where Odin drank from the grail, in a manner, defining the trail that we're on.

PART III:
VIKING VALHALLA

NORWAY AND SWEDEN

Two corvids take flight, a sheen of ebony-indigo feathers glinting in angled sun. From the centre of the world they loop upward, wings nearly touching, and with a unanimous caw they depart, heading in opposite ways. The story's the same. The location, however, varies. When Zeus released his black birds they flew under southern Greek sun, the heat of the hills around Delphi. The birds there were crows, though some mistook them for eagles, contour feathers taking similar curves in flight. One mighty ley line away past one or two prime meridians, Odin did the same, in Scandinavian frost just outside of Uppsala. The birds Odin released were ravens, larger than crows, but the birds were clearly kin. They spoke the same language, shared the same tales and were present at the earliest moments, the first memories known to the world.

Now, however, we're not circumnavigating the planet like those ravens or crows. What I'm doing is taking a break to rewatch *Excalibur*, to see if I missed anything in that particular grail interpretation. Late in the story, Percival, rather than Galahad, appears to be the last of the knights on the quest, surviving where all others have failed. Tricked and captured by Morgan and Mordred (Arthur's vengeful half-sister and son), Percival hangs from a blackened branch, having been strung up to suffocate, slowly. From the limbs of trees all around, fellow knights, his friends, hang dead. Ten years have passed since they set forth from Camelot on that sea-riled Celtic coast. Percival gasps for breath, holding on for the sake of the quest, his love for the king and the land.

When Percival was a young squire, Arthur saw in him what he saw in himself, someone in need of a mentor, a leader, and as with so many who seek purpose, his intention was good, his heart pure. Now a seasoned and war-hardened soldier, Percival fights for life while the rope that secures him to a weathered old oak groans as he swings, ever so slightly, side to side. The visual's identical to that of Uppsala, home to Scandinavian kings, where horses and men, soldiers and dogs would be hanged to appease the gods. It's where Odin himself was hung by his neck alongside the sacrificed, to swing and choke for nine days, the same creak of rope as he struggled for breath and for sight. It was then that he gained infinite knowledge, the price of that wisdom an eye. One eye for profundity. An eye for the truth of the grail.

If you want to see for yourself if, or how, Percival gets out of that chokehold you'd best skip this paragraph. Consider it a spoiler alert. If you don't plan on tracking down that old film, read on. What happens is that a spur from the armoured boot of another body swinging above gradually severs the rope that Percival hangs from, allowing him to drop to the ground and resume his quest for the grail.

Which brings to mind all those threads, lines and tributaries we've discovered and followed, some frayed, others sewn together like path-plotting songlines. And in thinking it through I'm now struck by the *shape* of our quest. Which feels like a twinkle of insight, but clarity I haven't had to sacrifice an eye to attain. In analyzing our journey so far, I find myself seeing it in layers and textures, like topographical globes where you can *feel* mountain ridges and ocean trenches beneath your fingers. If we laid it out flat, we'd have a diamond-shaped chessboard design, solstice and equinox lines cross-hatching our grail terrain, where we've been and places we still need to go. We'd have latitude and longitude slicing through solar paths, the whole becoming triangular columns and rows. We also have pilgrimage trails and mythological paths paralleling straight Roman roads. And through each geographical triad we see a spin of Celtic wheel, a turn of druidic swirl, directing us forward like globe-spanning birds in flight.

Now we're again on a plane, up with those birds, in a way. Unconcerned for the moment with topographical bumps, ley lines or the path of the stars. This particular plane's a big one, and new. Gone are the blinds you pull down to cover windows and block out the light.

NORWAY AND SWEDEN   185

This one's automated, and based on the time of day windows self-tint, turning a warm and calming sea blue, like eyeglasses that darken in sun. I'm wide awake, mind you, enjoying a view washed in lapis, everything becoming artistic, as though the whole world's embracing the blue of Picasso.

While the rest of the passengers settle in for a cramped, snore-filled snooze, I gaze through the colour and smile, reminded of a flight Indy and his dad endured on their search for the grail. The two are airborne in a rickety biplane and for some reason the pilot is gone and Indy's in the cockpit, having taken over the controls.

"I didn't know you could fly a plane!" his dad says, as they roar over mountains and forest.

"Fly? Yes," Indy replies. "Land? No!"

Beneath us, all I can see is cloud, but it's lovely, bright and topaz. I'm left to imagine where exactly we are. Sure, I could turn on that little monitor that estimates airspeed, altitude and where we are in space and time, but where's the fun in that? So instead I treat this gently undulating ride as an opportunity for a dreamy recap. Which makes me feel we're drifting through the pages of ancient Sagas, each turn of weathered papyrus and cracked leather our shared vignettes: history, myth, footpaths real and imagined. From the birthplace of Arthur we've been to a handful of Camelots, followed Vikings and Templars to places of raiding and ruling, praying and hiding the grail. We've leapt through the ages to follow the earliest voyagers, Celts, Romans and Greeks, even peering into the afterlife. But one thing remains, irrespective of hue, and that's a perpetuation of light, and I find myself remembering the word play of sages.

I'm tempted to say it was a time of transition, but of course that's always the case. As usual, the gods were changing, a result of movement, people travelling by choice or necessity, and, like legends, cuisine and design, deities too evolve into fresh iterations. I no longer recall where I saw this next quote, or who said it. Possibly Immanuel Kant or Ari the Wise. It might even have been Wayne Dyer. Regardless, the story goes like this. It was the early days of Christianity, with much of the world still pagan. And two people were speaking, a Christian and a pagan, exchanging viewpoints with inquisitive, open minds.

The Christian explains to the pagan, "I worship the Son of God."

To which the pagan replies, "Ah, we're the same! I too worship the gods' sun."

It's a story I like for a few reasons. The first time I heard it I wasn't sure if my mind should be blown or an eye-roll was more fitting. It's somewhat insightful, a bit clever, and no doubt would offend some people. In other words, there's probably a ribbon of philosophical meat on that bone. It might feel particularly resonant now as the sun's on my side of the plane, creeping its way through the blue, sky to sea, all viewed through a monotone cobalt as we bear north, I believe, at 800 km/h.

We're now above the North Sea. Norway lies ahead, Denmark and Sweden just east of us. To the west, the top half of Britain seems to have righted itself since Pytheas came through. Liberal pollsters would love it, Scotland no longer leaning to the right. Off the north coast of the old Pictish land are the archipelago scatters of Orkney and Shetland, hybrid Viking and Anglo-Saxon terrain. Despite my requests, our flight crew's unwilling to adhere to an equinox path, which would link us to Thor Heyerdahl's theoretical Norse–Asian homeland. But at least we'll touch down where we next need to be. Gradually our plane descends, curling its way into Oslo. Blue windows are clear once again, and below, along with the natural blues of fjord and open sea, I now have views of green, mountains adorned in timber. It actually looks a lot like the terrain Indy and his dad flew over, trying to figure out how exactly one lands a plane.

If we focus again on planetary lines, we've just reached 60 degrees north in latitude. From the equator we're two-thirds of the way to the top of the world. And in a nifty turn of math the globe's now half the circumference of where it's fattest. Sixty degrees north holds a unique appeal, its own mystique. Here we're encroaching on the Arctic Circle.

In Canada, this substantive, imaginary line separates northern territories from provinces, while here it slices through Norway before carrying on to bisect Sweden, Finland, Siberia and Alaska, then Greenland and Shetland as well.

The thick forests we're now flying unnervingly close to will thin further north, the transition from boreal taiga to tundra. But it's these southern reaches of Scandinavia that provided the wood for ships that explored so much of the world. Oak was preferred for boatbuilding, sturdy planks that could bend with the waves. From the stern of a longship a helmsman can watch as the bow of the craft behaves like the jet that we're on. Never actually travelling in a direct path but in fact constantly shifting, correcting, jogging to left and to right. It could be the world's subtlest serpentine, at times the most jarring. But pull back enough for a view from above and the journey resembles a straight, smooth line. The movement of planets and stars.

It was on the pilgrimage path of Saint Michael, meandering along a Camino offshoot, where we encountered England's Order of Saint Michael and Saint George, the military award based on Arthurian honour. Here in Norway there's similar recognition, also based on chivalrous conduct. It's the Royal Norwegian Order of Saint Olav, created by King Oscar in the 19th century in the name of King Olav II, the king known as Saint Olav. The Order rewards individuals for "remarkable accomplishments on behalf of the country and humanity," either civilian or military, a nod to the conduct and honour exemplified by Jomsvikings and grail protectors.

Awards vary based on classification. There are collars, stars, badges, ribbons and bows. Collars are adorned in gold, enamel and silver, with crosses flanked in weaponry. Military awards have crossed swords, while badges feature the Maltese Cross, familiar from Templars' tunics, along with a monogram O with a crown, symbol of Norway's monarchy. Stars resemble eight points of a compass, as though once again we're finding our way in the world, while the nation's coat of arms centres the medal, a gold lion encircled in white around blue and another white ring. Knighted women wear their badge on a bow while men wear the badge on a ribbon. In rare instances an award will be ringed in diamonds, a gleam consistent with the luminous eight-pointed star, the look of a sun god placed on the heart.

I admit it feels like we could be a planeload of solar deities, descending through blue into what's now become dazzling sunshine. From the airport we make our way to the centre of town, and I spend the next stretch of time in museums, on boats, and eating my fill of reindeer. A short ferry ride from downtown is the Viking Ship Museum, part of the University of Oslo's Museum of Cultural History. It houses three unearthed longships, archaeologically excavated from boat burials at Tønsberg, Sandefjord and Tune. All of these communities are nearby, along the fjord snaking north into Oslo, all close to Sweden and boatbuilding forests of oak.

Along with these ships are artifacts from the Borre Mound Cemetery, now part of Borre National Park, which is just south of us by the mouth of the fjord. Borre represents the largest accumulation of kings' graves in Scandinavia, home to 28 burial mounds, seven of which are enormous. The oldest date back to the year 600, two centuries ahead of the Viking Age, a proto-Viking cemetery on the largest scale imaginable. Despite past kings plotting an Olympian path to Valhalla, each tomb here is chthonic. This place could well be a door to the underworld, Herakles taking the occasional shift as a bouncer to keep hounds and hydras at bay.

The longships displayed in Oslo, the *Oseberg* and *Gokstad* in particular, are a remarkable blend of art and function. Although it's unlikely the *Oseberg* ever set sail, the boat still looks seaworthy, as though all it needs is its sail unfurled and a breeze, or possibly some of those shapeshifting swans that seem keen to pull boatloads of royalty. I feel privileged to be here, gawking at the *Gokstad*, as Oslo's Viking Ship

Museum will be closed for a number of years to rebuild and rebrand, reopening as the Museum of the Viking Age.

It was some time later when I chatted with Kris Frostad, Norwegian builder of the *Gokstad* replica *Munin*, our visit taking place over platters of herring and meatballs. (Munin is an alternative spelling of Muninn, same as Odin's raven.) The original ship (Kris's inspiration) is 24 metres in length, while the *Munin* was constructed to half that size. Rather than metric, Kris used imperial measurements.

"You know the original is eighty feet," he said, his smile warm, almost impish with enthusiasm. "So I thought, okay then, we'll make this one about forty." Then he squatted a bit, as though he was taking an imaginary seat. "And I figured the oars should go about here, you understand," he said, mimicking the action of rowing. Building the boat never felt like a job, he explained. "I loved doing it." He didn't work from set plans. "Just go by feel," he said, breaking into another smile.

Although artisanal in design, Kris's *Munin* is more than seaworthy, sailing for years in Salish Sea inlets around Vancouver. I was aboard it one time near Granville Island, part of a wooden boat festival. Now it's been pulled from the water, preserved at Burnaby's Scandinavian Cultural Centre. We had a view of the *Munin* while we ate one more course of herring. But it seemed to me, and Kris no doubt too, that the boat's oaken beams belonged on the sea.

A bottle of aquavit was set on our table and we spent time talking oak, as you do. Strong and durable, it's been a preferred construction wood forever. Booze connoisseurs know it from barrels used for ageing whisky and wine, while Viking Age soldiers knew it was best for making shields: heavy, brightly painted rounds that would hang from the gunwales of longships. When fashioned into hulls and keels, oak has the strength to endure Arctic waves, yet the flexibility to work with the sea and not fight it.

In another geographic and time-bending link, we see Druids again. Oak was a sacred tree to the augurs, its burls and knots inspiration for Celtic design, the loop of the wheel, stone circles and calendars linked to the gods. The word *druid* itself comes from Celtic Ercunian, the root-word being dru, which means oak. In Old Welsh the word's derw, meaning oak tree. And in Britain's ancient forests, the largest and oldest trees are still known as druid oaks.

Along with birch and conifers, alder and rowan, oak still thrives in the fields surrounding the kings' burial mounds in south Norway. The topography varies but the feel of the place is the same as the Kings' Graves at England's South Downs, chalk hills facing the Solent and the Channel. There the land's high, giving the buried a view, in a way, over tides and the sea. And like here in Norway, graves have been there a very long time, preceding the rowers of longships. In Britain the mounds, sometimes called Devil's Humps, are dated to the Bronze Age, before Pytheas travelled through. Like the barrows of Arthur's terrain and beyond, the interred from different eras were often buried together, reusing sacred ground. Scandinavian jarls were laid to rest in the same shared terrain in south England, given kings' burials far from home, a sign not only of respect but the integration of voyagers from abroad into local culture. These weren't smash-and-grab raiders. These were immigrants, making a home for their clans. The graves, by the way, are built on a solstice path, another southwest–northeast line.

When we hiked to the mounds in Wessex we had to weave through ancient forests of yew, the wood used to make English longbows. The fact that the venerable stand had survived harvestings through the Hundred Years' War was astounding and left me suspecting the copse had always been sacred. One gnarly specimen I traipsed around was 2,000 years old, its bark like weathered elephant hide. Somehow the old trees swallowed the light, and although the sun was high in a cloudless sky, the forest was dim and spooky. The twitch and scrape of branch overhead sounded like the rub of calloused fingers, a presence watching and plotting. People insist there are spirits in there, and I couldn't fathom making that trek after sunset. It felt not so much like the middle earth outside Miklagard but the one of Tolkien, where goblins and trolls reside. The oldest yew, however, isn't there, but across the Bristol Channel, a 5,000-year-old giant near a sheer-sided rock on Welsh moorland, a hill known as Arthur's Stone.

Most of the oaks here in Norway grow for a few centuries, often up to 500 years, although some have reached the age of 1,000. The largest specimen lies just over the fjord from the Borre Mounds and is known as the Mollestad Oak. It's about 13 metres high and nearly as big around at ten metres circumference. It grows on its own in a grassy field and looks like a heavy-set troll doll, a shock of hairy branches sprouting from a pot-bellied trunk.

But let's put a pin in our timber tracking for now as there's still more to see here in Oslo. I'm keeping this sojourn in a maritime vibe as we ferry and walk the Bygdøy Peninsula, a tidy cluster of museums for researchers and sightseers. A high yellow A-frame indicates a museum built to accommodate a tall-masted ship, and this one houses the *Fram*. It's known as the *Fram* Museum but also features the *Gjøa*, Roald Amundsen's boat he sailed through the Northwest Passage, the first ship and crew to accomplish the feat, which they did over three years concluding in 1906. The *Fram* (which means "forward") explored both the Antarctic and Arctic regions for a 20-year period, 1893–1912, led by Amundsen and fellow Norsemen Otto Sverdrup and Fridtjof Nansen.

The *Fram*'s first expedition into the Arctic was never intended to be one of sailing. Not exactly, anyway, as the North Pole's covered in pack ice. But the seeming solidity does in fact shift with the tides. The plan, therefore, was to take the *Fram* as far north as possible and simply freeze it into the ice sheet, allowing the natural movement of floes to then direct the ship over the pole.

A hundred years later the same technique was used by the MOSAiC expedition. In 2019–2020 a team of international scientists spent a year at the pole, conducting the most extensive research ever on global climate change. For this endeavour, the German research icebreaker *Polarstern* sailed from Tromsø, on Norway's northwestern tip, to wedge itself into the pack ice, same as the *Fram* in the previous century.

The museum has been here for nearly as long, about a hundred years. It's a place where you can clamber aboard the *Fram* and the *Gjøa* and envision yourself on shifting ice, hoping the food will last. There are interesting tidbits on penguins and polar bears, and if I remember correctly from TV ads both animals like northern lights and icy bottles of Coke, especially during the holidays.

The King of Norway has a home nearby, here on the peninsula, more of a summer retreat. With sharply rising hills and the fjord's icy reach, it does seem awfully Norwegian. I can appreciate a sense of national pride one might feel around here, irrespective of being a monarch. The terrain exudes what Canadian geographer Louis-Edmond Hamelin called nordicity, exemplifying this part of the planet.

When we eventually leave the *Gjøa* and the *Fram*, with their frigid polar history, it feels like a break in the weather, as we'll now explore warm-water tales of Thor Heyerdahl at the *Kon-Tiki* Museum. As I understand it, his family was gifted a residence upstairs, and a grandchild lives there now. Out front of the museum is a massive, blue-backed photo of Heyerdahl in 1947, climbing the mast of *Kon-Tiki*, his trans-Pacific raft of South American balsa logs. In the picture he resembles Robinson Crusoe. Heavily bearded in well-weathered shorts, he clings to a rope ladder, his hair blowing in ocean breeze. Behind him, billowing in the sail, is a likeness of the raft's namesake, Kon-Tiki, the old moniker for Viracocha, sun god of the Incas. Heyerdahl's route wouldn't follow a solar path, however, not quite a solstice or equinox line, but instead the drift of oceanic swirl, curve of wind and the Humboldt current. Written on the banner is perhaps the explorer's most famous quote. "Borders? I've never seen one. But I hear they exist in the minds of some people." Spoken like a true Viking.

Inside the museum is a separate exhibit of his boat *Ra II*, a ship of papyrus reed he sailed from Morocco to Barbados, proving transatlantic crossings have been possible since ancient times, when these boats were built by Egyptians. The first *Ra* excursion sank in the eastern Caribbean, but by the time of their second attempt, the crew had figured out a key design detail, something not obvious when you're building from etchings off pyramid walls. The key was to keep the stern high, more so than the bow, a feature prevalent in the ocean-going longships Vikings sailed and rowed across the North Sea, Atlantic and Arctic.

The main exhibit here of course is *Kon-Tiki*, Heyerdahl's raft of nine Peruvian balsa logs, equipped with a stout mast and sail. The exhibit recreates the boat on the water, lumbering across the Pacific. His book of that trek is still a great read, the film documentary as well. Unlike the modernized Hollywood version, which for some reason depicts the journey like the movie *Jaws*. The *Kon-Tiki* excursion was nothing like *Jaws*, by the way, although the crew did encounter whale sharks in the South Pacific, something they were unfamiliar with. And I suppose it might be easy to mistake the big plankton eaters for carnivorous monsters from weathered old maritime maps.

It was Heyerdahl's hypothesis that migration across the Pacific was in fact east to west, like the sun, following the natural flow of the currents. He cites kumara, or sweet potato, the starchy staple of South Pacific diets, which he states originated in South America, linking the Americas to Polynesia, Melanesia and Micronesia. Partially in response to Heyerdahl's claims, the Polynesian Voyaging Society spent the past 50 years proving the opposite, that Pacific Islanders have been sailing the globe wherever they chose, following planets and stars, not simply drifting with currents. One of the Society's primary pieces of anthropological proof is the *Hōkūleʻa*, a sail-driven, double-hulled ocean canoe that circumnavigated the globe on a three-year journey concluding in 2017, covering 47,000 nautical miles. Pilots are trained in the ancient art of reading celestial signs like prescient Druids, a means of triangulation and navigation that effectively supplants sextants, clocks or longitude lines. The term used is wayfaring, not unlike mapping techniques of the songlines.

When I think of the work of Heyerdahl, hypotheses he'd draft through speculation and extended periods simply watching the sea, I'm reminded again of the times on our quest where we've witnessed both intersection and exclusivity of fact and truth. I suspect Heyerdahl too knew how to walk that line, like the slivers of land and sea we've traversed on our travels. But he backed up each hunch with a daring excursion, the result being newfound lines of reasoning. Not necessarily plotted on maps but in paths of human movement, findings that redefined the sociological and anthropological status quo. For that I admire the modern-day Viking. His articles, diaries, photos and journals now comprise the Thor Heyerdahl Archives, part of UNESCO's "Memories of the World," housed at the museum and Norway's National Library. It's here I learned a story of the explorer I hadn't heard before. As a child his favourite book was Darwin's *On the Origin of Species*. And while the other kids in his hometown of Larvik, just down the road from the Borre Mounds, were probably rolling a tire with a stick, young Thor created a museum, and booked times for his friends to visit. The main attraction was a venomous adder he'd caught and kept in a cage. I wonder what he charged for admission.

But the main thing that's brought us back to Norway is that approximate equinox line from a mythical Scandinavian homeland far to the south and the east. Since he first theorized that Nordic people came from west Asia, Heyerdahl refined his hypothesis, saying instead the migration began further north, near the Sea of Azov, a brackish blister attached to the northeast corner of the Black Sea. Which is what ties this whole thing to our grail quest. As well as being a stopover for Herakles as he laboured his way across Europe, it was there, across the water from Miklagard, where Albrecht von Scharfenberg states with certainty that a few pilgrims spotted the grail. And while von Scharfenberg's work focused on Merlin and Parzival, it was his references to the chalice I found most intriguing. The grail, according to a small group of westbound pilgrims, was being transported around the Black Sea's north shore. It could've been bound for Miklagard, but at that junction, where the Black Sea meets the Azov, we're more or less on the equinox line that would direct migrants northwest, looking to make a new home for themselves in the forested fjords of Scandinavia. Which is precisely the path Heyerdahl claims author Snorri Sturluson describes in the *Ynglinga Saga*, delineating the history of Nordic kings, when he wrote, "Odin came to the North with his people from a country called Aser." Not unlike Moses leading Israelites from the Sinai to the promised land of Canaan. But before Heyerdahl was able to complete his "Search for Odin," he passed away in 2002. It was during a vacation in Italy, visiting relatives, when somewhat remarkably he died nearly on top of the Genoa grail.

A great many linguists and historians have discounted Heyerdahl's work. Place names in particular were key to his "proof" of locations and timelines, along with longship cave art around the Black Sea. Utilizing Norse mythology and Saga passages, Heyerdahl points out examples like Azov for Æsir, Udi for Odin, and Tyr, he explains, was Turkey. Other experts say these are merely coincidence. Which struck me as a classic rivalry, classroom academics versus those in the field getting their hands dirty. I'd love to hear Indy's opinion.

Although Heyerdahl seemed unconcerned with solar paths, the route he insisted Scandinavians followed would indeed place those emigrants under a Kon-Tiki equinox sun as they made their way north and west. Sól, however, was the name these migrants used for their goddess of light. Odin called her "the shining god." Appearing in Bronze Age accounts, she was worshipped across Europe and Scandinavia. Something I like is that this is a goddess of sun in lieu of a son of a god. And in Norse, Sól is pronounced like "soul." Make of that what you will.

But according to Heyerdahl, these future Scandinavians didn't go directly to Norway or Sweden. He claims that they moved in gradual steps across northern Poland and Germany, pivotal points in our tracking the grail, before settling in Denmark's fertile peninsulas. And it's from here, over time, he states, that these fair-haired wanderers moved from the lowlands of northwestern Europe into Sweden and Norway. Whether following Odin or Sól, what we have on our path is a thriving population of travellers making their way to another land's end.

Fog creeps from the east, past Riga perhaps, hugging the north Baltic coast, slithering deep into long-frozen fjords, an ice serpent in shapeshifting swirls. Same as the moment the father of Arthur rode mist over Cornwall to Wales or when Odin released his two ravens. Other than the cambion Merlin, only one other sentient being was here to witness the conjuration. Outside of Uppsala's swales and rises in stone, the place between humans and gods, is a clearing of bedrock and lichen the ancient spruce thought of as home. Stooped with the passage of 10,000 years, the tree could pass for an elder, a slight crook to its limbs, with a shock of green foliage up where the breeze blew clear. The spruce was here when the first tribes arrived, Celts and Teutons migrating from Alps. It watched as the pack ice moved in, and moved out, a turquoise-tinged blanket of white. It witnessed pods of balena at play, heading north to the rock shores of Thule. Not to mention the day a kraken passed through, rising from icy black depths. Some believed that the spruce was a seer, whose needles predicted the future. Others feel that the tree must be Yggdrasil, centre of all the nine worlds. For this reason, no mortal dares tread by its roots, for fear it will summon the serpent.

Or so the story goes. What I'm referring to is the world's oldest tree, which goes by the name of Old Tjikko, and it's where we are, in Sweden. Old Tjikko's a Norway spruce, nearly 10,000 years old. It's actually 9,600, according to dendrochronology (counting tree growth rings), but you get the idea. It's very, very old. By car it's a few hours north of Stockholm, almost on the border between Sweden and Norway. Lillehammer's nearby on the Norwegian side, while here in Sweden, the spruce is part of Fulufjället National Park.

After witnessing the regal presence of druid oaks and sprawling yews, I was expecting something much grander. But the ancient spruce is surprisingly slender. Almost withered. Apparently its venerability is a function of adaptability. (A nice reminder in there.) Exterior bark continuously regrows, effectively replaced with newer versions of itself, but rather than simply getting bigger, it's a somewhat mystical regeneration called layering. Trees within trees, in a way. It stands on its own on a small rise in rocky ground where the terrain looks like the polar ice sheet's only just receded. I think of those books on trees that state they need a community, why lone specimens die in the city. But this wizened old thing resembles a hermit, maybe by choice, or it's simply outlived its friends. Arctic moss seems to be its only companion, and as far as I can tell, the lichen's not much of a conversationalist.

What brings us here lies to the south, close to Stockholm, a bit inland from the Baltic. Uppsala. Home to the gods. It's also a university town, and has been for half a millennium. I've read descriptions of Uppsala likening it to Oxford and Prague, ancient yet youthful cities. Uppsala Castle is here, site of key moments from the past six centuries. It's the residence of monarchs, and still considered by many to be the heart of the nation. Rebuilt a few times, the castle tops a hill and is now a broad slab of warm-coloured stone, the look halfway between fortification and a bland but stately hotel.

Down the slope from the castle is the Fyris River, passing through the city in a series of canals that lead to Lake Mälaren, which worms its way to the Baltic. In the lake is the "birch island" called Björkö, location of Birka, a Viking trading hub from the eighth to the tenth centuries. And on the nearby island of Adelsö is the archaeological site of Hovgården, home to kings and jarls, and another place of burial plots going back through the ages. Both of these islands are UNESCO World Heritage Sites. For some reason, near the turn of the first millennium, these Viking sites were abandoned, in the same way Norse simply vanished from Greenland and the forests surrounding Old Tjikko simply faded away, leaving you to wonder if these things ever really existed.

The Fyris River, originally called the Sala, had its name changed in the 17th century to commemorate the battle of Fyrisvellir, which took place nearby late in the tenth century, the same time once-thriving sites on Lake Mälaren disappeared. Recent burial ground excavations at Hovgården have unearthed new perspectives about the people, place and time. Over 120 graves have been discovered, including five prominent mounds called Kungshögar, Old Norse for King's barrow or mound. One of the "royal mounds" was excavated early in the 20th century, and what was discovered was a treasure indeed. It was a burial from the year 900, but unlike a warrior's grave in which weaponry would be included to ensure safe passage to Valhalla, this tomb had no weapons. It does, however, represent an unconventional combination of Olympian *and* chthonic interment, as the body was burned in a boat and then buried as well.

So here we have the pageantry and honour of a ship burial, plus the cremation aspect of a boat burning, but the deceased had no weapons. He was, however, fabulously dressed (pre-cremation), accompanied by freshly killed corpses of cattle, horses and dogs. Which means we can be fairly certain in this bustling centre of trade this was a prosperous businessman. Which leaves us to wonder if he was beloved and sent off with fanfare or one of those self-aggrandizing blokes who buy themselves the biggest mausoleum. I like to believe it's the former.

Birka is considered Sweden's oldest town. Historians tend to agree the site was home to wealthy landowners, like our unarmed friend from the burned boat burial. These are the people who financed royalty. No doubt influencing policy too, as we see amongst gentry and nobility everywhere. Here it was called Uppsala öd, royal estates that supported the king.

There's a runestone nearby, at the Hovgården site on Adelsö, which some experts feel supports the theory of Uppsala öd, while others claim it does the opposite. Funnily enough, the rock looks a lot like Arthur's Stone near the giant old yew in Wales. Again, one side of the stone is flat, and it comes to a natural point, like a small, less snowy Alp. Only this one's covered in intricate runes, the look of illumination from ancient texts. The runestone has the rather unimaginative name U11, which is its Rundata designation, part of a Scandinavian runic-text database used to catalogue and standardize runes for research purposes.

The stone was carved around the year 1070 and placed close to the royal mounds. Unlike the Halfdan runes at Hagia Sophia, there's no signature as such, leaving us to wonder as to the author's identity. There is, however, reference to a king and the carver, as you'll see. The left side of the stone has neatly curved runes set between lines like a student's ruled notebook. But the rest of the stone could be Celtic. There's a series of swirls with interlocking, unending knots, the whorls we see in oaks and Celtic crosses. But you can tell from some eyes and a tail or two that these are serpents, stylized creatures with a flow like the timber of longships. The snakish S-shapes resemble the serpent at Rosslyn, doing its best to devour the World Tree of Yggdrasil.

Despite exhaustive research, runes remain open to interpretation, even by experts, so each runic discovery retains an element of mystery. Consensus on this stone, however, has translated the writing into Old Norse and from Old Norse into this, more or less: "You read the runes! Right let cut them Tolir, bailiff in Roden, to the king. Tolir and Gylla let carve these runes, this pair after themself as a memorial Håkon bade carve."

And here's my take on *that*, based on what we know. Gylla and Tolir were spouses, and Tolir was a craftsman who likely worked the hammer and chisel. There's another interpretation that states Tolir was a server, which could be a polite term for slave, or he could've been like the guy who poured wine at the pre-crucifixion supper. And despite what seems like a typo, we believe Håkon is King Håkan, who ruled here at that time. So perhaps royal assent was required to carve a stone like this and position it on prime real estate, or it may've actually been *commissioned* by the king, and Gylla and Tolir were well-liked locals. Again, an element of mystery remains.

Later, I visited with a runestone reader named Richard Hanson. He's considered a vitki, a modern-day Druid. Some might use the term sorcerer, but the alternate definition of "wise man" seems fitting. He's studied runes for three decades but admits even his mentors, some of whom have 60 years of research experience, still don't consider themselves experts. It's all about ongoing learning, he explained, as new interpretations and discoveries continue to surface. "GPR, ground-penetrating radar, for example," he said. "We keep finding things and have to figure them out. Then we hope it fits with what we think we already know."

He opened a small leather drawstring satchel and told me to draw out a stone, which felt a bit like the time I pulled tarot cards from a fortune teller. I let my mind go (even more) blank, reached in, and selected one, making a point of not fishing around, simply letting it happen. There were differing textures, but most were similar in size and shape to Scrabble tiles, each stone cool to the touch. But for an instant I thought I could feel the slightest electrical charge.

The carved script on the runestone I drew was shaped like a flat-ended hourglass, the look of a sharp-sided figure eight. Richard smiled and shifted it in my hand, giving it a quarter turn. The symbol's called a dagaz and is actually a butterfly shape (a sideways hourglass). It's been interpreted as meaning "day," "dawn," or "awakening." In the same manner a hieroglyph can mean something akin to an entire word, so too can some runes be translated into concepts rather than single letters.

"Ah," said Richard, as though unsurprised. "This means you're full of ideas, energy, potential. You'll surprise yourself with what you can accomplish. You just need to find focus."

Despite fighting an urge to joke about my mind having drifted, I appreciated and understood precisely what the vitki was saying.

Where we are now is home to Uppsala Cathedral, Scandinavia's largest church and Sweden's ecclesiastical centre. From a Scandinavian perspective this spot was, in a way, an island, a bastion of independence.

While other Nordic countries – Norway, Denmark, Iceland – shifted to Christianity at roughly the same time, Sweden did not. Yes, there were followers of the new "nailed god," but most of the country was pagan for another 200 years, an example of what I like to call collective individuality.

I suppose it could be the area. I've read that religion is born in dark places. I tend to agree, although I'm hard pressed to see Sweden as darker than Norway. People of the north speak of sila, the spirit of wind and all things, that can scream through the nights that last for three months. And I think of those dim, murky places that kindle unease, dark recesses that make hackles rise. As kids we might pray to something we can't yet define, to protect us from what's under the bed or behind a closed door. For me it was the basement, down the hall to Dad's unfinished workshop, where a concrete floor led to the cobwebbed pocket of black behind the furnace, a terrible humanoid shape that moaned and wept as though enduring an Inquisition. Even Thor Heyerdahl, who wasn't a churchgoer, said once or twice as they bobbed on the raft through a storm, when he truly feared for his life, he found himself muttering something akin to a prayer.

Although there were no borders for Heyerdahl to see dividing these Nordic nations, there *was* a divergence of faith, not unlike the pull of tectonic plates separating the globe under Iceland. As well as a region of proud identity, this remained a place of opposing beliefs. And it's this conflict that represents much of the studies of Ben Raffield. Ben's an archaeologist and professor at Uppsala University, having travelled the north following Vikings and burial digs. For me he represented a walking, talking, amiable research library. We met to share findings over coffee, giving me a chance to glean more from an expert. Specifically, I wanted to learn about Uppsala's past, similarities between Vikings and Celts, and maybe revisit the Baltic, in case Pytheas made it this far. And of course I wanted to see if he could point me directly to the grail. Funnily enough, for a couple of authors, our conversation focused on the work of two other writers. And what I quite liked was the fact that these particular travellers came from opposite parts of the world. Two scribes I now think of on a first-name basis. Ahmad and Adam.

Ahmad ibn Fadlan was a Muslim scribe from Baghdad, while Adam of Bremen hailed from Meissen in Saxon Germany. Ahmad was born in 879 and lived 80 years. Devout in his faith, he was an expert in Islamic law. He knew the Koran intimately and took offence at anyone saying their prayers "incorrectly." There's a copy of a page from one of his manuscripts at the nearby university. The handwriting says a great deal, with a certain neatness to the script. Tidy and organized but not flawless, and not particularly attractive. It's the work of someone who wants to do a thorough job, more concerned with content than presentation. On one corner of the page he's added an addendum, tightly packed words at a slightly cramped angle. What seemed most important was accuracy in his writing, ensuring all the information was there.

In part because of his knowledge and attention to detail, ibn Fadlan became an ambassador's secretary, part of the Abbasid Caliphate, their political influence extending from the Mid East around the Black Sea. And in 921 he was named religious advisor to a diplomatic party tasked with venturing north and west from what's now Iraq through the heart of Varangian Miklagard into eastern Europe. The objective of their expedition, a combination of politics and religion.

At the time, fighting was rampant amongst nomadic Black Sea tribes, predominantly Bulgars and Khazars, effectively Turks and Bulgarians. Ahmad and his team served as a kind of diplomatic peace-keeping corps, detached from the fray to be observers and advisors to policy makers. But here's an interesting wrinkle. When I was in the area I was acutely aware of standing at the cusp of Christian and Islamic worlds. Ibn Fadlan knew this as well, even then. Bulgars west of the Black Sea were shifting toward Christianity, representing a threat to Islam. So as well as peacekeeping and diplomacy, it was obvious ibn Fadlan also had an eye to convert as many infidels as possible.

From records of his trek we learn much of what we know of Scandinavians in that part of the world, specifically Varangians and

Rus, also known as Volga Vikings. Ahmad's detailed account offers us a pictorial glimpse at these Mid East Northmen. He describes their physicality, most being strong, healthy and bigger than locals around them. Each carried an axe, knife and sword. Which tells us these were affluent soldiers, respected and well compensated. In most of the world a sword was a luxury item. He also describes Viking tattoos in detail, which were clearly striking to the "unmarked" religious man, what he calls "designs in dark blue or green, from the tips of their toes to their neck." We can assume they weren't nude so the account likely has a hint of embellishment or speculation. I've often thought of Viking tattoos like those of Polynesians and Picts, parts of the globe where lineage stories were oral, with visual aids added by needles and ink. Storytellers themselves *were* the tale, open pages of muscle and skin.

Ahmad states that most Norse in the region wore long wraps or togas, which would cover one shoulder, leaving a sword-arm exposed. And he notes with a bit of disgust how these northerners weren't too concerned about privacy for sex. But there's another account from another Ahmad, the Persian scribe Ahmad ibn Rustah, who indicates Varangians' behaviour was in no way offensive, leading us to believe perhaps ibn Fadlan was prudish.

Ibn Fadlan also gives an account of a boat-burning funeral and describes human sacrifice. But I'm left to wonder if cremation might also be considered a form of sacrifice. Another line of reasoning is that if others *were* put to death to accompany the already deceased, it could be seen as a privilege, something the "sacrificed" were all too happy to do, joining the honoured and fast-tracking their way to an afterlife. Not unlike Cathars climbing the pyre at Montségur.

In a rather fun postscript, Antonio Banderas plays the role of ibn Fadlan in a Hollywood movie based on a Michael Crichton novel. Although it's derived from Ahmad's account, in the film he has to fight vampires, so some artistic licence to say the least. And of course I can no longer read the writing of ibn Fadlan without hearing it in a rolling-tongue *Puss in Boots* accent.

Raffield and I then talked about the other prolific writer of that time, Adam of Bremen, born a century after ibn Fadlan. Unlike Ahmad, Adam only lived 40 years, although records of birth and death are spotty, so we're left to approximate dates. I consider ibn Fadlan more of a field researcher, travelling further, immersing himself in new places, interacting with "foreign" people (even when it struck him as gross). Similar, in a way, to Indy. Ahmad was also unafraid to include personal sentiment in his accounts, giving us rich, opinionated insight.

Adam of Bremen, on the other hand, strikes me as the methodical researcher, similar perhaps, to Indy's dad, with the brunt of his writing being composed indoors over library texts and scriptorium scrolls. Much of his work is compiled from external accounts, what was said, seen and experienced by others. He is, however, considered "one of the foremost historians and early ethnographers of the medieval period." His most famous chronicle is the *Deeds of Bishops of the Hamburg Church*, in which he includes details of Leif Erikson's Vinland settlement, making it the first European account of the Americas.

Although not journeying as extensively as ibn Fadlan, Adam still ventured a good distance for the time, travelling as a missionary between Bremen and Hamburg, across northern Germany through the Schleswig-Holstein region into Denmark, giving the writer a taste of Scandinavian life. He wrote of Viking sailings across the Øresund Strait, and worked for a stint in the court of Danish King Svend Estridsen in the mid-11th century. Along with Ahmad ibn Fadlan, Adam of Bremen remains one of the earliest and perhaps best-informed Viking experts.

I tracked down a sample of Adam's handwriting as well. Unlike that of Ahmad, Adam's work is immaculate. It looks typeset, text in flawless straight lines. Paragraph breaks include decorative drop caps (an extra-large letter at the start of a word), scripted in colour, reminiscent of the illumination in Columba's *Book of Kells*. Adam's writing is the work of a highly trained monk, a thing of visual beauty intended to please the eye as much as convey information.

Over refills of coffee I asked Ben to discuss the Baltic, and he described the Estonian island of Saaremaa. Across the sea from Stockholm and due south of Finland, Saaremaa is Estonia's largest island, like a moored boat tied to a northerly bulge of the country. Equidistant from the Baltic capitals of Tallinn and Riga, this site is best known for the Salme ships. Salme is a village on Saaremaa, its shoreline resembling the fingers of fertile green that comprise south Nordic coasts. It would certainly feel familiar to Scandinavians from over the water.

What's been unearthed at Salme are two early longships. One's the size of Kris Frostad's *Munin*, the second is larger, at 17 metres in length. These ships were built in the seventh century, a hundred years prior to what's considered the start of the Viking Age. Both ships were at least 50 years old, with signs of numerous repairs, and neither was equipped with a sail. These were long-distance, open-water rowing boats, similar to the gigs we encountered on the Isles of Scilly. Some historians speculate rowing was done between navigable shores and islands, while others say ocean rowing was part of the Nordic experience. In the same manner Romans delineated distance in terms of a marching army, Scandinavian voyagers too had a method for managing miles. In Old Norse it was referred to as "vikusjö, vikja," the distance travelled between rotations of rowers, about four nautical miles. By alternating shifts, rowing and resting, these boats could move forward forever.

While the Salme ships muddy the waters in determining the Viking Age, they also present a mystery as to why they are there. The ships were buried with 42 soldiers' bodies, most were aged 30 to 40, and all died in battle. The amount of weaponry indicates it was an army and not simply a raiding party. Along with the human bodies are corpses of hawks and dogs, which may've been used for hunting or battle, but may have been part of a regal or diplomatic entourage. If that's the case, then these envoys didn't fare nearly as well as ibn Fadlan amongst the Rus (irrespective of vampires). Another noteworthy fact is that many of the swords in the boats were bronze, the high-end weapons of wealthy nobility.

The bodies in these Estonian ships were neatly aligned, some stacked, given what appears to be an honourable ceremony. But there was no burial mound, as though this laying to rest was done in haste or completed by others, showing respect for the dead but perhaps unwilling to put *too* much effort into the burial process.

The boats show signs of heavy fighting, both riddled with arrows. Researchers believe the arrowheads were tri-pointed, indicating a kind of heavy artillery almost certainly used for incendiary weapons like Byzantine Fire. And I think of the dead being honoured abroad, like the Kings' Graves in Sussex, Volga Vikings that Ahmad watched burn, and these bodies on Baltic shores. In Snorri Sturluson's *Ynglinga Saga*, he refers to Swedes fighting not only Danes but Estonians, and sure enough, isotope analysis performed on the Salme ship corpses confirms these men came from Sweden.

Feeling as though I'd taken more than my share of the archaeologist's time, I thanked him and paid for coffee. But it was only after we parted that I remembered questions I'd meant to ask. Like, did he know how to fly a plane? And *land* it too? Did he get along with his dad? Oh, yes, and where exactly could I find the grail?

Due north of Uppsala's centre, past the castle, university and southerly flow of the river, sits the old town of Gamla Uppsala, mythological and spiritual crossroads of the rulers and gods that brought us here. In Adam of Bremen's writings of this site we gain vivid insight into Viking paganism, and perhaps why this part of the world wasn't yet ready to banish old gods.

Writing in the 1070s from the king's court in Denmark, Adam describes the eyewitness account of a pilgrim who made his way here for a gathering and solstice ceremonies at the Temple of Uppsala. According to Adam, the traveller was a Christian, which may be true, or it could be that because Adam wrote for the church he wanted his source to sound credible. Regardless, we have an insightful, observant chronicler in attendance at some of the most intriguing proceedings to occur within the sacred temple of Gamla Uppsala.

The pilgrim says that the temple was "adorned with gold and three gods: Thor, Odin and Freyr." He describes hills rising around the temple in the shape of an amphitheatre, where those present could sit on sloped banks to watch the ceremonies unfold. Next to the temple was an ancient and solitary tree. Adam writes, "Near the temple is a very large tree with widespread branches which are always green both in winter and summer. What kind of tree it is nobody knows." But they "considered it to be divine." Some believe this was Yggdrasil, the tree Odin hanged from, same as the knights in *Excalibur*. And like Percival's, Odin's survival resulted in new insight and wisdom, like taking a sip from the grail.

Adam continues, "There is also a spring where the pagans are accustomed to perform sacrifices and to immerse a human being alive. As long as his body is not found, the request of the people will be fulfilled." Meaning that if a sacrificed body vanishes, it's assuredly gone to Valhalla. Which strikes me as a rather conclusive baptism. The pilgrim then describes a pagan practice accompanying sacrifice, the custom of bithja and blóta, a prayer-like ritual that represents an ask and appeasement. In other faiths it might be considered manifestation and subsequent gratitude, asking for things and giving thanks for what you receive.

An additional ceremony reported by the pilgrim was the Midvinterblot – what became Yuletide and Christmas. The pilgrim speaks of the winter solstice celebration and feast on the year's shortest day, another cycle of blessing and gratitude, in which animals – cows, pigs, horses and sheep – were sacrificed, boiled and eaten with generous servings of brewed mead and beer. It actually sounds like a pretty good party. In an interesting side-note, the pilgrim said that those who'd converted to Christianity and no longer wanted to partake in the pagan festivities didn't have to attend, so long as they "bought themselves free." In other words, they had to pay *not* to go. Like the old joke, "Christmas Recital, Free Admission! ($5 Exit Fee)." And in one of Adam of Bremen's rare snippets of opinion, he says the music the pagans enjoyed – belting out song while cavorting about – was "disgusting," and could only be tolerated once "transferred to silence." Which *really* made me wish I'd been there.

But the history here at Gamla Uppsala might best be encapsulated in its burial mounds, or tumuli. Three prominent royal mounds centre the space, with another 250 barrows dating back over 2,000 years. Evidence indicates at one time there were 3,000 mounds in the area. The three largest are believed to be where Ynglinga kings are interred, specifically Aun the Old, Adil and Egil. These kings are considered semi-legendary, as sources vary and are somewhat speculative. But it's believed they reigned here in Sweden in the fifth and sixth centuries, noted in Snorri Sturluson's *Heimskringla* as well as Old English sources. These are actually the Scylfings that make an appearance in *Beowulf*, their name a phonetic translation of Ynglinga. Now these three tumuli are simply referred to as the eastern, middle and western mounds. And yes, they're aligned with the sun.

It was here that the Thing of All Swedes would occur, an annual assembly or legislative gathering. Called a Gulating in Norway and an Althing in Iceland, it's where, aptly enough, all things (of importance) would be discussed and decided. Iceland's took place at Thingvellir, by the rift in the tectonic plates. Ironically, people coming together at the spot where the whole world's coming apart.

As with every Viking Age Thing, or legislature, laws would be written, disputes settled and decisions made with respect to assembling fleets for the new season of trading, raiding, emigration and war. The Ynglinga Dynasty reigned from here, and it's where Bjorn Ironside returned from the Med to rule. This was also seen as the home of the gods. In Old Norse it was known as Asgard, Nordic equivalent of Olympus.

(Valhalla is one realm within Asgard.) Here people considered the gods to be "regular" people, albeit with extraordinary powers. More so than the deities of Herakles's time and those Pytheas worshipped, believed to live in the clouds drinking wine above Delphi.

Snorri Sturluson claimed Freyr lived here, at the top of the Ynglinga family tree. According to Sturluson, "Freyr built a great temple at Uppsala, made it his chief seat, and gave it all his taxes, his land, and goods. Then began the Uppsal domains, which have remained ever since." Freyr was also god of fertility, one of the idols in gold the pilgrim saw upon his arrival. But a 12th-century Danish historian with the superb name Saxo Grammaticus said this was the home of Odin, which meshes with Heyerdahl's theory of this being a Nordic promised land. Sturluson, however, believed Odin lived down the road at Lake Mälaren, near the mounds and Bjorn Ironside's grave.

This passage from the *Ynglinga Saga* relates to a law set down at one of the earliest Things held here, "Thus Odin established by law that all dead should be burned, and their belongings laid with them upon the pile, and the ashes be cast into the sea or buried in the earth. Thus, said he, every one will come to Valhalla." Which seems like a pretty clear directive, a combination of burning and burying required by law. Some might say cremation was also a means of sanitation or impeding disease, and as we know, rules established by gods tend to be followed.

But as Christianity gradually became a national norm, family ties to the ancient gods no longer fit with church sermons. In the 16th century Johannes Magnus, Uppsala archbishop, revealed some "newfound history," indicating the city was actually founded in the Bronze Age by a Swedish king named Ubbo in 2300 BCE, and that Uppsala represents Ubbo's Hall rather than that of Odin, Freyr and Thor. Many scholars, however, feel Magnus invented facts to support his theories and create a more suitable Christian narrative. But in a rather neat twist, in 1989 Pope John Paul II came here and held mass at the royal mounds. His rationale, he explained, was that not only was this

Sweden's first archbishopric, but it represented an ancient Norse centre of faith and spirituality. Which I consider not only diplomatic but rather inclusive as well.

In much the same way our tour bus parked on former ocean at Ephesus, Gamla Uppsala too was once next to the water. But unlike the barrows of Scilly, submerging over time, here in Sweden, as on the west coast of Turkey, the land has risen, separating it from the sea. And in another intriguing twist, this locale is also considered by some to be Atlantis or Avalon.

The three royal tumuli here at Gamla Uppsala sat pretty much undisturbed for the better part of two millennia. Until the early 19th century, when a handful of academics began publishing papers saying the entire thing was made up, and the mounds were simply natural bumps in the land. Which offended not only historians but much of the population as well, as it effectively undermined the very fabric of the nation's lineage and royal history.

In 1846 King Karl x v (also known as Charles) commissioned Sweden's National Archives director Emil Hildebrand to excavate the royal mounds and remove any doubt as to what exactly they were. From a cultural perspective it felt like a dig for the grail, with an eye to answer not only historical questions but those dotted-line traces of heritage that just might connect with the gods.

Publicity, hype and fanfare surrounded the dig. It was technically complex. If you've watched archaeology documentaries or the movie *The Dig* you know how these things can play out. (*The Dig*, by the way, is the story of England's Sutton Hoo excavation, proto-Viking Anglo-Saxon remains that some believe validate historical elements of *Beowulf*.) The trouble is, invariably differing motives and interests arise amongst those involved, and with that the potential to mess things up. Not to mention the engineering complexities involved with the actual excavation. More often than not, what's found in the earth are outlines of things, timber lines and traces of artifacts. It's never as seemingly simple as Howard Carter cracking open King Tut's tomb to find roomfuls of treasure, along with a curse or two. (Reminiscent of Indy's adventures.)

Here at Gamal Uppsala, the first dig was done on the eastern mound. It began with excavators burrowing into the grassy bump from one side. Twenty-five metres in, they found a clay pot. Surrounding the pot were the charred remnants of talismans believed to be grave offerings. And in the pot were burned human bones. Removing more earth revealed bits of bronze, pieces of artistic panels, embossed with a spear-wielding warrior. Experts believe these metal panels adorned a helmet, similar in style to the one found at Sutton Hoo, with protective side pieces and cheek protectors (called *grima* if you care to get technical). They also found bits of gold believed to be from a belt or, according to the inventory, a scramasax (a doctoral studies word for knife, a fairly big one). Along with these items was a sharpening stone, a comb, drinking glasses (made of actual glass) and a board game called tafl, an ancient Celtic game similar to chess or a warlike version of checkers. Further examination determined the mound contained two bodies, one of a woman and one of a young man or boy. This, Hildebrand concluded, proved that not only was this a burial, but assuredly one of royalty. He then made a careful list of items, made a few sketches, bundled everything up and reburied the lot, where it's remained undisturbed ever since.

A few years later, in 1874, Hildebrand was tasked with conducting another dig and having a go at the western mound. Unlike with the first tumulus, this time his team dug straight down from the top of the hill, carving out a great yawning cavity. If there was something of interest to find, they were determined to lay their hands on it.

What they found first were stones. Not simply rocks in the turf but a kind of layering, like paving stones they referred to as cobbles. Beneath that was ash, clearly the remains of a funeral pyre. The layout was reminiscent of a roasting pit, how one buries meat on a fire under rocks, then covers it up with earth. And in this mound were the remains of one man, along with animal bones possibly intended as food for the deceased, similar to what we saw at the grave of the merchant at Hovgården. But here there were plenty of weapons as well, along with exquisite trade goods from around the world.

The grave contained a Frankish sword (from what's now western Germany), set with deep-red garnets and finished with gold. There was also a tafl-like board game with playing pieces carved from ivory. The interred was dressed in high-end, finely woven cloth inlaid with gold thread. And there were four cameos of a Mid East design, believed to be decorative pieces from a casket. These items show the global nature of travel and trade predating Viking voyagers, and just how far afield this Scandinavian dynasty reached.

By the time of the Wendish or Northern Crusades, Sweden was officially Christian, specifically Roman Catholic. Scandinavians as a whole were wading into the fray of crusades, religious skirmishes often seen as a fight for the grail. As Germans and Danes battled Baltic pagans (conveniently accessing trade routes), Swedes and Finns had their own borderland type of crusade going on, perpetuating a kind of east–west rivalry based loosely on faith. In addition to Teutonic Knights, one of these amalgams of Saxons and Scandinavians fighting for Rome was known as the Order of the Brothers of the Sword, or the Livonian Order. On their coat of arms was another Maltese Cross, with a broadsword in red suspended beneath, like its own separate crucifix or a dangling drop of blood.

Fighting continued around the Baltic with armies composed of an array of Scandinavian knights, similar to the diverse makeup of Byzantine Guards. Meanwhile, Finns and Russians had been fighting for the better part of a century in what was known as the Novgorodian wars. To ensure Christians prevailed, Pope Gregory IX sent Swedes to "defend" Finns from expansionary heathens in Russia. And in a tidy two-for-one, Sweden conquered Finland while fighting for Rome in what's considered the Swedish Crusades.

While this real-life game of tafl was being played around the Baltic, King Valdemar II of Denmark ensured he got in on the spoils. In 1218 he aligned with the quasi-Templar Livonian brotherhood, constructed some castles and made Estonia (including the island of Saaremaa) part of Denmark, a duchy known as Danish Estonia, which lasted a century until being sold to the Teutonic Order, another Templar offshoot, in 1346. The newly established land was known as the Ordensstaat, or State of the Teutonic Order. Two hundred years later it was Danish again, and for a remarkable stretch, from the mid-16th to mid-17th century, Denmark was ruled by only two kings, Frederick II and the long-living Christian IV, who reigned from 1588 to 1648.

This coastal Baltic enclave resembles a cut-and-paste version of Templar Jomsviking terrain in north Poland. The kind of topography where one expects to find fortifications and longphorts, a place you might bury or hide a grail. So let's go from here to where, according to Heyerdahl, Odin first led his migrating Scandinavian Asians, to the home of that venerable king Christian IV. It's time to cross the Baltic once more and see what we find in Denmark.

10

DENMARK AND GREENLAND

Our plane descends into Copenhagen, the city fanning westward like rippled sea in expanding concentric rings, a rock disturbing a pond. It's no surprise this is a maritime hub. There's water everywhere. We've just crossed the Skagerrak, a North Sea arm separating Norway from Denmark's Jutland peninsula. As the Skagerrak veers to the south, it's known as the Kattegat, running between Denmark and Sweden. The whole wash has been called the Norwegian or Jutland Sea, and to bring it together like a gift with a neatly looped bow, these bodies of water are referenced in the *Knýtlinga Saga*, meaning knitted or tidily tied.

Also called the *Kings' Saga*, the *Knýtlinga Saga* covers 200 years of Danish history and lineage, starting with our possible grail protector King Harald Bluetooth, carrying on through the royal bloodline to Harald's grandson Canute and beyond. It was written by Ólafur Thordarson, nephew to Snorri Sturluson, author of *Heimskringla*. Ólafur writes much like his uncle, piecing together snippets of history from fireside tales, oral legend and ancient skaldic poetry to give us a window onto Danish royalty. Many accounts of these times remain in poetic form, like the anonymous *Poetic Edda*. From this, Uncle Snorri wrote the *Prose Edda*, a blend of stories and myth, while his *Heimskringla* reads more like a historical textbook. Between uncle and nephew, we have the most comprehensive record available of Scandinavian royalty and the Ynglinga Dynasty, including their ties to the gods.

The last thing catching my eye before we touch down is the massive Øresund Bridge, a sea-crossing structure for cars and trains jutting from Sweden into this bit of sea called the Øresund Strait. What's most striking is that the bridge seems to truncate partway, ending abruptly mid-strait between Sweden and Denmark. Here the bridge transforms to the Drogden Tunnel, plunging into the blue of the strait at the artificial island of Peberholm to appear again on the Danish side at the island of Amager. It's an impressive engineering feat, reminiscent of the English–French Chunnel, with the addition of a high, sweeping bridge and an island connecting this chunk of Scandinavia to continental Europe. I wonder what Adam of Bremen would've made of this as he worked on his letters and watched dragon ships go by.

From the airport we have a short drive to central Copenhagen. Our accommodation gives us easy access to the pedestrian-friendly downtown and scenic canal system of Nyhavn, with its multicoloured maritime buildings from the late 17th century. The canal pulls the sea into the old city centre, with commercial and pleasure craft lining marina slips and moorage. Today there's a light sea mist, muting the paint of the buildings, and it feels more chill than it is. With its nautical history, this was a gritty part of town for an awfully long time, the clamour of pidgin and drinking houses and all that goes with it. Hans Christian Andersen lived here for nearly two decades, saying it inspired his writing. Although a great writer of poetry, plays and travelogues, he's best known for his children's stories like "The Little Mermaid" and "Thumbelina." A few of my favourite lines of his appear in his autobiography, *The Fairy Tale of My Life*, in which he poetically writes, "To move, to breathe, to fly, to float / To gain all while you give / To roam the roads of lands remote / To travel is to live." It would seem Andersen too was a Viking in his way, an eye forever on the horizon.

The water here does indeed conjure images of voyaging, and I imagine Pytheas doing the same, if he made his way here from that floppy top half of Britain. I make a mental note to see if I can't track down some amber, which would add a neat postscript to this Baltic leg of our journey. We'll be here for a week, so Deb and I fuss with unpacking and settle in, before visiting a design museum, the grounds of Tivoli Gardens, and exhibits at the National Museum of Denmark.

There's a remarkable new piece on display, part of the museum's Viking exhibit. The exhibition is called "The Voyage," and the item's believed to be a direct link between Denmark and Varangian Miklagard. If we aligned that equinox line with the theoretical path Odin took to get here, we'd be spot on.

"But wait," Andy says in *Detectorists*, "Can't *any* two points be connected by a straight line?"

"Yes, of course, but not all are aligned with the sun at specific times of the year," I'd reply, if asked the same thing by that fictitious person in an imaginary world. So, it's *different*, you see, and clearly more meaningful!

The item on display is a gorgeous piece of Viking Age jewellery, likely crafted in Syria or Egypt, and unearthed by a recreational detectorist much like Andy. Sweeping his metal detector in a gentle east to west arc, weekend history hunter Frants Fugl Vestergaard was combing a field in Bøvling, West Jutland, on Denmark's northwest coast. The signal was faint, Frants admitted, and he felt lucky to hear it at all. But he dug up a small bit of earth and rubbed at the mud to reveal a gold-coloured earring.

"Hey, it looks like gold," he thought, feeling his heart notch up a few beats. "And I think *wow*, and then time stands still for me." Almost immediately he realized he had a special find. What makes it more remarkable is that it's entirely on its own, far removed from any notable sites and nowhere near any burial grounds.

"I'm humbled and puzzled as to why I should find that piece, and then even in West Jutland, where it's so far between other finds. It's like getting a text from the past." Which is a quote I find endearing, an echo of sentiments common amongst field archaeologists. That there's an immediate, almost jarring sense of connection through time. One that leaves even the most seasoned treasure hunters a little weak-kneed. The same feeling I had as I clutched the 4,000-year-old adze made of greenstone, that evening with the archaeologists in Falmouth.

The jewellery Vestergaard found here in Denmark is the only piece of its kind ever found in Scandinavia, and one of perhaps only a dozen anywhere in the world. Vikings were known more for silver and gold coins. Jewellery tended to be items like necklaces or armbands, essentially currency that could be worn, or if need be cut into hack for barter and trade. This earring, however, is art, intended to showcase design and beauty beyond its intrinsic value.

The earring is gold, shaped into a small plate, almost a pointed crescent, set in a gold-threaded frame and surrounded by gold balls and bands. The plate-like piece is coated in enamel, made of opaque, melted crushed glass. Using additional bands of gold, a design similar to a fleur-de-lys is inlaid on the enamel. But rather than a flower, the shape is the profile of two birds, possibly doves, perched in a tree, believed to be the tree of life. It could be an olive branch or the outline of Yggdrasil.

The craftsmanship is exceptional. Experts suspect this was a gift from a king, and given its origins, believe it was presented to a member of the Varangian Guard, possibly for retirement, a Scandinavian heading home. Of course, it could've been transported by traders or thieves, but that's highly unlikely. This is an item almost certainly touched by very few hands, from craftsman to royalty to esteemed recipient. This piece could underwrite a castle. And not only does it connect a swath of the globe, but directly links Scandinavia to the Holy Land and domains where the grail originated.

Another day of misty sea grey. I know it's not always like this, as we've enjoyed the occasional glimmer of sun. But it feels, dare I say, more like a harbour than Oslo or Stockholm. Maybe it's the fact that Copenhagen is somewhat secluded, tucked in like a watery bed with an easterly view, while the capitals of Denmark's northern neighbours have more direct lines of sight to the full force of the sea. I might be overthinking it, or it could be my imagination. Regardless, in Oslo and Stockholm, coastal views struck me as vibrant, open and blue, the colours of the two country's flags. Whereas in Denmark each national flag that I see, white and red, reminds me of Templars' mantles.

A popular tourist spot here is the Little Mermaid, a statue in bronze commemorating Hans Christian Andersen's story. Nearby is the commanding presence of the Kastellet, Copenhagen's citadel, one of Europe's best-preserved fortresses. Built on raised ground with ramparts, bastions and double-walled fortifications, it's an intimidating structure that still looks impregnable. Exterior walls are constructed in a pentagon, giving it the look, in a way, of an Order of Saint Olav star. At one time the Kastellet encircled the city. Now it's a park, and its best-preserved section is in the community of Christianshavn, or Christian's Harbour. This neighbourhood is a series of artificial islands just outside of downtown. Founded by our venerable monarch Christian IV, it was built as a business centre for well-to-do merchants, reminiscent of Birka in Sweden. It feels like the market canals we traversed in Bruges and is said to be modelled on the layout of Amsterdam.

Christianshavn went through a few iterations. Last century it was a working-class neighbourhood, taking on a bohemian vibe in the 1970s. A tourist brochure states it was a hippy commune, which makes me chuckle. All I can envision are nudists and a whole lot of weed. Now it simply feels like a vibrant city neighbourhood: a few hipsters, coffee houses, families with pets, and young professionals.

A short train ride west takes us to Roskilde and the Vikingeskibsmuseet. Denmark's Viking Ship Museum. As well as being a tourist draw, the museum's an active research centre for maritime archaeology. The main exhibit is what's called the Skuldelev ships, five Viking Age craft from the year 1070, excavated in the 1960s. Skuldelev is on the Roskilde Fjord, a finger of water that points roughly north toward Oslo. The boats on display are five of nine found here so far, making this northern Europe's biggest discovery of prehistoric ships.

A thousand years ago the vessels were scuttled to create a blockade, a defensive maneuver to seal up the narrows. This helped, in a way, to preserve them. Although they've deteriorated, we do get a glimpse at their craftsmanship. Each ship on display is distinct, from warships to cargo and trading craft. Amongst the remaining boats still being excavated is the largest Viking ship ever found, *Roskilde 6*, a whopping 36 metres in length.

Inside the museum is a wall-mounted map detailing the northern hemisphere. Wide, sweeping arrows in red show the primary voyaging routes of the Vikings, paths of raiding, trading, emigrating and ruling. For another moment I felt what the detectorist described, that near-dizzying glimpse into timelessness. It's the sensation that triggered my first eight-year trek in the wake of northern explorers, "viking" my way around the top half of the globe. The wall-mapped arrows encircle most of the planet, effectively a series of pilgrimage paths. I could almost hear roaring props on that flight path, hauling Indy across the Atlantic.

"I want to go to there," is what I thought. Meaning all of it. But as I gazed at the map, destinations imagined, I also thought of *Moby Dick*'s Ishmael referring to mythic Kokovoko, stating, "It is not down on any map; true places never are." Leaving us to wonder what more lies in murky grey swash just beyond our map's edge. In a way it felt like spinning a globe, closing eyes and pointing a finger, a traveller's version of pin-the-tail-on-the-donkey, if the donkey's the world and the pin is your pack and potential. Little did I realize that instant would redefine my life.

I spent a long time engrossed in the map. It wasn't particularly attractive, no illumination or sea monsters. No references to "here be dragons," and Thule didn't even make an appearance. But in the wave-like curl of red arrows I saw Celtic knots and oak whorls. I saw the circular motion of currents like the Humboldt that shoved Heyerdahl's crew across the Pacific. And I saw the determination of weather-lined faces, wayfaring Polynesians in double-hulled wakas, mutton-chop sails bent in the wind, going the opposite way. I thought of the path of Erik the Red, then the trek of his daughter and sons following a similar curvilinear line across the North Sea, Atlantic and Arctic. And, being where we are, I thought of a man named Rasmussen.

Knud Rasmussen was a polar explorer, writer and anthropologist. His house is just up the waterway from the Viking Ship Museum, where the fjord yawns into the Kattegat. The house is roofed in thatch and looks like two buildings were combined into a single, lopsided structure, one large, one small, as though both halves were an afterthought. The explorer didn't actually spend much time in the house, as he was usually trekking and dogsledding the Arctic. He returned to write, pulling together journal notes and accounts he'd scribble down after hearing the stories and songs of people he met and lived with while he made his way around the polar North.

He was born in Ilulissat on Greenland's west coast, his parents Danish and Greenlandic. The community faces Disko Bay, known for its icefjord and massive bergs that drift toward Newfoundland. Now the area's a busy spot for sled dog breeders. Rasmussen did some advanced schooling in Denmark, where he pursued singing and acting. Apparently he wasn't particularly good at either, although that hasn't kept others from making a living at it. But Knud chose different paths, specifically his passion for exploring the north and study of Inuitology. This field of research, part of the humanities, focuses on the culture, history, folklore and language of the Aleut and Inuit nations. Rasmussen grew up among Kalaallit, Greenlandic Inuit, and spoke Kalaallisut, the Indigenous language. He also learned from an early age how to live in extreme conditions, drive a dog team and hunt, and not just survive but thrive in a harsh polar climate.

In 1902 he embarked on his first expedition, joined by fellow researcher–explorers Harald Moltke, Jørgen Brønlund and Ludvig Mylius-Erichsen. They called it the Danish Literary Expedition, their objective to learn as much as they could about Inuit culture. The team returned two years later, Knud wrote *The People of the Polar North*, and then hit the lecture circuit. The book's essentially anthropological travel literature. Perhaps from his background in acting, or possibly following months of hearing tales in igloos by fires on ice, Rasmussen writes like a true storyteller. Prose occasionally morphs into poems, while many passages feel like word paintings.

This excerpt was written as he and the party made their way up the west side of Greenland, climbing the Ilulissat Glacier: "The dark blue precipices at the edge of the glacier itself stood out like walls against the soft, red blush at the summit; but the ice on the sea, out beyond the glacier, gleamed pale green in the daylight. This was the Polar day in all its splendour. It is good sometimes to feel the power of Nature. You bend in silence and accept the beauty, without words." Which leaves me feeling we're there, next to the author, sharing in that shivering silence and beauty of frozen sea colours.

The book was a success, and Rasmussen was in demand. His lectures were popular and the western world hungered for tales of exploration and vicarious adventure. Perhaps because of this, in 1910 Rasmussen established what he called the Thule Trading Station at Qaanaaq on Greenland's northwest coast, across from Ellesmere Island. I doubt that's what cartographer Olaus Magnus had in mind when he placed Thule on his *Carta Marina*. Regardless, it's near the top of the map and a fitting name for what was then the world's most northerly trading post. As a business it did well, attracting fur traders and hunters from across northern Greenland, and it served as a last stop for sealers and whalers. In addition to being a business venture, Rasmussen's Thule Station became a base for further expeditions, a well-supplied cache of all they might need to provision themselves and their sled dogs.

That sense of remoteness, one last shot at food for the foreseeable future, was what I felt in a way when I found a few dusty rations and black seal meat in a small supply store in west Greenland. With a couple of tins in my pack, a few clothes and a journal and bedroll, I'd made my way past the farmstead of Erik the Red and over a ridge of low mountains separating two fjords. Beyond lay the remains of the lone bishopric that served Greenland's Viking community, a scatter of holdings dotting icy rock hills, north of the 60th parallel.

It was the third time on the trek I'd crossed that latitude, back into Arctic terrain. And on a particularly frigid afternoon, with oceanside mizzle that seemed eager to sinter to hail, I came upon a shallow cave home, carved in a patch of red earth beneath a blanket of turf that glistened with hoarfrost. The dwelling was dated to around 3500 BCE, possibly ancestors of the Dorset (proto-Inuit) people.

There was nothing stopping me from crawling in, other than the size of the opening. It was the diameter of a basketball hoop and plunged a long way underground, claustrophobic to say the least. And there were certainly no supporting beams like they had in old mines. It felt like the cramped, deep chute of the chain locker I was forced to shimmy into, under the windlass of that pilot cutter we sailed to Scilly. The anchor chain had knotted and I got the miserable task of crawling and dropping my way into the tight oily cubby as we were tossed about in a gale. I had to work hard in that space not to claw at the walls and scream, concentrating on breathing and doing the job at hand. But there I had six other people topside to help if I got hurt or stuck. In the deep, snake-like cave of rock and loose earth in Greenland I was utterly alone, and felt any blind subterranean exploration would be beyond foolhardy.

When Rasmussen happened upon a similar dwelling near Thule Station, this was what he wrote. "It is all so primitive, and has such an odour of paganism and magic. A cave like this, skilfully built of gigantic blocks of stone, makes one think of half supernatural beings. You see them, in your fancy, pulling and tearing at raw flesh, you see the blood dripping from their fingers, and you are seized yourself with a strange excitement at the thought of the extraordinary life that awaits you in their company."

Yes, I suppose I felt some of that, although my mind didn't leap to blood spatter and ripping of flesh. But at the risk of quoting Van Morrison, I felt, in a way, as if I might sail into the mystic. Or more accurately, plummet into the mystic. There was a definite mysticism about the place. The same sensation I had amongst the gnarly old yews by the Kings' Graves in Sussex. Or the palpable veneration in the shuffling queue at Mary's Ephesus home. No doubt what the pilgrim felt as he peered through midwinter gloom into firelit halls at Uppsala.

Rasmussen continued to explore and to write, eventually being the first recorded person to make it through the Northwest Passage by dogsled, traversing land and ice, which he completed in 1924, considered by many to be the "Holy Grail" of exploration. In part a changing environment made the trek possible, but more than that it was Rasmussen maintaining a local mindset, learning from Indigenous voyagers, applying techniques that worked. Unlike British polar expeditions that had insisted on men wearing tweed, hauling sledges on cracked, rugged ice with supplies that included grandfather clocks and silverware.

But even before Knud mapped a trans-North American route through the water and ice, he dogsledded from Greenland to Alaska, which apparently he relished. He was known for maintaining a sense of humour, even in the toughest conditions. Being hungry and cold, it seemed, was simply part of the experience. In what were called the Thule Expeditions, Knud continued to learn from Inuit Elders, healers and shamans, what I consider northerly druids, while exploring the top of the planet. He was employed at one point to resupply Amundsen and his crew aboard the *Fram* as they inched their way north in the pack ice, like a very slow drain spinning north, what's referred to as polar drift.

For another 20 years Rasmussen continued to travel the Arctic, study Inuit culture, write books and give lectures. The Thule Expeditions continued to 1933, and it was then that Rasmussen contracted vicious food poisoning, it's believed, from a bad batch of kiviaq, a meal of auk fermented in seal skin. He passed away as a result, at the age of 54.

Books were still written about Rasmussen by polar companions and other biographers. He was granted a medal from London's Royal Geographical Society and did more than anyone prior with respect to educating the rest of the world on Inuit culture. Another fact I like is that while clearly enjoying the spotlight, Knud was quick to attribute his success to the sled dogs. Despite being outside my sightline here on the Roskilde fjord, it's not beyond my vision, and I like to believe I can see all the way from these museum ships over Knud's home, across the North Sea: past Orkney, Shetland, over the Faroes, all the way to Ultima Thule. Although what I see at the moment is solely imagination, I know we'll be there straight away, "north of sixty" again, for another Icelandic trek to continue our quest for the grail.

11

ICELAND

When Hrafna-Flóki Vilgerðarson, known as Raven Flóki, sailed these northern waters he did much the same as Odin and Zeus, releasing reconnaissance corvids. But rather than sending the feathered voyagers to circumnavigate the globe, this was a mariner's trick, letting birds fly from the ship. If they returned to the boat, you knew land was still distant. However, when a bird didn't return, that was the direction you sailed. Apparently these Norsemen weren't wayfarers in quite the same way as Pacific Islanders. But like those ebony birds released by the gods, here too they mapped lines of migration, determining where people might seek independence and new opportunities. Eventually one of Flóki's ravens did not return, and that's the path that they chose. It so happens the raven flew to that spot on the *Carta Marina* just past the spouting balena and a serpent-like dragon in red. Known to both the mapmaker and Pytheas as Thule, it's what would eventually be named Islandia. Now it's our next destination.

As our flight banks toward Reykjavik, I'm rereading Malachy Tallack's *Sixty Degrees North*, and it's as though the author and I are gazing out the very same window. He writes, "Below, the land stretched out in a patchwork of brown and green, studded with scraps of white and blue and grey. And then, suddenly, the sea."

Sure enough, there's a thick, smoky fog hanging over the harbour, in fact what "Reykjavik" means, referring to its ever-present blend of volcanic mist and sea fret. Although it casts weird shadows on shorelines and hills, in places where sun does break through, colours are vibrant, the same cobalt blues we experienced in Sweden and Norway, only here I see more rock and ice. There's a blackness in the unvegetated ground cover, the telltale shades of old lava. At a glance it resembles desolate volcano fields we crossed in the tropics on other *Gone Viking* excursions.

Beyond a cluster of buildings in Icelandic flag colours – whites, reds and blues – I see hills rise into mountains, some steaming, others with deeply scraped snow resembling claw marks, residual icefall and avalanche. Author Gretel Ehrlich describes what I'm looking at now. "Arctic beauty resides in its gestures of transience. Up here, planes of light and darkness are swords that cut away illusions of permanence." It's that lack of permanence I associate with the pull of tectonic plates ripping Eurasia from the Americas, now happening directly below us. For the first time on a flight, I feel the temperature *drop* as we descend, as though ice in the upper atmosphere is more temperate than the environment we're about to enter. I can't help but feel like Raven Flóki at sea or Knud Rasmussen mushing a dogsled.

Arctic's defined in a number of ways. Some say it's that ring of the planet above 66 degrees latitude that is considered the Arctic Circle. Others say it's everything beyond the treeline, or anywhere summertime temperatures average below ten degrees Celsius. Another definition more in keeping with our trek incorporates celestial paths, delineating the Arctic as the southern range of polar nights and the midnight sun. If we let Pytheas weigh in, he'd no doubt point out all of this comes from the Greek word *arktikos*, meaning close to the northern Bears, Ursa Major and Minor, home to the astronomical north pole.

We've arrived in Iceland just ahead of midsummer. Days are long. And although it's unlikely we'll see northern lights, the capital exudes its own spectrum of colour and pulsing electricity. Once again I'm invigorated, pleased to be back on our grail path, here at the edge of the Arctic. So, you may ask, how does Iceland fit into our search for the grail? Well, a decade ago an archaeologist named Hansjörg Thaler delivered a paper at the International Conference on Cultural Heritage held in Vienna (theoretical homeland of Celts). Research utilized georadar and drones that scoured the tectonic rift here in Iceland, specifically the Thingvellir region, where Viking Althings were held. It was high-tech, sophisticated research, a far cry from weekend sleuths with metal detectors, and it revealed not only new findings but a fascinating possibility that could realign the path we're on.

Following the researchers' comprehensive aerial analysis, ground excavation unearthed a sword. Which may not seem like a big deal, as quite a few Viking Age swords have been found in the area. But this particular blade is a Romanesque short sword, one almost exclusively used by Templars. These swords, usually carried along with a shield, were weapons for fighting in close combat, in phalanxes and shield walls, used for stabbing and thrusting rather than the wide sweeping slashes of longswords and broadswords. This was the weapon of choice for Knights Templar, most often fighting on foot in pairs or small units.

The sword is dated to the early 1300s, the period Templars were on the decline, renounced by the church, with most of their assets seized. From the Holy Land the knights had retreated (as we saw in the Med) or joined new orders that slowly moved north. It was its own migration, in a way, emigration of a faith-based trade. A number of facts align with this new theory that Templars came to Iceland. One pertains to the knights' final supreme commander, the last Templar Grand Master, who was not among those knights who withdrew to fortified islands or reinvented themselves in new orders. His name was Jacques de Molay, and he headed the Templars for two decades, from 1292 until the order was finally disbanded in 1312 by Pope Clement v.

For his final five years as Grand Master, de Molay was under arrest in France, being interrogated, in an attempt to force him to hand over the order's records, known as the Templar archives. It's believed these documents not only listed holdings, but details of lineage along with treasure and ancient maps. It was a book (or more likely books) that could well reveal not only where the grail had been but in fact where it currently was. De Molay, however, refused to talk, and the secret as to where the archives were hidden died with him.

Some theorists claim Dante was a Templar, and that his epic poem *Inferno* shares clues as to where the archives might be. Which strikes me as a bit Dan Brown-ish, dancing the line of conspiracy theory. But a medieval researcher by the name of Gianazza, considered an expert on Dante, claims that he extrapolated a specific location from the poet's writings that places the last of the Templars in Iceland. He backed this up with documentation from early 14th-century Althings which states that at "the turn of that century there was a constant presence of a large group of continental knights." The exact place where the Templar-style short sword was found.

Yes, it's speculative. But time and again we've found clues pinpointing people and places as though this journey's been planned for us. Historical bread crumbs continue to coax us forward, a bit further, leading us to where we ought to be. Or perhaps *need* to be. And I'm reminded of Rasmussen, who spent much of his polar travels with angakkuqs, Inuit healers who share magic and myth through their actions and religious stories. It's believed they speak with the gods. These are the seers I see as druidic, peering through smudges of fog and smoke mist, where sila howls in north winds. And not for the first time I feel like an ivory pawn being moved across squares in a global-sized game of tafl.

With all this aswirl in my mind, we venture out, on a bus, across Icelandic tundra. Everything here seems enormous: mountains, lakes, glaciers, volcanoes. I can almost feel the lip of that deep, growing gorge, a Dante-esque glimpse into earth's core, another underworld gate. And I keep an eye peeled for a demi-god bouncer with a southern Greek accent.

Today it's as bright as it's been on this trip so far, a lapis lazuli sky with cream-frothing breakers smashing the coast. As we crest a long hill with a sweeping vista of blues – rugged mountains, ice, snow and sea – it feels like the Hebrides Cuillins, if those hills were still in the Ice Age. Our destination is Thingvellir, home to the Althings, where our missing link short sword was found. Although the sword's not on display, I think of a blade I saw thrust in a stone nearby, on Iceland's southwest peninsula, yet another land's end pointing roughly to Greenland. It was at the museum at Reykjanesbær, a modern sculpture made to look ancient. It could've been Arthur's stone, which itself just might be the grail, if we buy into Templar code and Wolfram von Eschenbach's *Parzival*.

I'd gone to the coastal museum not only to research Vinland but to get aboard the longship Íslendingur, another *Gokstad* replica, but one built the same size as Oslo's original. The sword in the stone took me by surprise. It's not a featured exhibit, and I almost tripped over it on a small stairwell landing. It was also a replica, a compact version of an Arthurian installation at a Reykjanesbær roundabout on the highway I'd navigated to get there.

I spent half a day in that space, learning of Vinland and longships and whaling. I lunched on hearty lamb soup, almost a stew, with thick buttered bread. I had a seat by a high glass window, triple paned, but still a cold breeze blew in off the fjord, permeating the space. The soup helped. Maybe it was the setting, but it tasted to me like the savoury fin whale stew I ate in Greenland, which had made for interesting dinner conversation. I was seated with five others and we spoke a pidgin of Danish, French, English and pantomime. Everyone had an opinion as we chewed on the gamey red meat.

"With one life taken," someone said. "Three dozen families are fed. But with chicken or beef, for example, many more lives have to be sacrificed to feed the same number of people."

The conversation bridged a range of subjects, from planetary preservation to metaphysical questions of consciousness, spirit and soul. It's one thing to visit in a language that isn't your own, exchanging pleasantries, asking directions. But it's quite another to philosophize about life and our interconnectedness within the universe while trying to remember things like linguistic gender and tense. All told, I think we did pretty well, each of us sharing our feelings as best we could. Opinions were strong, exchanges polite, inclusive and open-minded. It left me wishing it were this simple at every debate or legislative assembly.

I couldn't help but wonder what it was like at those Icelandic Althings. Apparently weapons were "left at the door," down the hill from the Thingvellir gathering. I've yet to come across any record of actual fighting. Heated debate to be sure. And arguments. But never a coming to blows. There was, it seems, deep-seated respect for the process itself. These were places and meetings not only for dispute resolution and creation of law but for spirituality and expressions of faith. Maybe elements of that, and those present, are what linger here in the land, preternatural hidden people.

When we finally arrive at Thingvellir's sacred site, it *does* feel as though we're accompanied. Not just the scatter of tour groups, all managing to disappear in the vast open land. But something more. Energy deep in the ground. Maybe it's the plummeting chasms that link the surface to the earth's core. Or maybe it is in fact a collection of transcendental entities, whispers of past and people, a clatter of axes and swords at the base of the hill, while a procession of pilgrims in skins, furs and armour, maybe a mantle or two, trek their way to a high rocky wall by a river and lake, to convene and preserve the world.

Back in transit, for now. Leaving our path to fate, somewhat, direction determined by others. What author Bernard Cornwell refers to as "following a path without certainty of where it will end." But we don't have to rely on celestial routes, just a flight path taking us in the direction of where this all started, back toward Arthur's homeland. We'll be in the air for three hours, assuming no glacial volcanoes flare up to disrupt our airspace as they did in 2010 at Eyjafjallajökull, then again at Bárðarbunga in 2014.

While we're on the subject of the earth far below, there's a fresh but intriguing thread of geological research regarding not only the land but the seabed as well. New findings indicate that this whole stretch of polar terrain, encompassing Greenland, Iceland, Norway and the islands Vikings called home, may in fact have been one single land mass. Not simply the one-time supercontinent of Pangea, but subsequent to that. In their Geological Society of America research paper "Icelandia," researchers Gillian Foulger, Laurent Gernigon and Laurent Geoffroy believe most of this ancient Nordic continent sank into the Arctic and North Atlantic, leaving what we now see as Greenland, Iceland and that scatter of isles Magnus placed on his *Carta Marina* near Thule and those fierce looking monsters with dagger-like teeth.

It may even undermine generally accepted theories of tectonic plates and the manner in which they move. Needless to say, there's plenty of opposition to the new theory. But the "Icelandia" paper backs up its theory with examples of core samples and ocean floor fossils. The earth's crust around Iceland, they say, is eight times thicker than anywhere else on the planet, indicating this polar region isn't so much a rocky plate but in fact may be solid, connected to the Earth's very core. Samples of fossilized plants indicate these Arctic islands did indeed connect Greenland to Scandinavia, but there aren't yet any indications of animal remains, which would better support the claim. It's believed the land mass sank about ten million years ago, its own Atlantis-like submersion.

What makes this particularly controversial relates to seabed resources, specifically which nation can claim submerged bits of the Earth as their own. In other words who "owns" the content, specifically mineral and mining rights, not to mention potential drilling for oil and gas. Once again we see belief and some science get muddied where money's involved. Another age-old dilemma of who owns what, the type of conflict that can trigger a holy war.

For now, however, the Arctic's hidden from view and all I can see is cloud. But the flight gives me a chance to catch up on notes, recapping treks over Greenland and Iceland, these places that may be disputed. In Greenland I felt a connection with Rasmussen, as I too spent time learning more of the land from an Inuit hunter. We talked about seals and blubber and fur, when to shoot and when not to, and the importance of hides and meat.

I then spent a day on a barren expanse of lichen-covered mountain, a berg-dotted fjord far below, a glacier rising above me. Later, I'd read a passage in Stephen Bown's *White Eskimo*, a Rasmussen biography, which felt much like my own journal entry, our experiences nearly the same despite taking place in two moments that spanned a century. "Only when the sun is out is there heat, bathing the silent landscape in a wistful peace. Hour after hour without hearing any sound, without seeing any living thing, and you work in these solemn surroundings so long that you stop and wince at the sound of your own footsteps. In each mountain ridge I saw only hope."

Yes, it was hope I experienced too, scrunching along to the sound of my footsteps, alternating from gravel to dirt and scrub grass. I had no idea where exactly I was, somewhere in a big green blob according to Google Maps, if and when I could get a signal. And there in the green, at a lag, was a tiny blue dot, my location, seemingly frozen in time. Despite utter isolation, I felt close to euphoric. I *was* in a way frozen there, in place, time, and temperature too. But the sun did come out on that long, lonely climb, and despite the cold, my face was pleasantly warm when I eventually crested the ridge. Land still rose to one side, while ahead and behind, it dropped to two fjords, the world's largest peace sign in blue.

I had similar feelings on previous Reykjavik flights: colours vibrant and crisp, icy blue sea, ebony rock and chalky-white glaciers. One last Rasmussen passage from Bown struck me as somehow familiar, a mutual glimpse at the land through fresh eyes, with a nod to Norse legends we shared: "... this ocean of unshakable calm that has its own breath. It triggers the awareness of half-forgotten visions. Ragnarök! Now I understand the imagination and dreams in the old

Nordic mythology." A sentiment, I believe, that hints at the fact that we've had unseen travel companions accompany us throughout this journey, diaphanous guides and ethereal hidden people.

12

FULL CIRCLE

Our plane drifts toward London, and as I finish the last of my books on the Arctic I find an additional note, tucked in a bibliography. It mentions the very spot where I traipsed through a rubble of Greenlandic rock coloured red, no doubt iron-rich, up an embankment from the hobbit-hole scraped into permafrost. The quote's pulled from old Danish research, and refers to Inuit terminology for that spirit-infested terrain, the term used being Sermik-soak. Legend states that part of Greenland was inhabited by "fantastical monsters, crazed people who ate stones, and dog-sized rabbits."

I don't believe I saw any monsters, nor did I eat any stones (that I know of). And I certainly didn't encounter any dog-sized rabbits, although I did find a skull that was hard to identify. It probably came from a sheep, although it might've been from a dog, but was eroded enough to remain a mystery. Which got me thinking about Rasmussen's sled dogs, the stars of his polar excursions. In one of his journals he mentions a windstorm so violent it blew a team of huskies through the air "like flour in a mill." Which kept me from ever again complaining about a strong breeze. And you'll be pleased to know, as I was, that despite a fright and some disorientation, the windblown dogs were just fine.

As the plane screeches onto the runway and slowly taxis past planes to the terminal, I remember my last time through here, when I had a rather unusual encounter. I was making a tight connection and the moment I got off the first flight I was called aside by an airline employee. She called another man over, checked our IDs, and told us to follow her. The two of us were escorted down a long, ramp-like corridor to an unmarked door leading directly onto the tarmac. A couple of trucks towing luggage trolleys buzzed past, and there was a black sedan with open rear doors. We were told to get in, which felt a bit like VIP treatment but also like a scene from one of those action movies where the protagonist is "escorted" to the bad guy's lair for some reason, to be told the details of the villain's nefarious plan. The bad guy assumes there's no way the protagonist could possibly thwart the evil plan, so it always seems safe to confide in them. Of course it never quite plays out that way. However. The other guy and I exchanged a glance, shrugged, and got into the back of the town car. Which proceeded to race us across the blacktop, skirting the tails of jets just off the runway.

The other traveller was a hockey scout, visiting eastern European countries for an NHL franchise to throw money at talented young players and sign draft papers. It turned out we'd grown up a short distance from each other in southern British Columbia. Small world indeed. Our next flights weren't the same but our gates were next to each other and our driver dropped us at another unmarked door between two 767s. The driver, who never did introduce himself, swiped a card and directed us up another long ramp which spat us into the fray of departures. I shook hands with the scout and we wished each other well. The whole thing still seems surreal.

This time, however, I don't have to make a connection. I'll be in London for a few nights of museums, research and likely a pint at a favourite pub. From the airport, I train directly to Paddington and stroll a few blocks to a modest boutique hotel. Across the street is a compact park, leafy deciduous throwing shade onto wrought iron benches. There's a classic red phone booth and the street's lined with small stores and restaurants, the neighbourhood humming with the energy of commuters. Down the street are a couple of nondescript chain hotels with a queue of idling black cabs. Following a plane and a train, simply walking feels somewhat cathartic. Outside my hotel I'm accosted by a sex worker, and decide it feels rather nice to be found attractive, even for a price. Two guys standing nearby tease me for being solicited, and I suspect that despite my desire to blend in, my pack and no doubt everything about me screams *tourist*.

Having left the unusual little entourage out front, I check in and enjoy the hotel interior, which has the feel of a compact, inviting museum. From a small lobby, a tight stairwell snakes upward, decorated with artistic impressions of geometric shapes and arithmetic equations. For whatever reason, the place has chosen to accessorize with the work of Leonardo of Pisa, Italian mathematician from the time of the Templars. A man we now know as Fibonacci.

Considered one of the greatest mathematical minds of the western world, in 1202 he published *Liber Abaci*, his *Book of Calculation*. Fibonacci effectively took the Indian and Arabic numbering methods and made them accessible, utilizing the decimal-based system we use today. Perhaps his best-known work is what we call the Fibonacci numbers, or sequence. Dan Brown even used a Fibonacci sequence for a complex lock mechanism to hide the truth of the grail, something only Tom Hanks had the savvy to solve. The Fibonacci sequence, by the way, is a progression of numbers in which the preceding two are added together. For example, if we start from 1 the sequence goes: 1, 2, 3, 5, 8, 13, 21, and so on. Which may not seem like a ground-breaking discovery but in fact this nifty formula connects to math's golden mean or golden ratio ($a + b$ is to a as a is to b), which appears and recurs throughout science and math, nature and structural design.

What I like most about the work of this medieval mathlete is that his seemingly simple systems pierce the fog that swirls between numbers and magic. Specifically, it taps into the heart of the mythic wisdom of Druids and geometrics of ancient oaks. Fibonacci's numbers have been used to derive biological settings, such as plant branching, leaf arrangement on stems, growth whorls in tree knots, flowering, and the development of fruit, cones and ferns. It's the basis of design we've seen in the tattoo ink of Celts, Polynesians and Vikings, every seagoing, wayfaring nation. Long before the use of Arabic numbers, elders knew the significance of these shapes, the inherent math of nature and gods. I take my time in the stairwell, feeling as though I'm walking through well-known secrets, shapes that still boggle the mind and answer questions about creation. Not a Heraklean gate to the underworld but something far greater, like discovering the ultimate answer key.

Dropping my bag in my room, I brew a quick cuppa and head east from the hotel around the top end of Hyde Park through Mayfair and Soho to the British Museum to check on the Sutton Hoo hoard (it's still there). And, as always, I spend time at the collection of Lewis Chessmen, staring into wide eyes of tiny royals in ivory, carved by a Viking woman whose name we no longer know.

Leaving the museum, I make my way south to the Thames, stopping briefly at the Savoy Hotel for a mini-pilgrimage to honour one of my culinary school chef–instructors, a mean bastard but a hell of a cook. As a 16-year-old he made his bones, so to speak, in the renowned Savoy kitchen, learning the French craft from English mentors. His favourite story was from when he was an apprentice, grating carrots into soup, and accidently added some of his finger. Which he didn't dare draw attention to, lest he be screamed at or worse. So instead he said nothing, silently bandaged his hand, and gave the soup an extra good stir. Needless to say, I'm not stopping for lunch, and carry on with a chuckle, following the north side of the river into Blackfriars to the one-time home of the Templars.

From above, Temple Church resembles a key, a chunky round church (now the nave) with a long, straight-sided chancel, the whole structure facing east, in line with the sun. It's the same layout we've seen at burial barrows and mounds across our grail trail, even those from the Bronze Age, preceding the Bible by centuries. Solar paths, it would seem, have always been a natural means of alignment.

In 1185 the church was consecrated and became the Templars' English headquarters. The event was conducted by the Patriarch Heraclius (not to be confused with our demi-god Herakles). Heraclius was Archdeacon of Jerusalem at the time, a supporter of knightly orders and keen proponent of the Crusades. He'd arrived from the Holy Land the previous year, his travel companions then-current Grand Masters of both the Templars and Knights Hospitaller, Arnold of Torroja and Roger de Moulins. Despite Arnold dying en route in Verona, Heraclius and Roger carried on, following a tangential line to the equinox, crossing Italy and France before sailing to England. The shrinking entourage carried with them a near-priceless set of keys, each the shape of the church. They in fact resembled those elaborate city keys you see at ribbon-cutting ceremonies, usually accompanied by an outsized cheque held for photos by people in suits, hardhats and mayoral chains of office. In this case the big keys opened the gate locks to Jerusalem, the Holy Sepulchre and the Tower of David.

Heraclius and company met with King Philip 11 in France and then King Henry 11 in England, their objective to muster resources and troops for the holy war. Previously, Henry said he and his sons would personally join the fight, but instead he chose to remain in England and run his kingdom from home. Infuriated by Henry going back on his word, Heraclius stated publicly that the king was the devil. Whether Heraclius was just lashing out or had indeed confused and frightened Henry with a diagonal chessboard, we can't be certain. What we do know is that Heraclius didn't mince words. Interestingly, most personal details we have about him were written by those he defeated in church and civic elections, so every biographer tends to paint a miserable picture of the man. The hot-tempered, name-calling meeting between Heraclius and Henry took place just west of us at Reading, starting point for our first *Gone Viking* adventure. And I can't help but feel a tidy circularity to all of it, which I'm sure Fibonacci could prove mathematically.

Temple Church is now a hub of legal activity, home to the Honourable Societies of the Inner and Middle Temples, two of London's four Inns of Court, professional associations for judges and barristers. The exterior of Temple Church is largely restored, having been damaged by bombing in the Second World War. But the overall look and design is much like it was when Heraclius was here, rallying knights and trash-talking the king. The overall shape of the building's unchanged, a heavy-walled, circular church with medieval stone effigies. If a Templar strolled through I suspect it would still feel familiar to him.

The whole thing was designed to replicate, as closely as possible, the three sacred structures in Jerusalem: the royal palace of Al-Aqsa Mosque, the Temple Mount and Solomon's Temple – thus the significance of the city gate keys that Heraclius and the Templar Grand Master brought from the Holy Land. The recurrence of keys, not only those used to unlock portals but this building itself with its symbolic design and layout, leaves me wondering just how much of this place might itself be the grail. If there was ever a physical relic such as a cup, bowl or plate under protection of the Knights Templar, it almost certainly would've been here for a time. Even while other knightly strongholds across Europe changed hands, were repurposed, or simply vanished, this spiritual fortress in the heart of London remained, persevering both physically and symbolically. It's also worth noting this location is only a five-day march to Glastonbury, probably half that duration on horseback, even if riding two to a horse. Which leaves me feeling as though we're as close to the grail as ever.

While Temple Church had served as royal treasury under King John, when the Templars were officially disbanded in the 14th century King Edward II took control of the site, granting it to the Templar-esque Knights Hospitaller, who leased the space to the colleges of lawyers, much as it is today. Despite its transition from high finance to that of the judiciary and legal profession, the area still retains an aura of money along with the law. Just up the block from the key-shaped building and its Honourable Temple Societies sits Barclay's Bank and the Court Chambers, while across the intersection of Fleet Street and Chancery

Lane is the Old Bank of England, once the Bank's Law Courts. Now it's a welcoming, three-storey pub.

Making my way into the pub, I get comfy at a small table on the top level, gazing down at a wide atrium. Windows are tall and arched, letting in plenty of light. A few bushy ferns and vines grow from a central planter, giving the interior the look of a well-tended jungle. Round lanterns hang from the ceiling on chains and add a medieval feel to the space. I can't imagine who dusts them, ten metres off the floor. Probably no one.

A pint of London Pride is placed on my table, a round slab of wood with the look of a Celtic chariot wheel. This one, mind you, leans to the right, like Pytheas's map of Scotland. I rummage through my pack, dig out a journal and scan a few notes. Temple Church witnessed a few more key historical moments, its transition from church–bank to law society not quite as seamless as I may've intimated. In 1540 King Henry VIII did his part to repeat history, abolishing the Templar successor Knights Hospitaller, and in doing so snatching more land for the Crown. Henry also replaced the Grand Master with a priest whom he called Temple Master, then got back to what he did best, accumulating spouses and eating.

It was actually King James I (the Bible benefactor) who granted the Temple back to the Inns of the Law Societies in 1608, provided they kept the place tidy, which they have. Now the original Temple is used as the associations' private chapel. Shakespeare even incorporated the church garden into his play *Henry VI*, the scene where the Houses of Lancaster and York symbolically pluck two rose blooms, igniting the Wars of the Roses.

It was those gardens that came into play for a number of secret Templar initiation ceremonies, some of the activities that eventually undermined the order, leading to their demise. One of the rites required new recruits to enter the Temple at sunrise, by way of the western door. Same as the traditional Christian alignment of graves, facing east. The premise being that when the dead rise for the next life, they'll face Jesus as he approaches with dawn at his back. Following their eastward entry into the temple, a version of the Heraklean path, Templar initiates would make their way to the circular chapel, where they'd take vows of poverty, piety, obedience and chastity, similar to orders of monks and the equally secretive Jomsvikings. These rituals, incorporating both spiritual and natural laws, are akin to the time-less practice of mystics, healers and Druids. I've even found histor-ical references to Jesus being a Druid. In no way derogatory, simply a statement of fact, or perceived truth. The notion of a prophet, able to commune with the natural world, speak to gods or just one, and peer through Olympian windows into the underworld, Valhalla or heaven.

Done with notes for now, I crack open Graham Robb's *The Ancient Paths*, and find more links between where we are and where we've been. Remarkably, but perhaps unsurprisingly, it's our travel companions the Celts that provide the connection. When I look back on the map to the places we've been perhaps nearest the grail, or more accurately grails, most close encounters took place on the Iberian Peninsula, with more "authenticated" versions of the grail in Spain than anywhere else. Why is that? Clearly there's a deeply religious vein in the coun-try. But many scholars state that the nation's Christian faith had its origins west of where we are now. Not in the verdant green glass of a chipped grail from Italy but in the land across the Celtic Sea known as the Emerald Isle.

Specifically, Robb finds a number of threads linking Celts to Galicia, Spain's northwestern corner, where we trekked the Camino from the place of Saint John toward James's remains at Santiago de Compostela. On the Galician headland, near Spain's Finisterre, sat an ancient stone lighthouse that faced due north to Ireland. Legend states that from its top you could see the green fields of Eire. This was almost certainly an old Celtic route, a waterborne path no different than those leading voyagers to Iona and the homeland of Arthur, like the Spanish monk who sailed to the Isles of Scilly and told Crowbone his future. The name of this legendary lighthouse in Spain? The Tower

of Herakles. Since then, an archaeological dig in southern Ireland unearthed the skull of a Barbary macaque, the species of monkeys that
occupy the mysterious caves of Gibraltar; the skull is dated around
300 BCE, the exact time Pytheas sailed through.

Is it possible Pytheas had a pet monkey from Spain? And dropped
it ashore in Ireland? If I've learned anything from the *Pirates of
the Caribbean* films, it's that monkeys on ships can't be trusted. At
least that was the case with the one in the *Pirates* films. Her name is
Chiquita, by the way. She's a capuchin monkey and full-time actor
who lives in Los Angeles. Her screen credits are extensive, having co-
starred with Scarlett Johansson, Matt Damon and Bradley Cooper,
to name a few. And apparently Chiquita's a bit of a diva, once slapping
Ben Stiller on camera and tossing a poo at Jeffrey Tambor. It wasn't the
first time that happened. For either of them. But I digress.

Robb's research on these potential connections is extensive, and
he explores the high probability of Celts roving in a north–south direction between the British Isles and Iberia. The Brigantes, he says,
are a perfect example, ancient Britons who ruled northern England,
the Scottish Borders and parts of Ireland. Their domain was called
Brigantia, also the name of their Celtic goddess, considered the same
as Athena in Greece, goddess of wisdom, art and defensive warfare.
(Not to be confused with aggressive war gods like Ares or Thor.) Robb
points out that as well as places like Spain's Tower of Herakles (where
one could see Eire) there are regions in northern Spain *and* Portugal
known as Brigantia. But he leaves it to us to determine which direction those voyagers sailed. "Perhaps the Irish Brigantes had heard of
the city in Spain and imagined their Iberian forefathers crossing the
ocean with the stiff breeze of destiny in their sails." Like those who
crossed Gaul with the Greeks in the time of Pytheas, so too we find
watery footsteps of Celts at each westerly land's end. This theory may
better align with those who believe the Celtic homeland was Hibernia,
the Irish Isles, and that diaspora led migration not from the Alps but
toward them, another Heraklean path like that of Hannibal's army.

Done with my pint and the pub, I walk away from a setting sun, my own little trek to the east, where I stick to the Thames's north side. St Paul's Cathedral is off to my left, and I'm making my way to London Bridge. Some mistakenly refer to Tower Bridge as London Bridge, but the city's namesake is actually an unremarkable span of concrete with shallow arches that barely clear the muddy flow of the river. If we want to get technical, the "original" London Bridge now crosses Arizona's Lake Havasu. One of those historical oddities that trips up every player of Trivial Pursuit. That particular one that crossed the Thames was built in the 1830s. But in 1968 when, I assume, some huckster offered to sell it to American entrepreneur Robert McCulloch, apparently he was unfamiliar with the old joke (or scam), and *actually* bought the bridge, pulled it apart and shipped it to Arizona. (I imagine him chomping a cigar and waving a Stetson as he did it.) Regardless, the old bridge from the Thames was reassembled in the American southwest, while the city of London rebuilt the perfectly pleasant but architecturally bland replacement over the Thames. The current London Bridge does, however, offer a decent view of Tower Bridge, the striking, photogenic one with a rising drawbridge, just past the moored museum of HMS *Belfast*.

The engineering involved to disassemble the 19th-century London Bridge was impressive, a bit like taking apart a jigsaw only to put it together again on another continent. The pieces, mind you, were great blocks of granite. Prior to that, London Bridge was constructed of timber, a few iterations dating back to the Romans. It was even pulled down by Vikings at one time, allegedly. I found that nugget during a previous *Gone Viking* expedition as we tailed Norway's King Olaf Haraldsson, later known as Saint Olaf. "Using wrought-iron cables strung from longboats to bridge pilings, and timing tide with his army heaving on oars, Olaf II hauled London Bridge down, a cascade of cracking timber crumbling into the Thames."

In theory it was a defensive tactic, a maneuver consistent with the goddess Brigantia, not unlike the sinking of the longship flotilla at Roskilde. It was the only Thames-spanning bridge for miles, the one nearest the river mouth and open sea. Which prevented Anglo-Saxon reinforcements from defending the city against the invading Norwegians. Records of this event are scant but it appears in some lines of skaldic (Old Norse) poetry, which claim this took place around 1014. A fascinating wrinkle to this tale is that those Viking warriors were trying to unseat the Danish King of England, Canute the Great. So, we have Scandinavian rivalries flaring up here in Britain, each nation believing they had a claim to King Arthur's throne and perhaps its accompanying grail. (The TV series *Vikings: Valhalla* puts a different spin on the event, positioning Canute as the attacker and Leif Erikson, of all people, as the brains behind the daring plan. At least they didn't add vampires.)

Like everywhere on the Thames, both embankments are peppered with exquisite pockets of history and architecture. Across the way is The Clink, the old city jail that's now a prison museum, replete with torture devices and grisly stories of past inmates. It reminds me of the dungeon we crept through on the Swiss island of Chillon. Most tales here, however, are more tragic than anything, prisoners interned for unpaid bills or stealing a loaf of bread. Which reminds me of a scene I like from an old sitcom in which a mobster's explaining his actions.

"Is it so wrong," he asks, "to steal a loaf of bread to feed a hungry child?"

The man being spoken to thinks about it. "Hmm, I guess not," he replies.

"And supposing," the mobster continues, "that rather than bread, that child prefers cigarettes?"

The district I'm in now is The City of London (in the heart of Greater London), or simply The City. And it remains a hub of international finance, reminiscent of when Templars were here, introducing new banking techniques to the world. Just past The Clink is *Golden Hinde II*, a replica of Sir Francis Drake's galleon he sailed around the world, concluding the three-year journey in 1580. He actually renamed the ship mid-voyage. It was originally called the *Pelican*. The reason for the name change? Drake got a substantial new sponsor, Sir Christopher Hatton, whose family crest was a red deer, thus the golden hind (the replica's name is spelled with an E.) Traditionally, changing a boat's name is considered bad luck among sailors, and it would almost never occur mid-voyage. (A proper ceremony had to be conducted, revealing the new entity to effectively purge the ship's previous juju.) Which makes you realize just how big the sponsorship must've been.

If we carried on, following the Thames toward the sea, we'd snake past Canary Wharf and eventually see the *Cutty Sark* on display in dry dock on the south side of the river, next to the National Maritime Museum in Greenwich. The *Cutty Sark* is a tea clipper. Built in 1869, it was the fastest ship anywhere. Clippers were cargo ships constructed for maximum speed, built to "clip" the breeze, making the most of the wind. Slender in shape, they're equipped with three towering masts (foremast, main mast and mizzen) with multiple jib sails off a bowsprit or boom. Under full sail they're a thing of beauty, literally tons of canvas bending in gusts of wind.

Improvements in steam technology, however, made clippers obsolete as freighters. The *Cutty Sark* operated for a spell hauling sheep from Australia, then was used as a training ship. It spent a few years at Falmouth, the port where our cutter excursion to the Scillies began. Now it's perched on a neat glass encasement, somewhat skeletal without sails, bare masts and spars resembling crosses awaiting crucifixions.

Just past London Bridge (the current one), I have a direct line of sight over the river to the stern of *Golden Hinde II*, which looks freshly painted, the amber-hued deer on a royal blue background, framed in red filigree. Here on the north side I've now arrived at the Tower of London, where I recall the words of historian Peter Ackroyd: "You can learn more about the human condition in a voyage along the Thames than on any long journey over the oceans of the world." But he warns, "Tread carefully over the pavements of London, for you are treading on skin." And, with a bit of a cringe, I continue.

Considered a castle, fortress, palace and prison, the Tower is as much a symbol of Britain as Buckingham Palace is, or possibly Wallace and Gromit. The crown jewels are here, including the renowned orb, sceptre and crown. The crown's made of platinum, silver and gold, studded with diamonds, pearls, rubies, sapphires and emeralds. The star gem (no pun intended) is one of the Stars of Africa, known as the Cullinan diamonds. The one in the crown is Cullinan II, a whopping 317 carats (63 grams).

An array of guards patrols outside: the Queen's Guard in red tunics and tall, furry black bearskin hats, as well as the Yeoman Warders, known as Beefeaters. Technically, the Queen's Guard protect the jewels (as well as the palace, fortress and prison), while the Yeoman Guards mostly serve as informative tour guides now. These ones smile, visit and make jokes. While the ones in the towering bearskins remain professionally stoic. Of course, tourists take photos and see if they can't make the Queen's Guards crack a smile. (They won't.) I wonder if Swiss Guards go through the same rigamarole or if Viking Varangians had to endure this as well, some joker standing alongside them, making a face while sketching a selfie on papyrus.

But beyond the intrigue and appeal of the palace, the jewels and their protectors, I'm here to see the Tower's "true" guardians, its resident ravens. At least that's what people believe. Unlike Odin's Huginn and Muninn or Drake's *Pelican* (sorry, *Golden Hinde*), these ravens won't circumnavigate the planet. At least it's unlikely. They're merely here to uphold the realm.

In the latter part of the 17th century, Charles II was King of England, Scotland and Ireland, part of the House of Stuart. And Charles was warned that, should the ravens ever abandon their Tower-grounds home, the kingdom itself would fall. So began the process of ensuring the resident ravens remained, and with them the British Empire. John Flamsteed was the king's astronomer at the time and had the most to say to King Charles regarding the ravens. But John wasn't, as you might think, analyzing planets and stars via corvids to interpret the future. In fact, Flamsteed begged the king to get rid of the ravens, as they kept interfering with his telescopes at the royal observatory. Charles, however, wouldn't hear of it, leaving the astronomer to record celestial signs through the frustrating flap of black wings.

Exactly who told Charles the ravens had to stay seems lost to history, but we do know how many are needed. The number of ravens required to maintain the Crown is six, as well as a spare (the corvid bench, if you will). As I write this, there are nine, so things look promising for the monarchy. There's an official Ravenmaster, who tends to the birds, although they come and go as they please (the ravens, that is). But there's no mistaking this is the corvids' home. If any tourist is stupid enough to interfere with or try to feed them, the ravens attack. It seems they aren't bound by the same rules of decorum as the Queen's Guard.

Although it's a tad cutesy, each one is named, though not nearly as mythically as Huginn and Muninn. The seven ravens currently on the roster are Harris, Erin, Gripp, Rocky, Poppy and Jubilee, with Georgie warming the bench, offering caws of encouragement to his teammates. Every so often they put on a show of sorts alongside the Ravenmaster, taking an occasional snack break and solving puzzles, as they do. It wasn't long afterward I'd be strolling through a residential neighbourhood when I saw a crow turning earth with a stick, using it like a spade to dig up worms after a rainfall. No dirty beak for that one. Apparently, many corvids are smarter than dolphins. I admit the one with the little shovel looked awfully clever to me.

Another legend of the Tower ravens goes back even further than Charles, to the year 1536, when Anne Boleyn was being shortened by a head. The story claims that at the moment of her execution, "even the ravens of the Tower sat silent and immovable on the battlements and gazed eerily at the strange scene." But this was written by a playwright named George Younghusband early in the 20th century, so where he found that nugget is anyone's guess, unless of course he made it up. It does, however, acknowledge the fact that these birds have always had a mystique.

I can't help but feel that one or more of those ebony birds are guiding us too in a way, having come from that pocket of Arctic, the tip of submerged Icelandia perhaps, where Flóki's raven directed his longship. What else might that extrasensory bird have been trying to communicate? If in fact that entire northern land mass sank like Atlantis, could it be another diluvian tale, a biblical flood like the one in King James's Bible?

Most cultures have a version of the deluge story, water rising to cover the earth, usually associated with a purging of humanity to facilitate new creation or a global rebirth. In China it's the Gun-Yu, across the Mid East the Mesopotamian flood. In Old Norse it's linked to a jötunn or troll named Bergelmir, while in Greek mythology it's tied to Pandora's daughter Pyrrha and her husband Deucalion. Flood myths are also part of Australian Aboriginal culture, and are found in Polynesia and the Americas, from the South American Cañari to Mesoamerican Mayans and the Ojibway in North America's geographical heart.

If we utilized the research garnered from the icebreaker RV *Polarstern* and the MOSAiC team, we'd see what appears to be another inevitable flood. As our polar ice melts, not only from carbon dioxide but more menacingly by methane, where I'm standing on the bank of the Thames will once again be part of the sea, perhaps in a lifetime or two.

In Islam, Judaism and Christianity, the original story plays out through the actions of Noah. The Bible gives us details of his monstrous, life-saving ark, measured in cubits. Not unlike the *Munin*, Noah's ark was constructed more or less by approximation, going by eye, as a cubit was based on the length of a forearm, specific to every builder. The Bible also states that the ark was constructed of gopher. Which paints a hilarious image if you think only of the dancing rodent that starred in *Caddyshack*. But in fact, gopher was a type of wood, although no one's yet determined what gopher wood was, or what kind of tree it came from. Based on the dimensions of Noah's ark (which translate to the size of an aircraft carrier), there must have been an awful lot of it on hand. Naturally, I like to imagine it's similar to oak.

In the Noah version of the flood myth (as you're probably aware), he eventually sent out a dove, which returned to the ark empty-handed (or empty-beaked, I suppose). A week later they repeated the process and the dove came back with an olive leaf (or branch), indicating water had begun to recede. And following another week's wait, when they did it again, the dove didn't return, letting Noah know there was finally, in all likelihood, a decent expanse of land to be found. But a part of the story that doesn't tend to get top billing is that prior to the dove, Noah released a raven. From *Genesis* 8:6–7: "After forty days Noah opened the window he had made in the ark and sent out a raven. It kept flying back and forth until the water had dried up from the earth." In other words, Noah started the process in the same manner as Raven-Flóki, no different than Odin or Zeus. Another interesting feature of Noah's ship, as described in the Bible, refers to the boat being built in three separate levels, symbolizing heaven, the material world and the underworld, reminiscent of the realms Herakles trekked, and the multilayered approach of Olympian and chthonic interment. An additional twist to the ark's design is that each level supposedly represented a Temple of Jerusalem, like the Templar Church in London.

If we follow the tale to its conclusion, Noah's ark came to rest on Mount Ararat, a high point of land in Armenia, which is actually two peaks. On a clear day, one side's identical to Mount Fuji, while the other resembles one of the looming Alps just past Chillon that continue to appear in our tales of Celtic migration. In another neat little link, it happens to be on the border of what Heyerdahl claimed to be Asir, starting point for a Scandinavian exodus.

In Celtic lore, a version of the flood tale appears in the 11th-century *Lebor Gabála Érenn* (*Ireland's Book of Invasions*), which I consider an Irish Saga. The book has a few iterations, and like so many Viking Sagas is a collection of prose and poetry, a blend of narrative history, myth and speculation. It details how Ireland came to be, from the world's beginning to when the text was written in the Middle Ages. The tome describes how Eire, or Érenn in Gaelic, was "taken" or settled six times. The first four iterations of ancient seafaring settlers (the Cessair, Partholón, Nemed and Fir Bolg) gradually vanished, were wiped out or emigrated en masse. These nations were replaced by the gods, known as Tuatha Dé Danann, who were followed by the Milesians, present-day Celts. A great deluge or flood was said to have taken place following the fourth wave of inhabitants, paving the way for gods and humankind.

It's the only history I've encountered that doesn't start (at the very beginning) with the gods, but instead places deities in the middle branches of the populace family tree. It's a particularly intriguing blur that blends not only Druids and gods but *all* people, a tidy Fibonacci formula to unravel virtually every oaken knot. Which is consistent with what we've learned of spiritual places like the forests and lakes of Uppsala, where deities are part of the nation's lineage. Bringing us back to the notion of godly bloodlines, and what exactly the grail might be.

We've touched on this previously, but here by the Tower of London seems an ideal place to further explore the ravens' significance. In addition to appearing throughout history, religion and lore, ravens, along with their corvid kin crows, rooks and magpies, are believed to be capable of moving through time. Not like the time travel of Doc Brown and Marty McFly (with their flux capacitor) in *Back to the Future*, but rather the notion embraced by many Indigenous North American Nations that these regal birds concurrently see past, present and future. Similar to augurs inhabiting Eire with the gods, their offspring the Celts who migrated along with the sun, not to mention spanning the seas of each western land's end. Whether or not these winged seers might be Merlin-esque cambions, I couldn't say. But it does bring into question the plotting of timelines and these birds' perspective onto the world.

Ravens are known to see the world in a manner we're incapable of. For example, humans are trichromats. We see only three colours: red, blue and green. Every hue of a rainbow or crown jewel sparkle that we marvel at is simply a faceted blend of those primary tones. Ravens, however, like most birds, are tetrachromats, and see each colour we do in addition to ultraviolet light, what scientists call the fourth colour. In other words, ravens see a more vibrant world than we're capable of, spotting things invisible or incomprehensible to us. And that's simply one bit we know.

If time too is an interpretive unit of measure (like cubits), more of a guideline than definitive, it stands to reason that to ravens and crows the grail's not only hidden but still being crafted and used. With an aerial view from the Tower, Harris, Erin or Gripp (Georgie too for that matter) might not only see Temple Church but a Templar or two in the garden, balancing chequebooks of vellum. They might even see Glastonbury and its possible underworld portal, or the assortment of Arthurian circles and stones past the tin mines and cliffs facing Wales. They might see Merlin pacing his crystalline cave while a fleet of oak longships goes past, making their way to Uppsala. From the perspective of ravens, Arthur both sits on a throne and has lost it, while Excalibur rests in a stone and a lake, as well as the king's calloused hand.

But for now, ironically, I feel pressed for time, so I'm heading back in the direction of my Fibonacci "formulaic" hotel. Still on the north side of the Thames, a few other trivia nuggets come to mind. I'm doing my best to forget the frightening MOSAiC graphs and disturbing computer-generated pictures of the Thames rising to consume London districts and boroughs, symbolic S-curves swelling to swallow the city like a python consuming a hog. Images that resemble the Midgard Serpent gorging itself on Yggdrasil, concluding one of our realms as it descends in a watery underworld.

To make the most of my stroll I walk all the way to Westminster, where I set my watch to Big Ben. A short distance north of where I am now is the suburb of Mill Hill, once the county of Middlesex, now part of Greater London. The significance of Mill Hill? Well, for me it's the place where Doctor Henry Jones, Indy's dad, had his home. At least the one filmed by Spielberg. And I can't help but feel reassured, knowing we're close to our fellow grail hunters.

Big Ben starts to chime, breaking my recollection. And gets me thinking once more of the concept of time. If we hopped a train or got on the M40 heading northwest, in an hour we'd arrive at Oxford, home to the Ashmolean Museum and King Alfred's Jewel, pivotal points on previous *Gone Viking* excursions. But what brings the scholarly town to mind is the story of two Oxford instructors, Anne Moberly and Eleanor Jourdain, both teachers at St Hugh's College.

It was between semesters, 1901, and the two friends were vacationing together in France. Referring to a classic Baedeker guidebook, they trekked to Versailles Palace, gave their tour group the slip and meandered through the grounds to the small garden chateau known as the Petit Trianon. King Louis XV had it built in the 1760s, then Louis XVI gifted it to Marie Antoinette as her private retreat. A chateau in a palace. Not a bad playhouse or fort.

It was during Anne and Eleanor's 20th-century exploration of the place that they allegedly happened upon a small group of 18th-century courtiers, including Marie Antoinette (head still attached, very much alive) seated and sketching the chateau grounds. The two teachers were transfixed, gazing into what they believed could only be a portal through time. It lasted a few vivid moments, then apparently the tour group caught up with them, the guide gave them a shout, and when the teachers looked back to what they'd both seen, Marie and her long-dead companions had vanished.

It took some time (and courage, no doubt) for the two to share what they'd seen. They were respected members of their college, both having served as principal, and neither cared for publicity or what might be considered bizarre. But they did come forward, in a manner, publishing an account of their experience using pseudonyms in a book called *An Adventure*. It was doubted by some, accepted as true by a great many more, and became known as the Versailles Time Slip. It remains one of the best-documented (albeit alleged) examples of individuals catching a raven-like glimpse of the world and one of its wonderfully ambiguous, ghostly and perhaps infinite representations.

Where we are now, just past Temple Church, is again at the cusp of a great blend of history and joining of timelines. Following the Romans this pocket of city, called Lundenwic, was predominantly Anglo-Saxon. In the sixth century the settlement expanded to the west of the walled city, future home of the financial core. With an absence of Rome it thrived, in part due to easing taxation. The river port grew, in its way a commercial transition from gamma to alpha level, although industry remained cottage-based – small farms, individual crafters, artisans and tradespeople – and the city prospered for two-and-a-half centuries. Then the Norsemen arrived, raiding riverside sites, each community easy pickings from the shores of the Thames, resulting in the ninth century seeing economic decline and unrest as Viking assaults increased. King Alfred, however, is said to have kept "the Danes" at bay and "refounded" the city of London, which entailed moving people and industry back within the old Roman walls.

The city's rebirth came not solely by thwarting Scandinavians with reinforced walls but also through peacekeeping and a form of international cooperation, or more accurately, coexistence. In 886 King Alfred and Viking Jarl Guthrum established the Danelaw, relegating about half of Britain to an amalgam of Nordic settlers, leaving most of the geographically fat part of the island to Alfred's people. This in part was what was considered the Anglo-Saxon "refounding" of London, and with it a peace that enabled the port on the Thames to prosper once more. At least until the bridge got hauled down in the following century.

It brings to mind those ravens seeking out land, whether sent by Flóki, Noah or Odin, and their time-bending view of the world. The pair released by Odin, as you know, were Huginn and Muninn. The two birds would occasionally ride on Odin's shoulders, his familiars, like a pirate's parrot, or perhaps a seagoing monkey. (Not to be confused with a sea-monkey, which is actually a shrimp, but that's a whole other thing.) It's said Odin could speak with the corvids, like a Druid conversing with nature. In Old Norse they were considered kin to fylgja, supernatural spirits accompanying travellers to determine their fortune. In mythology they're known as hamingja, or guardian angels. More than merely acting on fate, the female hamingja influences luck, and in Iceland the word still means happiness.

Both of Odin's birds appear in the Sagas called the *Prose Edda* and the *Poetic Edda* as well as in the *Heimskring*. One account even refers to Odin as Hrafnaguð, meaning raven-god, a Norse Ravenmaster if you will. Likenesses of his corvids have been found on an array of archaeological pieces, from brooches to armour and bracteates, a kind of gold medal worn as jewellery, essentially Viking bling. These medallions have been found across Europe, from the Holy Land to Scandinavia, with some of the largest collections coming from the Vendel or proto-Viking era. Most, however, were made during what's called the Migration Period, the time frame following the "Roman interlude," when Celts resumed their continent-wide paths of transhumance.

Depictions of Odin with Huginn and Muninn like those on many bracteates go back to the time before Jesus. When Romans first expanded into Germania they encountered images of the god and his birds from central Italy (Viking Langbarðaland) all the way to the Baltic. Their likenesses have been found on British Isle runestones as well, the best surviving example being on the Isle of Man by the village of Andreas.

The Manx runestone known as Thorwald's Cross is now at the town's compact kirk. The writing's almost worn off, adding another layer of mystery to runestone readers' interpretations. But what can clearly be seen is the raven-god, a bearded man thrusting a spear at a wolf as it chomps at his foot. Despite the viciousness of the melee, one of the birds sits stoically on Odin's shoulder, as though knowing full well what's going to happen. The stone's deterioration even baffles the ability to determine its age. Rundata says it's from 940, while another method of dating claims the stone is from a hundred years later. The wolf, by the way, is Fenrir, sibling to Jörmungandr the Midgard Serpent (both offspring of Loki), all of whom were present at Ragnarök, foreseen as the end of the world. The two beasts do their best to finish off Odin, and with the god's destruction so too is the world expected to end.

The stone on the Isle of Man also contains transitional imagery like many from the turn of the second millennium, bridging faiths from pagan to Christian, what's known as syncretic art. In this instance, while Odin is doing his best to put Fenrir down, there's also a cross crushing a parallel image, what scholars believe to be "Christ triumphing over Satan." In other words, one last winner-take-all tafl match in which Michael and George slay the dragon *and* Thor finally kills the serpent.

Beyond the mythic symbology, what I find most relatable to the legend of Huginn and Muninn is what they represent, not only to Odin but to all of us. The ravens were considered embodiments of mentality and emotion. In Old Norse, Huginn translates to thought, while Muninn means intention or memory. Thought and memory, searching the globe, returning at day's end to rest and reflect at our shoulders.

Another facet of the tale rich with metaphor is that most of Odin's encounters with the material world take place when he's in his alter ego persona, a nomad named Grímnir. In other words, what he presents to the world is merely an image and not his true self. (Insert personal introspection here.) When not spending time battling a wolf intent on destroying the planet or helping Thor fight the world-swallowing serpent, Odin remains in many ways utterly relatable. He refers specifically to his reliance on his two ravens, encapsulation of cognitive thought and recollection, and the sense of vulnerability that accompanies the potential loss of those human traits.

In the poem *Grímnismál*, taken from the *Poetic Edda*, Odin assumes the role of narrator and shares his growing concern, expressing his fear that one day his birds won't return. "O'er Midgard, Huginn and Muninn both / Each day set forth to fly / For Huginn I fear lest he come not home / But for Muninn my care is more." In other words, he accepts that one day the ability to think clearly will go, but he truly dreads losing his memory. It would seem aging, mental frailty and even dementia have been part of the human condition for an awfully long time. Not to mention the fear of that process.

In addition to the Sagas, Odin's ravens appear on many Viking Age flags, known as hrafnsmerki, or raven banners. Numerous jarls, chieftains and Scandinavian royalty flew the flag from ramparts and ships, and hrafnsmerki would often be carried as standards on a battlefield. The raven banner is another compelling connection between cultures, places and times. Its design is considered totemic, the symbology sacred. It feels linked in a way to the anthropological moieties of Indigenous North American cultures, where the raven is often one of two ancestral deities that began not only the world but subsequent family trees. More spiritual bloodlines to gods.

The banner, now a frequent icon in Norse mythological artwork, usually sports tassels or tags, said to resemble windsocks or vanes used on Viking longships. In a neat linguistic link, the Old English word *fana* meant both flag and vane. Another interesting feature (fun with flags) is that the traditional raven banner was shaped like a triangle with rounded edges, as though being mapped by triangulation, with a druidic nod to the curve of branches and leaves, all of it bending in wind. Perhaps another golden mean ($a + b$ is to a as a is to b).

Today's a travel day, but an easy one. No customs to clear, planes to board or taxis to hail. I walk a couple of blocks to Paddington Station, where I'll catch a train and sit for six hours or so. I have time to stroll around and can't help but look (yet again) to see if there's a Platform 9¾ like the *Harry Potter* one at King's Cross. If there is, it's still invisible

to this Muggle. I grab snacks from the shop in case the onboard selection's lacking, and wait at the departures timetable until a train to
Penzance blinks onto the board.

The train's enormous (12 cars) and I have reserved seating, so boarding feels relaxed, not the scrum of holiday free-for-all routes. I settle in
by a window, facing forward, and take stock of my books and notes.
Although I've felt it before on this rambling quest, I have another sense
of pending conclusion, which I suppose makes sense, as we'll soon
reach the literal end of the line. Fitting in a way, as I feel there's only
one direction we can possibly go, and that's back to the very beginning.

A half hour out of Paddington the train rolls into Reading, a key
spot on the map for a lot of the country's history. It was here that Harald
Bluetooth's son, Sven Forkbeard (Canute's dad) went toe to toe with
Alfred and his brother Ethelred, who was king at the time. A series of
bloody battles ensued, hastening establishment of the Danelaw, draw-
ing a line through Britain to establish a new Viking home. My first time
here, which effectively started two decades of viking-voyaging, I strolled
around town as though peering into a fresh little portal through time.
Beyond the area's significance to Viking history, Reading has been a
prominent town for centuries. Built on the Thames, it has access to
London as well as inland, making it a critical trading and transport
hub. The tidal pull of the river eases through here, symbolic S-curves
less pronounced, as the land undulates more than it does near the sea.

Reading was also a medieval ecclesiastical centre, and the 12th-cen-
tury Reading Abbey ruins are a powerful, haunting site to explore.
Sun-bleached brickwork stands like a sandstone shoreline, resembling sea-caves and cliffs crumbling to an unseen coast. This was one
of England's richest, most powerful monasteries, with a royal residence
just across town. Which was one of the things that brought Heraclius
here for his less than amiable meeting with King Henry 11 and their
squabble regarding crusades.

The might of Reading continued into the 17th century, when it was
one of England's richest towns. But the English Civil War triggered

the city's decline with a siege, crippling trade as fighting took place in the streets that now run past the station. But a century later a new commercial boom began with manufacturing, ironworks and a hugely successful brewery industry the area's still known for.

When I stayed here, I walked from Abbey Square to the Reading Museum and its Thames Water Collection, an exhibit of treasures and junk pulled from the non-tidal part of the river. Centuries worth of archaeological artifacts have been hauled from the silt and riverbed mud, everything from rubbish to priceless votive offerings. There are items from Pytheas's time, spanning the Bronze and Iron Ages. A highlight is a fabulous Viking Age longsword, the smith's insignia hammered into the steel near the guard by the base of the blade, at what's called the fuller. When I first saw it I wrote, "How did this sword affect history, how it was or *wasn't* used? Somewhere in the forged metal, pommel and grip we're left to fill in the story, a weapon from the water, like the Lady of the Lake relinquishing Excalibur."

If we go back to a time before Romans, this was the capital of a Celtic kingdom, a crossroads for trade not only across Britannia but beyond the river, across the sea to the Mediterranean. When Rome arrived they called this place Calleva Atrebatum, translated from Celtic, meaning woods of the Atrebates tribe. These Druids in forests of oak and yew emigrated from Gaul, a path not unlike that of Pytheas. But these migrants came directly from Belgium, led by a Celt named Commius. Those first Romans uncovered coins that were old even then, minted by the Celtic king from the continent.

A few miles south, near the edge of South Downs National Park and the Kings' Graves tumuli, a find known as the Winchester Hoard was discovered, believed to be diplomatic gifts from Caesar to Celtic King Commius. It was found on an overcast weekend in 2000 by Kevan Halls, another soft-spoken metal detectorist. Kevan was a florist by trade, and enjoyed getting out with his detector not only to be in nature but to see some of the flowers he knew so well growing wild, like animals freed from a zoo. If I've heard the story correctly, it happened after lunch, approaching the time most detectorists may've called it a day, when Kevan's sensor emitted a strong signal, indicating he was onto something. That something was one of the greatest buried treasures ever found.

The hoard consists of ten pieces of gold jewellery: brooches, bracelets, a neck chain and torcs, which are solid, heavy rings worn like a necklace. The amount of gold Kevan found in the sod-covered dirt weighed in at over a kilo. He was awarded £350,000 for the find, the highest reward under the Treasure Act. It's described as "the most important discovery of Iron Age gold objects in over fifty years." Now it occupies a raised, teal display under glass at the British Museum, just down the hall from the Lewis Chessmen and Sutton Hoo pieces.

The splendour of the gifts to Commius were apparently well earned, as he effectively brokered a peace accord between Rome and his Briton countryman the military leader Cassivellaunus, a fighter by all accounts, who had no desire to live alongside "foreigners." But from what he'd witnessed in Flanders, Commius knew battling endless legions was no long-term strategy to effectively lead a people. And in much the same way as King Alfred determined how best to live in relative peace with the Vikings, the Celts of Commius chose a logical path of order, one that saved countless lives.

The currency of Commius offers another window on a time when Celts were in charge around here, rather than those few centuries they spent patiently waiting for Rome to go home. While some of the Celtic coins are stamped "COMMIOS," others are marked "COM COMMIOS," meaning son of Commius. Whether it was Junior or Senior who got the posh gifts from Caesar, we can't be entirely certain. All this was taking place during the final few BCE years and the start of what's considered CE. Commius, by the way, had three sons that we know of: Tincomarus, Eppillus and Verica, each known as Com Commios. Not unlike the legend of Celtic siblings leading their respective clans out of central Europe to Iberia and Italy, the Commius brothers ruled different regions of Britain. It's believed Tincomarus ruled the north (of this area) and Eppillus ruled the south, where the Winchester Hoard was found. While Verica, who was probably the youngest sibling, became sole ruler for a spell early in the first century, right around the time Joseph of Arimathea may have been making his way to this part of the world, transporting his own treasured relic.

A few passengers have boarded the train, a few disembark, and we resume our shimmying journey west by southwest. In my journal I find an old note of the first time I came to Reading. It was an overnight stop and I had a takeaway meal in a small apartment-hotel. I'd bought a bottle of Old Peculier, a favourite beer that's tough to find outside the UK. The brewery's a great supporter of literature, sponsoring their own mini crime-mystery writing contest. Stories can be no more than ten words in length, and select tiny novels are printed on the labels of bottles. For fun, I wrote my own ten-word mystery, which goes like this.

"Jurors know his guilt. And he theirs. He smiles. Free."

It's a story I'm still proud of. This time around, I come up with this, which I call "Unplugged":

"Dozing off, he wondered why she smiled at the doctor."

And with that pleasant image, I too have a smile as I close my eyes for a nap.

I end up napping longer than I'd planned, and we're now in southwest England, passing through Somerset. The train stops at Taunton, where Taunton Castle still stands, squat and chunky, built by Normans early in the 12th century, the heyday of Templars. Taunton too was a town of financial significance, being home to an Anglo-Saxon mint in the early Middle Ages. What strikes me as the most prominent structure in town is the square tower of the Church of St James, apostle from the west end of the Spanish Camino.

A side-note you may already know is that Santiago is Spanish for Saint James, as in Santiago de Compostela, the Way of Saint James. It's specific, in fact, to that "first" James, brother to John and son of Salome and Zebedee, and has been a popular boy's name across the Spanish-speaking world for centuries. I find myself grinning each time I hear the name James, informally Jim, as it's oddly personal.

Apparently my dad wanted to name me Hamish, a Scottish version of James. According to family lore, my mom and sisters vetoed the name. Had I ended up being Hamish, I'm not entirely sure how I'd have fared on the playground, growing up in a community not particularly well versed in Gaelic. However, I feel it's a wonderful name. My dad was William, by the way. And as I understand it, after some back and forth, it was decided I would be Billy. Legally. No middle name, tidy and simple. Which I like. In Grade 7 I became Bill and remained that way, apart from a few who still call me Billy, which I like as well. But here's the thing I find fascinating. When I meet people for the first time, I introduce myself as Bill. (Which is in no way interesting, I realize, but stick with me, we're getting there.) When I see many of those same people again, they invariably call me Jim. Which seemingly makes no sense. If it was misheard or forgotten you'd think it could easily be confused with Phil, which makes sense. One time on the phone I was even called Dill (short for Dhillon). But I've been called Jim by people I've only just met dozens and dozens of times in my life. Now I just smile and file it away, knowing on some parallel plane I suspect I've always been Hamish. For all I know there's a Scotsman named James somewhere in that cartographically unstable north part of Britain who wonders why the hell people keep calling him Bill. I'd love to meet him one day.

I pull up an image of Leonardo's *The Last Supper* for a visual reminder of the original James, known as James the Greater, as there are two apostles named James. Not sure how James the Lesser felt about his nickname, although I can imagine. In Leonardo's portrayal, *our* James, brother to John, is perhaps the most incensed at the table, his look one of incredulity. The theory is that these pivotal players in our grail cycle may've already known what was going to happen. All of it.

From the crucifixion to the resurrection. Which again conjures not only a time-bending perspective, but just how similar these spiritual individuals may've been to mystics and seers.

Of course, I can't help but click an additional link or two where people pose questions on Google. My favourite being, "How come everyone at the Last Supper only sat on one side of the table?" I wonder if the person asking the question thinks it might be a photo? In actuality, at a meal like that, attendees would most likely have lounged on cushions, with the table being low to the floor. I'll be sure to correct the inaccuracies when I get around to painting my own version.

Although still heading west, our train's now moving sharply south as we enter the county of Devon. Behind us to the north is the Bristol Channel, where pilot cutters and gigs were busiest in this part of the country, the arm separating England from Wales. And on the far side of that water is where some say Arthur was born, another landscape of Druids and Celts.

The train parallels the River Exe as we roll into Exeter, with Exmouth just beyond that, fronting the Channel. With its southern exposure and exemplary natural port, this part of Britannia (Belerion to Pytheas) was one of Rome's primary points of entry. It became a centre of the international wool trade, reminiscent of the fur industry that sparked the Baltic Crusades. The Welsh called this place Caerwysg, meaning Citadel on the Exe. And the earliest written records of the area speak to its resource abundance, particularly multitudes of fish that were said to have "filled the river."

This entire southwest toe of England fed much of the Mediterranean, with rich, oily pilchards being used to make fish paste integral to Italian cooking, a culinary staple the armies of Rome carted home. At the mouth of the Exe, excavations unearthed coins from the time of Pytheas (as well as Alexander the Great), clear indication of regular travel and trade between here and the Med. To Romans, this port was the terminus of the Fosse Way, a sharply angled, solstice-adjacent road running northeast 230 miles through the meaty centre of England to

Lincolnshire. Rome called this end of the route Isca, the same as the fortress in Wales. In a remarkable blur not only of time but place, these two fortresses on the south coasts of Wales and England appear to lie on a contiguous longitudinal ley line, two versions of a single locale.

Where we are now even makes an appearance in Ptolemy's *Geographia*, where he describes it as the capital of the Dumnonii tribe. These were early Britons who inhabited Cornwall and Devon, no doubt arguing over how to put cream and jam on a scone. In his cartographic notes, taken from travellers' records and tales, Ptolemy describes Exeter as an "unplanned community." (Not a mistake, mind you. We love you just as much as your siblings.) What this actually means is the town simply formed on its own. Once the fortress was constructed, soldiers' families began to arrive, followed by merchants and tradespeople to support and service them all. As the community grew, a bathhouse was built, then a basilica and forum. It feels like every port fronting the Med, river mouths and sea access for travel and trade.

With its wealth and appealing coastline, unsurprisingly, this spot also attracted the Vikings. In 876 Danes sailed into the Exe and captured the city, making it theirs for nearly a year until Alfred arrived and, with the help of local reinforcements, forced out the invaders, who retreated east under sail through the Channel.

I have a good view of Exeter Cathedral as we continue south and west. Out front of the church is a tall war memorial. Which seems apt. Although what I'm looking at was built around 1400, the original was completed in the 11th century, constructed in a manner to utilize previous iterations of fortification, from Roman walls to earthen burhs reinforced by Saxons, each rampart intended to defend against "pirates," which at the time meant Norsemen.

The train slowly carves into Devon, where we'll be inland for a while: pastures and paddocks in varying shades of emerald. Up ahead we'll cross into Cornwall, with the next large town being Plymouth. On a previous visit I wrote, "The bridge over the Tamar offers lofty views of bight and Barbican. Far below, the river resembles muddy tea.

Heavy working ships and jaunty pleasure craft are moored in tidy rows. The view's familiar, details new."

Plymouth's central station manages to drop travellers directly into medieval history, now adjacent to a university. A pedestrian through-way with trees and trimmed lawn known as Armada Way steers travellers south, past Drake Circus on to Hoe Park, a rise of land that resembles a pap, overlooking a yawning waterfront. The first time here I noted, "Drake, Cook, Nelson, the *Mayflower* – all viking in their way – came to or from Plymouth, one of the world's great harbours. Between river mouths of the Plym and Tamar, this former Roman trading post is still Western Europe's largest naval base." That trip was an overnight stay, a 24-hour treasure hunt with touchstones and milestones that could fill the better part of an encyclopedia.

This is where the Pilgrims set sail in 1620, off to America, where in theory the holiday habit of roasting a turkey began. A fun side-note to that story is that the original "Thanksgiving" supper on that eastern seaboard would've assuredly been eel, something the Indigenous Wampanoag Nation taught the settlers how to catch, one of the easiest forms of fishing, requiring no tackle or gear. The sustainable food source is rich in protein and fat. You can pretty much live off it, plus it's tasty no matter how you prepare it. But eels have a rather unappealing appearance some scribes compared to snake, which a great many Puritans associated with the devil, and the next thing you know, settlers stopped singing the praises of the delicious, nutritious eel. (They kept eating it, mind you; just didn't talk about it.) And that, in part, is why many western cultures tend to eat turkey to celebrate certain seasons rather than the more historically accurate (and sumptuous) eel. It's worth noting, however, that the meal took place at the spot the new arrivals (also) called Plymouth, in the lee of Cape Cod.

By spending time here in the original Plymouth, you can't help but find yourself in another raven-esque blur of eras. This was a pivotal revolutionary site, in both the English Civil War and the somewhat less violent Industrial Revolution, with the port providing volumes of import for manufacturing as well as the export of copper, tin, lime and kaolinite, the primary ingredient of fine china and porcelain.

Centring the green of Plymouth's Hoe Park is Smeaton's Tower, a squat lighthouse striped red and white like the world's chunkiest barber pole. It's a memorial to engineer John Smeaton and is one of a very few Eddystone lighthouses. These cutting-edge engineering structures were built on the Eddystone Rocks, a submerged stretch of jagged black gneiss that runs offshore along much of south Cornwall, the bane of shipping for centuries. It was the Eddystone Rocks, in part, that effectively defended this coastline from Scandinavian marauders.

At the west edge of the park, beyond shadow thrown by the lighthouse, sits the Viking Stone, a record of Norse raids on these shores from the year 997. Although Alfred got credit for thwarting Viking attacks in the previous century, it was stormy seas and the ship-ripping Eddystone Rocks that protected this coast most often. The runestone looks much like the one by the chapel on the Isle of Man, the syncretic stone with both Odin and Jesus keeping an eye on things. (Well, both eyes of Jesus plus Odin's one.) There's a Celtic-like cross in a circle, which resembles a Solar or Templar Cross, all of which is set on a looped ribbon, as though midway through giftwrapping, just waiting on someone to offer a finger to finish the bow. Beneath this image is a longship under full sail, a prominent high bow and stern with sturdy hull beams depicting oak planks. Funnily enough the ship looks like the *Mayflower* embossed on the Mayflower Steps on the other side of the park.

I always find a trek through Plymouth a kind of transition. The River Tamar separates Devon from Cornwall, England's last county before we reach the Atlantic. It's home to some of the richest, most plausible Arthurian lore, and for that reason remains paramount on our grail map. If we follow the meandering S-curves of the Tamar inland, we'll eventually reach Arthur's realm, from the moor to the cliffs and castle foundations beneath Norman rubble. And across the water in Wales, past the line joining both forts named Isca with the

Arthurian Court at Caerleon, we find the Nanteos Cup, believed by many to be the actual Holy Grail.

Unlike other alleged grails, this vessel isn't so much considered the Last Supper cup but is supposedly made of wood from the true cross. The cup, referred to as Cwpan Nanteos in Welsh, is a simple wood bowl, or mazer, "a wide shallow cup without handles," with a small flat base, similar to a rice bowl, and looks like it could've been carved from the burl of a tree. Over time it's been broken, possibly with bits being stolen, each fragment a relic of a relic. Now it's about a third of what it once was, and looks more like a spoon than a chalice. But what makes this partial cup remarkable is that, like the spring water at Mary's Ephesus home, this grail's been known to heal. A great many sick people have attributed miraculous recoveries when they consume any liquid (or food) from the cup. Even gravely ill individuals have attained full recoveries, most of which are well documented. Leaving us to wonder: Could believing it make it so?

Celtic folklorist Juliette Wood points out that the cup, also called the Nanteos Healing Cup, was only considered to be the grail at the turn of the 20th century, and no credible proof links it to Joseph or even the Holy Land. It's now on display at the National Library of Wales in Aberystwyth. Experts believe it's from the Middle Ages, which obviously makes a Last Supper appearance impossible but doesn't rule out the possibility that the wood might be from a crucifixion cross. Indications are the tree the wood came from was likely a sapling at the time of the Templars, but even dendrochronology is admittedly approximate. Some mistakenly call the cup olivewood but it's actually Scots or wych elm, a deciduous tree that grows across Europe from Scandinavia to the eastern edge of the Mediterranean. The carved vessel is simple in design, the kind of thing you'd expect a humble traveller (or perhaps a day-labouring carpenter) to drink from. The only indication of any ornamentation is a small groove near the lip of the cup, indicating it may've originally had a decorative metal rim.

It was first put on display by George Powell in 1878 at the University of Wales. George inherited the cup from his dad, William. But how William came to possess it is where the story gets interesting. At the turn of the 20th century, the poetically named Ethelwyn Mary Amery wrote *Sought and Found: A Story of the Holy Grail*, in which she relates the story of her visiting the Nanteos estate (the Powell mansion), where the oldest surviving family member confided in her. It's unclear if the family member (referred to as Ethelwyn's host) was a sister of George or possibly an in-law. Regardless, the story aligns intriguingly with some of our most plausible grail theories. According to the Nanteos host, the cup came from Glastonbury a few centuries earlier. But for the sake of security it was secretly taken to the Welsh abbey of Strata Florida in Ceredigion, considered the Westminster of Wales, where a small brotherhood of seven Cistercian monks were entrusted with its guardianship.

One by one the monks died of old age until only one protector remained. It was then that a villager informed the last monk that a plan was afoot to steal the cup from the abbey. And so once again it was shuttled away in the night, with the courier monk seeking shelter at the Powell home. William's family took him in and the monk lived there in hiding until, on his deathbed, he gifted the cup to the Powells, provided they kept it safe. There's an indication the monk may've even suggested the cup be returned to the church. But William bequeathed it to George, where it remained safeguarded by the family, and eventually the university library museum.

Amery's book, published in 1905, generated a wave of renewed interest in the grail. Strata Florida Abbey got on board once again as its place in the cup's provenance attracted new parishioners. And in a collaborative event held in 1909, the cup made a rare public appearance, part of a sermon and exhibition at the Welsh abbey. It was a bleak day of heavy summer rain, but despite the conditions, an enthusiastic crowd of 350 gathered on the church grounds. Everyone, it seemed, wanted a glimpse of the grail. They even endured the grandstanding of three different reverends, one reporter noting, "The event consisted largely of lengthy addresses," until it was time to reveal the grail. The correspondent then wrote, "The mood lightened considerably when the legendary Nanteos Cup worked its magic once more. To great astonishment and delight, when it was removed from its case and laid on a table in full public view, a brilliant ray of sunshine broke through the clouds and the rain stopped."

A hundred years later, in 2015, a fascinating addendum to the tale played itself out when the cup *was* in fact stolen. But in a rare approach for the local constabulary, the police went public, imploring the thief or thieves to just give it back, no questions asked. Apparently an intriguing bit of correspondence took place, all of which is publicly redacted. And in what can only be described as a spy movie scene, a clandestine "drop" was arranged, the cup was returned, no names were named, and no arrests were made.

When George Powell first inherited the cup, he simply packed a bag (steamer trunk, actually) and hit the road, possibly to grieve the loss of his father or maybe because he was now staggeringly wealthy, not to mention the fact that he may've actually just attained the Holy Grail. (So, *now* what?) The legend of the cup's healing properties, however, continued to grow, a kind of mythic, expanding provenance. Allegedly, some not only drank from the cup but took a small nibble of the wood as well, thus the cup's deterioration. Unfortunately, it's impossible to tell if the misshapen edges have teeth marks or not.

Speaking of nibbling, one of the other reasons I consider travelling through Plymouth a kind of transition is because it's where the train's crew often changes, with Pullman car dining service starting or stopping, depending on which direction you're going. Last time through I was eastbound, a late afternoon train, and I'd arranged a booking for supper. Designated seating was at capacity, but the accommodating crew set up a private table for me in the adjacent coach, where I dined at a table for four on my own. Which, between you and me, was close to perfection. Yes, I've had lovely visits with strangers and made friends at communal seating, but sometimes it's awfully nice to simply slide into your own mental space and just be, only occasionally having to break from your reverie to say "yes, please" to more veg or wine. Because it was an impromptu table, it had to be set while I stood in the bend between cars. A white linen tablecloth was laid out, starched napkin, cutlery, plates, salt, pepper and butter, and a selection of glasses. Settling in, I couldn't help but feel like an Agatha Christie character, the ambient sound a gentle rattle of silverware on china and rhythmic *ka-chunk*, *ka-chunk* of steel wheels on rails.

An attendant took my order before selecting glasses: beer, water, wine etc. Maybe a port to finish. Which made me smile again, as this was part of my very first job, working at my dad's jewellery store. We sold giftware as well: china and crystal, and as a kid I learned the difference between stemware for red or white wine, sherry or port, with a goblet for water, which of course in my mind was a chalice or grail. I took a moment with the big bulbous glass that was set on the table with its crystalline stem, feeling the weight of the bowl in my palm, the tapering stem between third and fourth fingers. The goblet was half-filled with water, and I gave it a swirl. Sun through the window caught the liquid, adding the softest hue. I could imagine it being turned into wine, even blood. Maybe washing down mouthfuls of meat ripped from bone, the way Rasmussen envisioned ghoulish creatures in frigid subterranean lairs.

I let my mind drift in dreamy imagery, like a raven on ocean updrafts, racing toward land, crossing places we've been so far, solar paths and pilgrimage trails, the routes of Druids and gods. From Heraklean pillars to the shores of the Med, where grapes were crushed into wine, and the place where religion was debated with swords, and a Holy Land turned into claret. Until the last orders of knights moved north in migration, following a road imagined by a modern-day Viking. Leaving us to wonder if those final crusaders, the last vestige of Round Table paladins, did in fact sail to Thule, to watch from the edge of an Althing, where new laws were written and new land created, in a way replacing lost kingdoms. No doubt those cavaliers knew the same tales, legends of bloodlines and grails. It could be they knew the source of those legends, inscribed into archives or runes. Or it may be that they, like the rest of us, were reliant on stories and faith.

I think of the Celtic folklore expert who claims nothing's been written to prove the Nanteos Cup came from Jerusalem, Jesus or Joseph, nor from any of our multiple Marys. There's not even a single Viking or Templar reference in the Powell family version of the cup's history. But of course, nothing was written, not really, until recent years. All the tales we've ever had, fact and fiction, have been passed on through stories. Which most of the time were spoken, pictorial too, like the swirl of tattoos and lineage. Those endless dotted lines that plot maps and familial trees, embrace religion and disprove it as well. The mathematics of mystics and modern-day science, all of it bowing to planets, stars and the paths of our ancestors, real, imagined and those we've yet to meet.

The train's now heading due west, toward setting sun and the Land's End that started this journey. As I watch fields of green and glimpses of shoreline roll by, I'm still processing all that we've seen. I divide scribbles and notes into lines and give it a title, "Solstice and Equinox," to encapsulate, I hope, a concise retrospective, a small saga concluding our quest.

I followed a solar- and faith-based trail
for nearly two decades to now
trekking east from the west, doubled back into triangles
seeking a chalice or cup

while I wandered, I wondered, with wonder and fear
what I'd find in a deity bloodline
a space by a sea where a saviour was raised
and a relative traipsed toward tin

to the westernmost reaches of shingle and earth
where the last of lands' ends gently sing

in a siren-song chorus of wave over beach, a splash of breaker on reef
calling pilgrims, the pious, the questers and questioners
seeking communion with gods

where the glimmer of future imagined once fell
in a crumble of moribund angels
at the place where a clandestine urn filled with ash
spilled the remnants, now charred, of the lords
with the blood of a saint on a rag dipped in gilt
imprisoned in crystals and gems

while across a few mountains, canals and a fjord
sat a dish carved in emerald hues
once secured, then stolen, now lost into time
in Olympian, Valhallan tombs

where time-bending birds on the wind circle earth
through a swirl of dimension and time
over ley lines and bylines, Heraklean paths
cobbled roads running rings out of Rome

while a ship of mahogany, druidic oak
sailed to isles that sank in the sea
past a spit of Atlantis, Belerion, Avalon
sought as the Ultima Thule

a spot on the map where an island in black
slides in silence through serpentine worlds
as the polar ice islets of frost-fractured floes
freely float and refuse to refreeze
and the Thing where protectors of grails still meet
with two ravens, the last of their kin.

CONCLUSION

The train's nearing the end of the line. It's not yet the last stop but I disembark just the same, simply wanting to walk for a while. Sun's creeping down in the sky and my pack feels good on my back. No longer ridiculously overloaded with books or a vinyl LP. Just some clothes and a journal that resembles a wedge. I've torn out a few pages, now rumpled bookmarks and discarded notes, including a partial grocery list. The artist in me wonders if these papery nuggets and scraps might be a worthwhile souvenir. Not for anyone else, of course. Just us, recalling our travels.

The evening looks pleasant and I might take the long way around, veering out to the shoreline, past shifting dunes, where the sea cliffs hang over water. The North Star is already gleaming, off to the right, reaffirming I'm still westbound. And I remember a Margaret Atwood line, as though retracing our route from the Arctic: "Turning to face north... we enter our own unconscious. Always, in retrospect, the journey north has the quality of a dream." Aside from some photos and dog-eared notes in my journal, a part of me is acutely aware of the subconscious imagery and inherent dreaminess of this quest. It was nearly captured for a moment, in the druidic swirls and oaken whorls of a billow of pearly cumulous that seemed to accompany us here, lingering over the tracks, where a few rainbow glints held a promise of rain. What I associate with in-between days of transience. Pull back far enough and we might see celestial lines and the triangulation of migrating Celts, globe-trotting Vikings, or knights clad in moons and sun-crosses.

It *was* in retrospect, the north now behind us, as I carried on toward setting sun. No longer in a subconscious drift, but vitally present. I recalled one final lone trek across Greenlandic hinterland, a hidden track revealed between fjords. The only sound was the soft scrunch of my boots on gravel, occasionally muted as I ventured into scrub grass, for no other reason than to change footfall sounds from pebbled staccato to a weedy and muted legato. Each step created a rudimentary score, the methodical four-four of marathon marches and legions far from home.

No doubt the fact that I'd been on my own for some time and was just coming off a fever played a part. And that I was grieving the loss of my dad. It was still early days since his passing. But I shouldn't be too quick to discount or explain away what occurred. As I traipsed my way up a rise in the land, another inlet of fjord pushing bergs into shore, the clouds overhead rearranged. Surrounding sky was topaz blue, softened in its brilliance as sun radiated on water, igniting jewel-like gleams in the ice. The formation stretched into stratospheric wisps, enabling me to see both cloud and clear sky, the same plein air effect as the statue of Arthur overlooking the moor and Tintagel. It was then that a face appeared in the cloud, or more accurately peered through the cloud. It resembled a bearded old man with white hair, a dead ringer for Merlin or Odin. To be perfectly honest, it looked like Santa as well. But of course at that moment, on my own, it could be whatever persona or gift-giving god I might want or need it to be. I stopped and gazed up. As it hung there, seemingly staring down, directly at me, the face somehow managed to grow, to expand. Whether imagined or real I no longer care. I savoured the visual, the connectivity, the sensation profoundly comforting. I'm still not sure if it vanished or I blinked, somehow making it disappear, one of those metaphysical cloud-making experiences, or in this case, disbanding the very same cloud.

Two quotes came to mind at that moment from authors who, in a way, accompanied me, both capturing what I felt in that space, geographically and emotionally isolated. Wilderness to be sure, but not entirely unexplored. Malachy Tallack describes the patch of Arctic I inhabited as a true "image of the north: bright and brittle, terrifying and intensely beautiful." While Robert Macfarlane refers to the experience I witnessed as "active expansiveness." I can think of no better way to describe it. Gaping awareness, and a lasting glimpse of something not only impalpable but profoundly and utterly real. Which leaves me certain that faith itself manifests a translucent bridge to divinity, an alignment of triads and spirits, some treasured, some holy, some lost to time. A seeming intangibility that creates its own druidic terrain, landscape where journeys begin and end in belief and imagination, the paths of planets, heroines, heroes and gods. In terms of our quest, I now realize, each grail we seek remains. Already in each and all of us.

EPILOGUE

So did we find the Holy Grail? Have we located, even handled, the physical cup, if such a thing really exists? I can't say for certain. Not that I'm keeping it secret, you understand. Just that I simply don't know. We covered a lot of terrain and witnessed a host of relics purported to be the grail. Not to mention those nebulous items, chalice-adjacent if you will, representing some alternative form or interpretation: dishes and plates, architecture and bloodlines, even parts of the human anatomy. In addition to these we've found sculptures, paintings and urns, some buried and burned, with perhaps a few smuggled from the material world to someplace beyond, home to more hidden people. If we were to release a raven or two, plot their path like a pilgrim or seer, we might yet find a new way, a dotted-line route off the map, beyond its borders and edges.

In their quest for the cup, Indy and his dad conclude their long journey with a feeling of certainty, confident they now know where the true grail is, what it represents and how to possess it, or rather, how to hold on to that notion. Which leaves me too with a satisfying sense of completion. That leap from faith toward knowing. When, at times, simply believing in something makes it so.

No doubt I'll always retain a sliver of treasure hunter mentality. A desire to once more feel that spark of unearthing something ancient, bending time and touching the past. Part of me still enjoys imagining a relic resembling a cup being physically cached somewhere. Maybe outside of Uppsala, or the home of chivalrous Vikings, buried or submerged in a bog.

Plenty of people still like to believe that a chalice is hidden in King Arthur's realm, near Glastonbury. Although some intriguing links place Joseph of Arimathea in the area, the notion of the grail in Somerset didn't arise until the 15th century, initiated by a handful of ambitious evangelists. But the theory gathered momentum in the 19th century by way of a doctor named Goodchild. John Goodchild (who I assume grew up to be John Goodman) was a British physician who split his time between England and Italy, maintaining a practice in both countries.

During one of his summers in northwestern Italy, a short distance from Genoa, the doctor happened upon a striking, gem-quality crystal bowl in a tailor's shop window. It refracted a shade of aquamarine described as shoreline hues of the Mediterranean, even the Sea of Galilee. According to Goodchild he was compelled by a vision to not only buy it, but return it to the spot he felt it belonged, that being its alleged former locale, the spiritual heart of Glastonbury. For a man of science it seems similar to the time-travelling teachers at Versailles, reluctant to divulge their experience, while at the same time feeling an obligation to do so.

When he returned to Somerset for the winter, Goodchild later explained he had another intensely strong urge, instructing him to bury the chalice at the base of a thorn tree growing in a serpentine bend of the River Brue. Eventually it was unearthed by local Christians and labelled a vessel of Jesus, reminiscent of grail cycle tales we've uncovered throughout our journey, relic provenance evolving only after an item's discovered. That confluent murk of fact and truth, melding, while remaining distinct. Which I find reassuring, even empowering, leaving us to decide for ourselves. What we desire, and what we want to be true.

ACKNOWLEDGEMENTS

The *Gone Viking* travelogues (*Gone Viking: A Travel Saga*, *Gone Viking II: Beyond Boundaries* and *Gone Viking III: The Holy Grail*) have been a pleasure and privilege to create and to share. The books' success is a result of the ongoing support of a great many people. A welcoming, fun-loving group we affectionately call our #GoneVikingCommunity. Despite my best efforts to personally thank everyone, I know I'm incapable, and for that I apologize. But please know that you are treasured and remembered, and I can't thank you enough.

With thanks to my publishing and distribution team: Don Gorman, Peter Enman, Jillian van der Geest, Grace Gorman, Geneviève Nickel, Chyla Cardinal, Gerilee McBride, Joe Wilderson, Kirsten Craven, Cory Manning, John Walls, Heather Read and Tom Simons.

To those who appear in the travelogues, people I've met and befriended along the way, including Kristian Frostad, Ben Raffield and Richard Hanson.

To my bookstore partners: Andrée Bizier, Barb and Tom Pope, Marianne Smith, Ryan Toso, Caitlin Jesson, Joy McLean, Jordan Minter and Neills Kristensen.

To my unfailingly supportive friends: Michael Averill, Mala Rupnarain, Helen Gowans, Chris Koth, Susanne Rasmussen, Laura Olufsen, John MacFarlane, Lorette Luzajic, Edythe Anstey Hanen, Linda Quennec, Antonia Colapinto, Patricia Sandberg, Barbara Black, Jeanne Ainslie, Anna Byrne, Irina Moga, Kate Bird, Annette LeBox, Cynthia Sharp, Gilles Cyrenne, Stephen Karr, Anita Daher, Janet Doane, Kerry Gilbert, Gray Lightfoot, George Dow, Ray Turner, Bob Devereaux and my dear friends from St Ives's Norway Square, Camilla Downs, Kyla Estoya, Gerald Chan, James Fisher, Allan Hudson, Linda Pearce, Paul Bennett, Steve Vanagas, Liz White, Stephen Bales, Terry

Leinemann, Ian Shaw, Adrienne Drobnies, Michael Seidelman, Lara
Varesi, Line Liblik Larsen, Robert Ramsay, Mark MacKenzie, Tom
Woods, Ian Cognito, Carla Stein, Janet Kvammen, Jude Neale, Thomas
Lundy, Jacqueline Carmichael, Neil Oliver, Sheilagh MacDonald,
Evelyn Lau, Jacob Steele, Jeremy Bassetti, Timothy Niedermann, Tor
Torkildson, Vin Maskell, Evelyne Valadon, Sarah Burke, Al and Todd
Imrie, Tammy Evans and David Skillen.

And to my extended family, loved ones, and of course to Deb, for
everything. Skal!